DEVELOPMENTAL BREAKDOWN AND PSYCHOANALYTIC TREATMENT IN ADOLESCENCE

DEVELOPMENTAL BREAKDOWN AND PSYCHOANALYTIC TREATMENT IN ADOLESCENCE: CLINICAL STUDIES

Edited by
Moses Laufer and M. Eglé Laufer

Ronald Baker
Marion Burgner
Donald Campbell
Janet Humphrey
Anne Hurry

Rosalie Joffe
Roger Kennedy
Kanwal Mehra
Ranald Urquhart

Yale University Press   New Haven and London

Published with assistance from the foundation established in
memory of Amasa Stone Mather of the Class of 1907, Yale
College.

Designed by James J. Johnson and set in Times Roman types
by G&S Typesetters, Inc.
Printed in the United States of America by Vail-Ballou Press,
Binghamton, New York.

Library of Congress Cataloging-in-Publication Data
Developmental breakdown and psychoanalytic treatment in
    adolescence: clinical studies / edited by Moses Laufer and
    M. Eglé Laufer; Ronald Baker . . . [et al., contributors].
       p.   cm.
    Bibliography: p.
    Includes index.
    ISBN 0-300-04437-2 (alk. paper):
    1. Adolescent psychiatry.   2. Psychoanalysis.
3. Adolescent psychopathology.   I. Laufer, Moses.
II. Laufer, M. Eglé, 1925–   III. Baker, Ronald,
MRCPsych.
    [DNLM: 1. Mental Disorders—in adolescence—case stud-
ies.   2. Psychoanalytic Therapy—in adolescence—case
studies.   WS 463 D489]
RJ503.D49   1989
616.89′022—dc 19
DNLM/DLC
for Library of Congress   88–38741
                                                      CIP

The paper in this book meets the guidelines for permanence
and durability of the Committee on Production Guidelines for
Book Longevity of the Council on Library Resources.

10 9 8 7 6 5 4 3 2 1

Contents

Acknowledgments

The work described in this book—the clinical studies and the theoretical formulations—has relied throughout on the goodwill and help of a number of people, public bodies, and trusts. We especially want to acknowledge the invaluable help of David Astor and Lord Goodman over some years and to thank them. The Sir Jules Thorn Charitable Trust has been exceptionally generous, and the work described was, in a large measure, made possible by their support.

When the idea of establishing a walk-in service and a research centre for adolescents seemed a possibility, we were greatly helped and encouraged by Anna Freud and Adele Morrison. Such encouragement early on meant a great deal to us. So, too, has been the help of Lord Ardwick and David Cohen, trustees of our research center. Albert Solnit has followed our work and our ideas, and we thank him for his early insistence that we publish our psychoanalytic clinical experiences.

The Centre gained many friends and supporters over the years, and we wish to acknowledge and thank them: Bridget Astor and the Wreford Charitable Trust; the John S. Cohen Foundation; the William T. Grant Foundation, New York; Irving and Joan Harris and the Harris Foundation, Chicago; Marks and Spencer p.l.c.; the New-Land Foundation, New York; the Rayne Foundation; and Lois Sieff of the Edward and Lois Sieff Charitable Trust. Other people who have helped us have asked to remain anonymous; nevertheless we thank them very much.

The Brent Consultation Centre, which has been supported for over twenty years by the London Borough of Brent (the Education Committee and the Education Department)—a unique support—might have had a much more difficult early start if not for the special help that came from the then director of education, Frank Wyeth, and from his successor, Gwenneth Rickus. The support and encouragement from both were critical in our ability to establish our walk-in service and to carry out our day-to-day work. So, too, was Peter Wheeler of the Brent Education Department, who was always there to help until his recent retirement and premature death.

Large numbers of professional colleagues have contributed to the life of the Centre—establishing the service and the research, working before there were funds to pay them, and participating in the present and past in developing the ideas that form part of our work and that are reflected in this book. We especially wish to single out Maurice Friedman, Mervin Glasser, and Myer Wohl who were there from the start and who actively shared the excitement and responsibility of establishing the walk-in service and the research center. We thank also Howard Bacal, Deborah Bandler, Geoffrey Baruch, Maria Berger, Barry Biven, Catalina Bronstein, Pauline Cohen, Rose Edgcumbe, Irmi Elkan, Jean Garner, Anne Hayman, Peter Hildebrand, Thelma Hillaby, Alex Holder, Sonia Holmes, Colin James, Michael Lapinski, Brendan Mac-Carthy, Baljeet Mehra, Peter Mond, Jack Novick, Kerry Kelly Novick, Dinora Pines, James Robertson, Frances Salo, Kenneth Sanders, Joan Schachter, Nick Spyropoulos, Harold Stewart, David Szydlo, Salo Tischler, Robert Tyson, Peter Wilson, and Marie Zaphiriou-Woods.

The administrative and reception staff, present and past, have been very important to us and to the work. Their care, both of the day-to-day work and in their contact with the many adolescents who have come for help, has been an essential ingredient. We thank especially those who have helped in the preparation of this manuscript, while making sure that the day-to-day work was not interrupted—Nancy Dunlop, Carol Hobden, Christina O'Leary, and Beryl Sontag. We thank Alison Huntley who was with us for many years and who took an active part in the early preparation of the manuscript. We thank also June Bell, Margaret Edwards, Marjorie Fleming, Lindy Frazer, Traudl Fritsch, Evelyn Pease, Dorothy Sibley, Sheila Stagg, Margaret Stark, and Connie Stephens.

Gladys Topkis, senior editor at Yale University Press, has been extremely helpful and resourceful throughout the preparation of this book, and we express our gratitude to her.

Finally, we gratefully thank those members of the center staff who have contributed the clinical studies to this book—Ronald Baker, Marion Burgner, Donald Campbell, Janet Humphrey, Anne Hurry, Rosalie Joffe, Roger Kennedy, Kanwal Mehra, and Ranald Urquhart.

MOSES LAUFER and M. EGLÉ LAUFER

DEVELOPMENTAL BREAKDOWN AND PSYCHOANALYTIC TREATMENT IN ADOLESCENCE

Moses Laufer and M. Eglé Laufer

Introduction

This book describes the psychoanalytic work with nine adolescents whose treatment was part of a clinical study of mental breakdown in adolescence, in progress at the Centre for Research into Adolescent Breakdown/Brent Consultation Centre. The main purpose of this study is to investigate the possible meanings of acute mental disorder in adolescence. The data are being obtained from the daily psychoanalytic treatment of adolescents who have come to the Brent Centre for help.

In undertaking this study, we were prompted by our view that psychopathology has a different meaning in adolescence than it does in childhood or adulthood and that the severe disorders of this period—some of which give the impression of the presence of psychosis, confused thinking, and distortions of the body image—may be more amenable to intensive treatment than they have been thought to be. We were aware that existing knowledge of mental disorder in adolescence is such that we rely too readily on opinion and guesswork in assessing the presence of psychopathology, with possibly disastrous results for the adolescent's whole future life. It has been our experience that such descriptions as psychosis, manic-depressive illness, personality disorder, and schizophrenia have often been used incorrectly for adolescents, with the added implication that little or nothing could be done to help them except to rely on medication. Some of these diagnoses seemed based on the meaning attributed to symptoms or on the long-held assumption that categories of assessment intended for adults are no less applicable to adolescents.

There has been, and still is, a widely held belief especially among psychiatrists that adolescent disorders are strongly influenced by genetic or organic factors, a belief that has greatly affected the ways in which adolescents are assessed and treated. Our view is quite different. For us, mental functioning and mental disorder need to be understood by the application of a psychoanalytic developmental model of the mind—that is, one based on the assumption that each period of mental life from infancy to adulthood fundamentally affects and influences the subsequent periods and that each developmental phase—infancy, early childhood, latency, adolescence, early adulthood—makes a specific contribution to the move toward normality or psychopathology. Although there are important differences in psychoanalytic thinking generally and among individual psychoanalysts about the significance of the contributions of the various periods of life—reflected to some extent in the varying emphases to be found in the clinical chapters in this book—there is broad agreement that the whole psychological development of the person needs to be considered in assessment and throughout treatment. But more or less emphasis will be placed on one or another period of life depending on the specific psychoanalytic theory adhered to—object relations, self psychology, Kleinian, developmental.

Although the clinical chapters in this book form part of our study of mental breakdown, they can also be read as individual descriptions of the psychoanalytic treatment of a number of adolescents. The members of the staff who have contributed these clinical chapters present their own views and ways of working; but it should also be noted that the analytic treatment carried out by each of the contributors was constantly discussed, and in this sense the shared views of other members of the staff may be indirectly included.

It will be obvious that the individual clinical studies taken together raise essential issues about the structure of some of the psychopathologies of adolescence and their assessment and treatment; these are addressed in the chapters that precede and follow the clinical chapters. Some of the assumptions about psychopathology and its treatment have already been documented and discussed in *Adolescence and Developmental Breakdown* (Laufer and Laufer, 1984), but the issues raised by the nine clinical studies present further questions: What is the relationship between perverse behavior and psychotic functioning or psychosis in adolescence? What is the nature of the transference in the treatment of these adolescents? What are the implications for altering the course of psychopathology and conducting an analysis of the severely disturbed adolescent? How can we differentiate between lesser or greater mental disorder?

Freud's "Three Essays on the Theory of Sexuality" (1905) contained his essential contributions to the understanding of the relationship between puberty, the period of adolescence, and later psychopathology. Although he made some subsequent references to this period of life, these are few and are not central to his writings. Following Freud, psychoanalysts expressed little interest for some years in this period of life.[1] It was only in the 1950s and 1960s that writings about adolescence by Blos, Erikson, Eissler, Anna Freud, Geleerd, Harley, Jacobson, and Lampl-de Groot began to appear. The tendency nevertheless was to include adolescence and the treatment of the adolescent as extensions of the study and treatment of the child. This development not only proved to be limiting both theoretically and clinically but had the added effect of delaying recognition of the critical contribution of the period of adolescence to mental health or illness in adult life.

Although contributions to the psychoanalytic and psychiatric literature on adolescence have continued to appear throughout the years, the concerns expressed have often had to do with problems of technique, psychotherapy versus psychoanalysis or other forms of intervention, and the role of the family in the treatment of the adolescent—concerns that seem peripheral to us—while the genesis and structures of the severe pathologies of adolescence have remained little understood. We felt that, as part of our work with very disturbed adolescents, there must be ways of understanding further what is really going on in the minds and lives of these people and of applying such understanding to helping them rather than compromising and silently acquiescing in the prospect of a lifelong severe and crippling mental disorder.

The Walk-in Centre and the Centre for Research

Our work in the community brought us closely in touch with the fact that many young people had no way of knowing how to get the help they urgently needed, even though many felt hopeless and knew they would not "grow out of it." At the same time, our psychoanalytic work with severely ill adults repeatedly demonstrated that during their adolescence and before, they had experienced serious trouble which was subsequently forgotten or ignored, with far-reaching consequences for them. We felt that a way needed to be found to apply psychoanalytic ideas so that help could be made available to adolescents, without expecting them to be aware of the nature of their problems and without requiring them to make use of formal agencies that might represent to them mental disorder, punishment, uncertainty about confidentiality, humiliation, or simply not being taken seriously.

This led to the founding of the Brent Consultation Centre, a walk-in service supported by the Education Department of the London Borough of

---

1. Exceptions were Bernfeld, Aichhorn, Jones, and Deutsch.

Brent. Adolescents learn of our service through advertisements in the local newspapers; notices in schools, libraries, youth clubs, and subway stations; talks by members of the Brent Centre staff in local schools; and our contacts with the probation service, the police, religious leaders, and youth leaders. The service, which offers interviewing, assessment, and nonintensive individual psychotherapy without cost, is intended for people between the ages of fifteen and twenty-three, but anybody may come in, with or without an appointment, and for any reason. We assumed from the start, correctly as it turned out, that if we were to be of help, the most essential factor would be the quality of the professional staff. They would bring with them training and skill, the ability to talk with adolescents in a caring and understanding way while at the same time assessing the presence of psychopathology or risk; they would be aware of the importance of prolonged contact and the seriousness of the undertaking.

The range of disorders for which young people have sought help has been extensive, and the adolescents have come from every part of the community, from various cultures and family structures, and with enormous variations in their ability to convey what is troubling them. As we met more and more seriously vulnerable young people, and as we were repeatedly forced to confront the limitations of our existing knowledge about the disorders of adolescence and their treatment, we decided to estabish also the Centre for Research into Adolescent Breakdown whose primary function would be the psychoanalytic study and treatment of some severely disturbed adolescents.

In the course of our work, an organizational structure evolved through which we sought to take into account both the anxieties and uncertainties of the adolescents who came to us and the needs and anxieties—spoken and unspoken—of the members of the staff. The original intention of the service was to make available help to adolescents who, for whatever reason, chose to come in. The walk-in nature of our service meant that we would most likely know very little, if anything, about those who came to us, and that the variety of problems—immediate practical ones as well as those of psychopathology—would inevitably be diverse. Our undertaking to treat seriously disturbed adolescents meant that the young person, his family, and the staff member responsible for the treatment had to be aware from the outset of the possible problems arising during treatment. This was especially so for those adolescents who, on our recommendation, accepted five-times weekly psychoanalytic treatment. As our experience accumulated, the organization of the walk-in service and the Centre for Research was altered appropriately. For example, we adopted a system whereby assessment and recommendations for further help are decided upon at weekly staff meetings. This procedure arose from our awareness of the many factors that have to be considered before an assessment can be made and suitable treatment offered.

Most, if not all, of the adolescents described in the following chapters would probably not have sought therapy on their own initiative, and certainly not intensive psychological help. When an adolescent comes to the walk-in service, he or the person who has advised him to come (teacher, social worker, family doctor, friend, parent) may have been aware that something was not right in his life, but it is usually only through the process of interviewing that the adolescent begins to realize the extent of his need for psychological help. As part of our initial contact with him, we find that it is sometimes appropriate to help in other ways, too. We may discuss future plans, give information about community services for himself or members of his family, or explore possibilities for obtaining medical or legal advice.

Individual weekly or twice-weekly psychotherapy is available through the service for the adolescent only. We do not offer family or group therapy because we feel that such help is not suitable for this age group, especially those over fifteen. The parents of the adolescents are sometimes interviewed, of course, but the purpose of the interviews is to help in our work with the adolescent rather than attempt to influence the structure of his family or the relationships within it. Free psychoanalytic treatment is also available to any adolescent who we feel needs such intensive and long-term help and to whom we can apply the simple diagnostic criteria of our study of mental breakdown in adolescence.[2] It is to that study that we turn in the next chapter.

---

2. Although free treatment is available, adolescents and parents who can afford it make agreed-upon contributions toward the cost of the treatment.

I.

Adolescent Breakdown and Treatment

Moses Laufer

1.

Adolescence and Adolescent Pathology: Clinical Issues

When we first set up the walk-in service, we considered our function to be a preventive one inasmuch as we believed that intervention during adolescence could be of help in times of crisis and might prevent serious disorder in adult life. Although the interviewing and treatment staff of the service are experienced in work with disturbed adolescents, we were quickly confronted with the fact that we did not understand much of what was being conveyed to us by the adolescents' behavior and by the extreme anxiety many of them were experiencing. But we often knew that we were probably observing the presence or potential of severe psychopathology, even though we might not at the time be able to explain why we felt this.

One simple observation prompted us to undertake a pilot study of the psychoanalytic treatment of a number of adolescents who had attempted suicide. We had been impressed by the fact that attempted or actual suicide seems to become an available form of action only following puberty. We were aware that an adolescent's decision to kill himself[1] cannot be used diagnostically except that, at the least, it must be a sign of an acute break with and distortion of external reality. At the time of our undertaking this study, we wanted to answer a specific question: what is it about the physical and mental changes that take place during adolescence that can bring a person to the conscious decision to attack his body with the intention of being dead as

1. When "he" or "him" is used in the text, the pronoun refers to both male and female adolescents. When we refer specifically to a female, we describe the "girl" or the "female adolescent." To ensure confidentiality, all names used in the text are pseudonyms.

the result of this attack? We assumed in the study that certain fantasies and gratifications must exist that make it possible for the person to deny the real consequences of his actions—that is, that such an attack on his own body is a sign of an acute psychotic episode. We also became aware that for the adolescent the unconscious motive for an attack on the physically mature body is probably even more far-reaching: he wishes to destroy what he considers to be the source of feelings and fantasies that have taken over his mind. We speculated that feelings of being abnormal, ugly, or dirty contain the adolescent's nonconscious conviction that his fantasies are of a perverse nature and that killing his body will be a way of removing their source.[2] During the treatment of these adolescents, the transference was replete with references to the destruction of the sexual body and to the adolescent's wish to give over his sexual body to the analyst—to disown his body—while at the same time maintaining an excited, threatening, but passive relationship to the analyst (Friedman et al., 1972).

Mental Breakdown in Adolescence

We were well aware that our efforts to understand attempted suicide concerned only one group of adolescents who were seriously at risk: those who needed to attack their sexually mature bodies. They did not yet supply insights into the psychopathologies of other adolescents who were coming to us for help and who had neither attempted suicide in the past nor seemed likely to do so in the future. Yet, the behavior, feelings, and fantasies of this latter group left little doubt that they, too, were in very serious psychological trouble. There were adolescents who had perverse fantasies and wishes enacted through the use of their own bodies or with another person. Others were compelled to use their bodies in a range of ways but were not obviously moving toward perversion; instead, they relied on cutting part of the body, compulsive eating and vomiting, drug taking, anal masturbation. Still others referred to behavior and thoughts that frightened them because they believed they were becoming insane.

Assumptions about Adolescent Development

These observations from our pilot study, together with further experience in the treatment of seriously disturbed adolescents and young adults over some

---

2. This followed Freud's idea in "Mourning and Melancholia" (*S.E.*, 1917) of the role of the superego in attempted suicide.

years, helped us formulate assumptions about adolescent development and psychopathology. These assumptions were then applied to a second study, enabling us to define those areas that we felt needed further understanding.

Freud began his essay "Transformations of Puberty" (1905) with the statement that "with the arrival of puberty, changes set in which are destined to give infantile sexual life its final normal shape." He then referred to the period up to puberty as "an important precursor of the subsequent final sexual organization." We would elaborate these statements to include the following assumptions: At puberty, a process of development sets in that is qualitatively different from what existed before. Having a sexually mature body forces every adolescent, whether his development is proceeding in a normal or pathological direction, to make unconscious choices that will result in an irreversible sexual identity by the end of adolescence. To state this in another way, *the main developmental function of adolescence is the establishment of the final sexual organization*—an organization that must now include the physically mature genitals as part of the body representation. Once this final sexual organization has been established, the opportunity for some kind of internal compromise, which may have existed earlier in adolescence, exists no longer.

It is only by the end of adolescence—at about the age of twenty-one—that the person has finally established an image of himself as having a physically mature body that can impregnate another or grow a child. Whether the outcome is normal or pathological by the end of adolescence, the developmental task throughout adolescence is to integrate the various earlier images of oneself with the ability to feel (unconsciously) responsible by the end of adolescence for one's own thoughts, feelings, wishes, and actions. The normal adolescent assumes ownership of his own body. But even in normal circumstances, ownership of one's body, which also means accepting responsibility for the consequences of one's actions, may bring about a range of regressive manifestations that result temporarily in the adolescent's giving up what he has attained. Ultimately, however, he wishes to regain the position of a sexually able person who is prepared to deal with the anxiety this arouses. These are the adolescents who are able, for example, to use masturbation as a kind of "trial action," the ones who are ultimately able to seek and find a relationship with a person of the opposite sex with whom they can feel sexually gratified and socially normal. The turmoils in the lives of these adolescents do not represent either a deadlock in their development or a break with reality; their anxieties are usually transitory, brought about by the continued wish for regressive gratification, which may represent some kind of sexual abnormality to them but which they are eventually able to leave behind.

During adolescence the image of the body has to alter or be altered to include the functioning genitals of the opposite sex. This means that during adolescence one must finally differentiate oneself as male or female, while acknowledging the different role of the body of the opposite sex. For the first time in one's life, incest is no longer a fantasy that can be kept safe and harmless; it now becomes possible because of having a sexually mature body, and every human being must find an answer for this, whether it is a normal answer or a pathological one. Again for the first time in one's life, all behavior, thought, and fantasy is now judged by one's own conscience as being a sign of either normality or abnormality. A boy aged seven or eight may be closely tied to his mother and may unconsciously feel gratified by his passive submission to her; but as long as he gets on well enough with his peers, does well enough at school, and does not raise the concern of his parents or teachers, his life moves along at a more or less uninterrupted pace. In adolescence, however, this same person will now have to contend with his conscience in a much more specific way, a conscience that may begin to accuse him of being homosexual or punish him for his masturbation, which now may carry the fantasy of submitting to a big and powerful woman. His earlier passivity has now, in adolescence, been transformed into a sign of abnormality, and he may now begin to accuse himself for his feelings and fantasies.

It is not uncommon for such adolescents to present themselves or be brought for help, but this usually happens only after an acute crisis, in which both the adolescent and his family may be surprised and bewildered by what has taken place. The adolescent's behavior may now contain signs of a *developmental breakdown*—that is, unconscious rejection of the sexual body, hatred of the body, and a need to maintain unconsciously the picture of himself as someone who is victimized or persecuted or made helpless by inner forces over which he has no control. By the time we see the adolescent, he has already found some compromise, and we may be confronted with a range of ways of coping with this onslaught from his body and from the internal persecutors. The breakdown in development is the pathology; the various manifestations of the disorder—whether attempted suicide, anorexia, delinquency, or drug taking—may help us trace the specific road he has unconsciously chosen to live out the fantasy expressed in his pathology and at the same time to attack his sexual body and the image of himself as a sexual male or female. By the end of adolescence, his distorted relationship to his sexual body will result in an image of the body in which the functioning genitals may be altered or even disowned, but which nevertheless represents and perpetuates the pathology.

When we refer to the road unconsciously chosen by the adolescent to live out a fantasy, we are referring to a fantasy that, in psychopathology after puberty, takes on the quality of "compelling" the adolescent to behave in a predictable way and leaves him with the feeling that he is no longer in control of some of his thoughts and actions. We are referring to the *central mastur-bation fantasy,* a universal phenomenon that itself has nothing to do with pa-thology. This fantasy takes on specific characteristics among adolescents who are developing in a pathological way; they have a compelling need to live out this fantasy in object relationships and their sexual life, feeling that this is the only gratification that really matters. The central masturbation fan-tasy is, we believe, fixed at the time of the resolution of the Oedipus complex and contains the various regressive satisfactions and the main sexual identifi-cations. But it seems that, with physical maturation of the genitals, the con-tent of this fantasy takes on new meaning and places the defensive organiza-tion under much greater stress. For some adolescents, the power of the fantasy, which may make them feel that they have lost touch with the conse-quences of their behavior, is frightening. The adolescent himself is not aware of what the fantasy is or means; its content and meaning are not readily avail-able to consciousness. Instead, he is primarily aware of feeling no longer in charge of some of his actions. The presence or power of this fantasy is not dependent on whether the person masturbates or not but may be expressed also through daydreams, various kinds of object relationships, or sexual activities.

Our assumptions about the developmental function of adolescence and the meaning of breakdown in development do not yet tell us anything about the severity of the pathology that is present. Breakdown in development de-scribes interference in a process; this may be a breakdown that does not dam-age one's relation to the outside world or it may represent a break with reality and indicate the presence of very severe pathology. How can we know more accurately? How can we apply our assumptions about development so that we can know more about the severity of the pathology, as well as about the choice and aims of treatment? To put this somewhat differently, we had to find out the ingredients of adolescent breakdown and what it was that differ-entiated severe from less severe breakdown.

We were also well aware that, although some adolescents seemed to be much closer to behavior and thought that might ordinarily be considered "psychotic," there was a difference in the nature and quality of the internal battle going on in these adolescents compared to some adults who are as-sessed as psychotic. We believed that this difference conveyed something specific about the timing of the final establishment of psychopathology, with the assumption that some psychotic activity and perverse behaviors become irreversibly established only by the end of adolescence. We also thought that a more precise understanding of the contribution of the period of adolescence to normal and pathological development and of the meaning of adolescent psychopathology could enable us to offer the adolescent a way of altering the direction of his development so that his life by the end of adolescence and during adulthood might be determined by nonpathological factors.

The Clinical Study

It was becoming clear to us that something beyond the attack on or destruction of the body needed to be understood if we were to make sense of other manifestations of serious psychopathology during adolescence. Some of the observations coming from our pilot study, we thought, might be relevant to other pathologies as well, even though we assumed that the different pathologies very likely represented different degrees of severity of disorder. For example, the analysts treating adolescents who had attempted suicide often felt intimidated by these patients and the inherent violence in their pathology and described how their own sense of reality was weakened by these adolescents.

We then undertook a second study, through psychoanalytic treatment, which would include adolescents showing signs of the likelihood of the presence of serious psychopathology—injuring part of the body, homosexuality,[3] compulsive eating and vomiting, drug taking, severe depression, isolation. We ourselves felt that the key to the understanding of their disorders would be in understanding their relationships to their sexually mature bodies, but as yet, we had no clinical evidence to substantiate this. In our pilot study we had excluded adolescents who seemed psychotic (because at the time we assumed we could not treat them psychoanalytically), but the more we saw very disturbed adolescents the more we became convinced that they might be helped by analytic treatment. By now, we also had come to doubt the usefulness of the diagnosis of "psychosis" in adolescence. We felt that these young people must be included now if we were to observe, study, and understand the meaning of the adolescent's relationship to his body and its link with severe pathological manifestations.

Our assumptions for the second study were (1) that a breakdown in development takes place *at the time of puberty*—at the time of physical sexual maturity—among a certain group of adolescents, and (2) that this developmental breakdown manifests itself through the adolescent's relationship to his

3. This view is at odds with the position taken in the American Psychiatric Association's *Diagnostic and Statistical Manual*, 3d ed. (DSM-III).

own body. These simple criteria have been the basis of much discussion among the staff, some of which will become clear in the chapters describing the adolescents' psychoanalytic treatment.

Three types of adolescents, distinguished by the way in which they use the body to express the pathology, would be treated: (1) those who had attempted suicide, (2) those whose relationships were of a perverse nature, as in homosexuality and fetishism, and (3) those whose behavior showed signs of severe disturbance in functioning (psychotic functioning)—that is, whose fantasies distorted their relationship to the outside world; or whose relationships to people were characterized by extreme suspiciousness, accusation, blaming, and violence; or whose fantasies were expressed mainly via the body itself, as in anorexia, bulimia, obesity, or drug taking.

The adolescents accepted for this study were to be between the ages of fifteen and nineteen at the start of treatment, ages that represented our view about the beginning and end of adolescence. We had observed that it is very unusual for adolescents below the age of about fifteen to seek help of their own accord. The decision to seek help might represent the adolescent's beginning ability to experience anxiety about himself, without having to rely on others to experience it for him; it might also represent the adolescent's feeling that he could now be responsible for his own body and emotions. We assumed also that adolescence as a developmental period ends at about the age of twenty-one; this seems to be the time when responses to anxiety become much more predictable, representing a more fixed internal structure and an established relationship to oneself as a sexually mature person. Thus we set the upper age at nineteen, assuming that this would enable us to intervene some time before the psychopathology had become fixed.

It was decided that a maximum of fifteen adolescents would be in psychoanalytic treatment at any one time as part of the study. This number was determined by the financial resources of the Centre for Research and by our awareness that we needed to keep the study small enough so that the extremely difficult problems of treatment could be constantly addressed by the staff in regular weekly clinical discussions. Such a decision also acknowledged, from the outset, the anxieties evoked in the analysts undertaking the treatment of such vulnerable adolescents. The theoretical bases of the treatment issues are discussed in the next chapter.

Moses Laufer

2.

Why Psychoanalytic Treatment for These Adolescents?

The nine adolescents whose treatment is described in part II were offered psychoanalytic help after information obtained during assessment convinced us that a developmental breakdown had taken place. This conviction was not mainly a theoretical formulation but represented the judgment of the diagnostic staff that the current mental state of each of these adolescents was precarious and his vulnerability for the future was extremely severe. In addition, each was assessed as fitting one of the three categories listed in the previous chapter.

The Adolescents

Sam was aged eighteen when he contacted the Centre. Subject to uncontrollable rages at home, he had attacked his parents and broken furniture. He spoke of his contempt and loathing for his parents, which was expressed in shouting, swearing, and taunting as well as in physical attacks. He teased and tormented his pet cat. Beyond this behavior, he also spoke of his fear that he was mad.

Cara was aged sixteen when she telephoned the Centre. She spoke in her first interview of binging and vomiting and of her wish to die. She had made a serious suicide attempt the previous year.

Charles first came to the Centre at sixteen because of his concern about his impotence. He was also acutely self-conscious and often felt deeply rejected. He then contacted another clinic but returned to the Centre for help at age nineteen. By then, he had attempted suicide ten times and was admitted to a hospital after each attempt.

Bill contacted the Centre at age eighteen, soon after discharging himself from the hospital to which he had been admitted following a serious suicide attempt. He was in a very disturbed state, feeling that he was going mad and that he could kill himself. He accepted the interviewer's recommendation that he return to the hospital, with the promise that when he was able to be discharged they would meet again to discuss the possibility of help. During the time Bill was in the hospital, he maintained contact with the interviewer by telephone.

Kevin, aged nineteen when he came, felt that something was physically wrong. He had dizzy spells, said he wanted to die, and once had thrown himself down the subway stairs. He was terrified that he might be homosexual. He had been cutting himself on his face and hands for the previous six months. He also spoke of his history of epilepsy but tried to make light of it. He had little ability to put his terror into words.

Mary first came at sixteen, with her mother. She was anorexic and seemed debilitated; menstruation had stopped. But she did not return for three years, until the age of nineteen. She felt hatred and feared madness. She had taken an axe to her father's study to retrieve a prized possession he had confiscated. She also had physically attacked her mother on a number of occasions.

John, who came when he was eighteen, had tried to kill himself several weeks previously. A year earlier he had tried to cut an artery and at the age of thirteen had tried to suffocate himself with a plastic bag. He had also been cutting himself, on his chest, abdomen, arms, and legs. By the time he came to the Centre, he had almost ceased attending school.

Mark came at age nineteen, accompanied by an older sister and two older brothers. By this time he was barely able to cope. He was afraid to leave the house and could not sleep alone. Before coming to the Centre, he had been referred to a psychiatric hospital, having been diagnosed as suffering from paranoid schizophrenia. In his initial interviews he talked incoherently, checked to make sure that the room was not bugged, and spoke of his puzzlement about people who accused him of being homosexual. He was convinced he was being watched by spies. He had no friends and rarely attended his college classes.

George came at the age of nineteen. For several months he had been attending a day hospital to which he was referred after a breakdown. Previously, he had stayed away from college classes and had contemplated taking a drug overdose. He had told the psychiatrist at the hospital that he did not like his body; although very overweight, he felt too small and thought his forehead was too high. At the Centre he complained that people were looking and laughing at him. He talked of tormenting the family cat and was afraid that he might attack and harm somebody. In the early interviews he brought complex diagrams linking thoughts and feelings to himself by arrows.

The Assessment Period

A characteristic shared by all the adolescents was the feeling of compulsion to behave in certain ways. They felt unable to alter their behavior, and a feeling of being mad or going mad was an integral part of their anxiety. They sought to be free of their mental pain, but usually did not express an acute wish for change when they first came to the Centre. Treatment for them meant the hope that they would not be alone with their pathology. Their vulnerability and anxiety were such that they would have been ready to consider almost any form of treatment that contained a promise of help.

The process of analytic treatment began during the period of assessment (even though the interviewer was not the one who would carry out the treatment). During this phase the interviewer helped the adolescent to acknowledge frightening fears, overwhelming fantasies, shameful wishes, or uncontrollable and incomprehensible behavior. This was the first opportunity for the adolescent to feel that he could talk openly about his mad feelings and that there might now be some hope for him.

By the time psychoanalytic treatment began, the adolescent and the interviewer were able to discuss his urgent need for help, his fears of madness, and his hopelessness. But he was not really aware of the specific nature of psychoanalytic treatment (except for Charles, who had had psychoanalytic treatment at another clinic). Instead, he relied primarily on his trust in the interviewer, on the interviewer's conviction of the severity of the adolescent's present mental state, and on the interviewer's expressed commitment to psychoanalytic treatment as suitable for him.

The initial assessment period varied in duration from a few weeks to several months. In each case the interviewer became convinced that the adolescent was seriously at risk—that there was evidence of the likelihood of another suicide attempt, of a perverse solution of some kind as in homosexuality or fetishism, or of behavior and functioning conveying that his fantasies and fears were seriously distorting his relationships and that his link with the external world was tenuous at best. There were times, of course, when clinical evidence was not available; it then became one of the tasks of the diagnostic meeting (attended by all members of the interviewing staff) to decide whether a serious risk existed and whether psychoanalytic treatment should be discussed with the adolescent. Often, the issue was not whether the adolescent was in serious personal trouble but whether psychoanalysis was the treatment of choice—whether it could reverse the process that was now actively distorting or destroying his development. We also had to try to establish whether the adolescent could make use of psychoanalytic treatment—whether there was evidence that he could take part in the process and in a commitment intended ultimately to reverse and undo the pathology.

When an adolescent came to the Centre, he usually had little if any expectation that asking for help might mean having the choice of psychoanalytic treatment. Although aware that something was wrong in his life, he did not know which treatment might help him. So the process of assessment and the decision about his need for psychoanalytic treatment also meant enabling him to begin to grasp the severity of his problems and their implications for his present and future life. Without the interviewer's commitment to the adolescent's need for psychoanalytic treatment, the adolescent was likely to minimize or deny the severity of the disorder. It was not uncommon for an adolescent to express the belief that nothing could change and that there was little purpose in agreeing to undertake daily treatment. We were aware that his struggle against treatment and his denial of his illness contained his panic in being made aware of his vulnerability. But we also knew that such a denial was an integral part of his pathology inasmuch as it represented his wish to destroy his sexuality. It was therefore essential to keep his present state and future vulnerability in the forefront of the interviews; among other reasons, the adolescent (and at times the parents as well) was often quite ready to adopt an attitude of "wait and see," an attitude that contained the unconscious wish to perpetuate the pathology. However difficult the task of assessment, we knew it did not allow room for error or failure because wrong assessment could affect his whole future.

Before psychoanalytic treatment was discussed, the adolescent had already been made aware of the interviewer's concern about the present and future risk in his life. Although it was essential for the interviewer to discuss and explain the purpose of psychoanalytic treatment and his own reasons for considering it necessary, there was also some evidence available to show the adolescent that risk existed: one or more suicide attempts, severe depression resulting in withdrawal from school or work followed by a feeling of bewilderment or confusion, secret dressing in clothes of the opposite sex, a recent need for hospitalization because of psychoticlike activity or behavior, the inflicting of pain or actual injury on himself or others. Some of these signs of risk had been present in the adolescent's life for some time, but until now he had avoided seeking help either because he had found ways of dismissing the significance of his behavior or because he was too afraid that it might be a sign of madness to discuss its possible meaning.

The Aims of Psychoanalytic Treatment

What is it about the psychoanalytic process that we think is essential for undoing the pathology that damaged the adolescent's relationship to himself and left him vulnerable to severe psychological disorder in later life (Dewald, 1978; M. Laufer, 1978; Ritvo, 1978)? Each of the adolescents described came for help at a time when he either was using his relationships as a vehicle for living out his abnormal sexual fantasies or had become aware that he was at risk of expressing these fantasies in ways that could result in his death by suicide. For the adolescent, a new kind of internal reasoning began when the treatment, through the use of the transference, addressed the constant projections that were distorting his perceptions and emotions and continuing to damage his relationship to himself. Treatment also had to enable the adolescent to acknowledge the violence and destructiveness contained in the developmental breakdown and in his present life.

The daily treatment sessions created a continuity that was itself essential to the process of understanding and change. Once the adolescent was able to get in touch with his pathological development, he could begin to risk experiencing again the (temporary) break with reality that had taken place at the onset of puberty and continued to act as a traumatic warning throughout adolescence. The madness the adolescent felt at puberty had by now been repressed, but it continued to act as a frightening reminder of the power of the breakdown. Reexperiencing the developmental breakdown in the transference could enable him to understand why he had to have the breakdown, and he could then begin to risk reviving his relationship to his body, which he felt compelled to reject or destroy at the time of the breakdown.

An essential characteristic of their pathology is the adolescents' need to maintain the rupture that has taken place with their pasts, a rupture that was acute at the time of puberty, when it was intended to strengthen the unconscious belief that they could maintain a relationship to their fantasized omnipotent image of themselves. Analytic treatment was threatening or even dangerous because it questioned their need to use this rupture defensively. Puberty and adolescence confronted them unconsciously with the reality of their "failed" sexual bodies and their illusory image of themselves as omnipotent, which they could maintain up to the time that they became sexually mature. Before puberty they could maintain the belief that they did not have to be male or female, that they could be omnipotent without being sexual. Physical sexual maturity suddenly shattered this illusion and forced them to acknowledge their bodies as being inadequate and dangerous at the same time. The fantasies they had harbored safely up to the time of puberty now took on a sexual dimension that had to involve the physical body. Their central masturbation fantasy forced them to a sexual answer which sought gratifications that were pregenital and safe but also removed them from the real world. The postpubertal world of sexual male/sexual female, the union of the male and female genitals, and the reality of their own maleness or femaleness shattered their prepubertal illusions.

If the adolescent's breakdown is to be understood and is to have a chance of becoming integrated as part of his history, the possibility must exist for him to risk allowing continuity between his present and past life. Instead of keeping his past isolated, populated by monsters that must never be confronted, the adolescent can begin, as part of his treatment experience, to question what he has done to the memory of his past and to understand his need to distort his experiences and perceptions. This is not an academic exercise; the experience and understanding of the transference enable the adolescent to confront the defensive reasons for the distortions of his relationship to his body in the present and allow him the internal freedom to claim his sexual body as his own rather than as something made up of violence, destructiveness, madness, or thoughts and wishes that perpetuate the attack on his genital sexuality.

Some of the adolescents seemed more ill than others at the beginning of treatment. We were aware during the period of assessment that whatever the aims, treatment might be of only very limited help (Mark, George), but we were convinced that it was important nevertheless to treat and investigate. It was as if the interviewer and later the analyst were confronted with the adolescent's hopelessness and his near-conscious awareness that he had few chances left to do something about his present life. It was as if he had either given up the battle with the existing disorder or was perpetuating it because of the gratification it yielded. Mark and George, for example, realized that their relationships to people and their expectations of themselves had not changed for a long time and that past gratifications had taken on a sexual dimension since puberty and had therefore become more dangerous without actually being altered.

We were aware at the time of assessment that there was a possibility of *developmental foreclosure,* a psychic giving up during adolescence and an acceptance of the pathology as deserved, irreversible, and gratifying. The danger was that the adolescent might come to believe that there was no possibility of a life other than an abnormal one—an established perversion, a psychotic outcome, or a less noticeable pathological solution, as in sadomasochistic relationships, impotence, frigidity, or incapacitating depression.

Nevertheless, analytic treatment was made available to these adolescents. Although we knew the outcomes were doubtful, we also felt that there might be a way, through analytic treatment, to avert crippling pathology. The dilemma was that this could be tried only with the cooperation of the adolescent himself. The battle is really within the adolescent; he may feel that to change now means giving up the only gratifications that belong to him (anal masturbation, transvestism, self-beating, homosexuality) and that, if these are taken away or questioned during treatment, he might be alone, isolated, and even more hopeless. In each of these cases we ourselves did not know whether the solutions the adolescent had found were fixed and irreversible or whether the developmental process of adolescence had not yet been halted.

In summary, in the course of the psychoanalytic treatment of an adolescent who has experienced a developmental breakdown, a number of essential aims can be fulfilled. If they are, they offer the adolescent the possibility of a second chance—of giving up his pathological solutions and becoming less vulnerable to severe mental disorder in his adult life. These aims can be defined as follows:

1. To establish that a developmental breakdown took place at puberty— at the time the body reached physical sexual maturity
2. To enable the adolescent to get in touch with the traumatic quality of his anxiety at the time of his breakdown, which may have included a loss of contact with external reality and a feeling of being mad
3. To understand why he had to have a breakdown at the time of puberty and why the breakdown took the specific form it did
4. To establish that his present pathology represents a psychological deformation or destruction of his sexual body
5. To enable the adolescent to revive his relationship to his sexual body and to allow for the active integration of his mature genitals as part of his image of himself as a male (or a female)
6. To establish or reestablish a continuity with his own prepubertal past and to remove the power of the distortions of the past

Resistances to Psychoanalytic Treatment

Some of the adolescents readily accepted the interviewer's recommendation of psychoanalytic treatment, but others needed an extended period of time to decide what to do. In addition to their feeling that accepting the need for such treatment might be equivalent to accepting the "fact" that they were mad, some of the adolescents were discouraged from agreeing to this help by the Centre's requirement that their parents had to be interviewed before treatment began in order to inform them of our recommendation of psychoanalytic

treatment and to convey the seriousness with which we viewed the adolescent's present life.

Some had earlier described their parents as being in some way responsible for their present crisis and feeling of failure. It became clear to us, however, that to respond to such a view as if it were totally accurate would be to confirm the adolescent's feeling that he was being persecuted, maltreated, or seduced. This, in itself, would have been a serious error during the assessment period because it could have perpetuated the adolescent's long-standing belief that he himself had little responsibility for his present crisis or that he was simply expressing, via his pathology, what he believed his parents had always wanted—a damaged, castrated, nonsexual child rather than a potent, sexual adult. The battle of "who is to blame?" unconsciously carried with it the fundamental issue of "to whom does my sexual body belong?"—itself an arena for living out violent, sadistic, punishing fantasies of union or destruction. Often this view had to be challenged before treatment could begin. Some adolescents did not want the interviewer to meet with their parents, and this issue sometimes required considerable discussion to avoid jeopardizing the undertaking of treatment.

It was not uncommon for parents to oppose a form of treatment that would expect the adolescent to attend five days each week and would probably continue for two to five years. This prospect frightened some parents, and we could work with their fear. But at times the parents' doubts, or their more active resistance to their child's treatment, contained their belief that they would be blamed by the Centre for his present mental state. Further, some parents feared that their own psychological problems might come under scrutiny or judgment, especially if there was a past history of mental disorder. Other parents remained doubtful or openly in opposition to the Centre's recommendation about treatment, but said they would not actively stand in the way.

Additional resistance to treatment sometimes came from professional people who had contact with the adolescent or his family. Although this did create difficulties, it did not cause us to reverse our decision to make treatment available.

The Framework for Treatment

The nine adolescents who are presented here came for help when they were in acute trouble. Some could barely function without active care, some were at risk of suicide, and others were behaving in odd and often uncontrollable ways. It was essential not to deny their vulnerability but rather to convey that

we were aware of it and that we had to plan for the possible consequences during treatment. It was mainly because of this need that the interviewer discussed with each adolescent and his parents various arrangements that might have to be made at the start or during the period of treatment.

The framework for treatment acknowledges the many difficulties that are *inevitably* encountered with the development of the transference and especially when the developmental breakdown becomes part of the experience of the transference. The framework does not itself help us understand the meaning of the adolescent's present disorder, but it can be an important ally during treatment. It is essential that this framework be addressed *before* treatment begins and the transference relationship becomes an important component. The adolescent and his parents must understand that certain arrangements are required as part of the Centre's recognition that the adolescent is at risk or ill and that the analyst's commitment to helping him work toward change can be carried out only within a certain context.

The framework for the treatment may have to include some or all of the following: whether the adolescent can attend school or go to work and, if not, how he will spend his day; where he will live; the need for an adolescent who has attempted suicide or is at risk to agree that he will not live alone, and for his parents to agree that he will not be left alone for any length of time; if the adolescent is in the hospital or has to be admitted, an agreement with the hospital that he can be discharged only with the prior approval of the analyst carrying out the treatment.

Discussing these arrangements with the adolescent and his parents has another important meaning. It conveys to the adolescent that the analyst is not hesitant to acknowledge the presence or risk of illness and is not frightened by the problems or crises that will certainly arise during treatment. It defines the analyst's attitude toward the adolescent and toward the undoing of his breakdown, recognizing from the start that treatment can easily be jeopardized.

Doubts about Treating Adolescents by Psychoanalysis

We were aware from the beginning of the study of the many opinions, including doubts and hesitations, about the suitability of psychoanalytic treatment for adolescents. One concern is that a treatment that expects attendance five days each week for two to five years may encourage a regressive relationship to the analyst that will perpetuate or strengthen the psychopathology rather than help undo it. Another is that treatment which makes such a demand and encourages such a regressive or passive relationship during adolescence is

itself contrary to helping the adolescent meet the age-appropriate social and psychological demands of that developmental period.

Our view has been that these doubts are mainly unwarranted. We believe that it is just such a controlled regressive relationship, experienced and understood within the transference, that can ensure that the pathology is undone or, at least, that its destructive potential is removed or lessened. The malignant force of the developmental breakdown that took place at puberty, a force given added power by the rupture with the past resulting from this breakdown, can be removed or lessened only when the adolescent can re-experience the breakdown within the transference. The process of psychoanalytic treatment—that is, daily sessions over an extended period of time; a constant understanding of the breakdown as experienced and revived within the transference; keeping the pathology and its meaning in the forefront of the adolescent's life; constantly confronting the meaning and the history of the pathology which is now contained in and gratified by the living out of the central masturbation fantasy—creates the chance of reversing the pathology. Not to undertake psychoanalytic treatment of such vulnerable adolescents is a chance lost and would forgo the possibility of initiating a process that could enable them to come into touch with the specific meanings of the existing pathology. Further, it would leave them open to more severe and crippling pathology in early adulthood.

The issue of psychoanalytic treatment for the adolescent should be related, then, to the problems of *selection for treatment*. We would say that such treatment should be limited to adolescents who have experienced a developmental breakdown rather than be considered suitable for a range of lesser crises. Special care must therefore be taken during the period of assessment to establish the severity of the present disorder, whether a developmental breakdown took place at puberty (even though its force may become manifest only later in adolescence), and whether the adolescent can acknowledge the presence of risk to his life or the possibility of more severe mental disorder. The clinical implications of what has been described here are discussed in part II.

II.
The Clinical Studies

Ronald Baker

3.

Sam: An Adolescent with Necrophilic Fantasies

Sam, a handsome, bespectacled young man, was eighteen when he was advised to come because of uncontrollable rages, which took the form of denigratory attacks on his parents that very quickly led to his smashing up furniture and other household objects. He showed no remorse for this behavior, and his parents put no pressure on him to repair the damage or replace the items he had destroyed; on the contrary, the father made good the breakages. This was an essential feature of the outbursts. At the time of his referral, Sam's contempt and loathing for his parents were absolute. He never attacked them physically, but he endlessly provoked them by shouting, swearing, nagging, taunting, and baiting them, so that they were at the end of their tether when they sought help for him. Deterioration had occurred over the previous six months, which Sam was later to relate to his feelings of humiliation and panic when he was unable to achieve erection in his first attempt at sexual intercourse.

Although the parents knew that there was something seriously wrong with Sam, it was evident that they had avoided seeking help for a very long time. Indeed, they had made considerable allowances for their son's disturbing behavior; the extent to which they were prepared to accommodate it without introducing boundaries for him was itself grossly pathological. For instance, the fact that he was never required to make any reparation for the damage he caused denied him some structure in his environment. Had this structure been present, it would presumably have reduced his fear of madness.

The father, a scientist, and the mother, a teacher, were a well-established middle-class couple. Sam was the younger, by six years, of their two children; their daughter was a qualified architect. Despite the parents' intelligence and articulateness, it was never quite possible to get a good account of Sam's early history. So far as we know he was a normal full-term baby but was not breast-fed. The mother had had no infant losses or miscarriages. It was not possible to ascertain whether she was depressed or disturbed during Sam's early months. In short, the mother could provide only sparse information about his early development, and that quite defensively.

When Sam was eight months old his mother was hospitalized for several months with osteomyelitis of her arm. During this time Sam was looked after by his maternal grandmother and also attended a nursery. For some time after she was released, the mother was unable to hold or carry him. She described herself as completely devoted to him at this time and emphasized her deep distress at having to leave him because of her illness. For her the separation was "like life and death," so much so that she eventually discharged herself from the hospital against medical advice, but agreed that Sam would continue to spend some time in a day nursery to ensure that she would not injure herself by picking him up. During his second year the family moved abroad; again he was cared for by others, this time while his mother worked. He was so distraught by this, however, that she soon stopped work so she could look after him during the day. Sam recalled having "hated" his mother for leaving him. He deeply resented his parents' closeness to each other from as far back as he could remember. The same obtains to this day.

He had a memory from about age six of his father's "strapping" him as a punishment for masturbating, but the details of this were vague. When he was seven his paternal grandfather died—a very traumatic event in his life. He recalled his shock that somebody close to him could die, and he reported an almost delusional early notion that "Jews do not die—only the others," which was shattered by his grandfather's death. The treatment took place under a cloud of dread that his parents or his analyst would die. This was an interesting contrast to his excited preoccupation with just these wishes and fantasies—a matter on which I will elaborate later.

He remembered with sadistic pleasure how at about the age of eight he had systematically pulled out the fur of his grandmother's cat. His later obsession was his need to torture his dog by strangling it or taunting it. He often locked the dog in a wardrobe and enjoyed hearing it growl. Recently, he had put the dog in a sleeping bag and swung it around repeatedly. He also admitted having masturbated against the dog. Many of these events occurred regularly throughout adolescence.

As Sam approached his twelfth birthday his already difficult relationship with his mother was further strained by her preoccupation with his schoolwork, particularly mathematics. Sam described how she forced him to learn and insisted that he not go to sleep until he had finished his homework. Sam remembered these events with consummate anger. It was, however, in the years that followed, when he was eleven to fourteen, that the drama of his relationship with his mother truly unfolded with lasting consequences.

It is not known whether the mother had a formal psychotic illness in these years or was simply severely hysterical, but it is extremely likely that her behavior was not just Sam's imagination. What is not certain is the extent to which he may have provoked it; certainly he was both frightened and excited by it, and, as we shall see later, it was very important for him to try to reestablish it in the transference, with me representing his mother "going mad."

Sam described these episodes as his mother's "fits." Following some provocation, or sometimes for no apparent reason, she would begin to scream and shout and then fall to the floor. Father would restrain her physically and threaten to call the doctor. Sometimes she would run out of the house with Sam and his father in pursuit. But Sam's prevailing image was of his mother lying on her back on the floor moaning deliriously. When this led to her locking herself in the bathroom, falling to the floor with a thump, and thereafter being silent and unresponsive to Sam's enquiries, he fantasied that she was dead. It seemed, too, that she was playing dead. On occasion he actually went to school not knowing the sitution while she remained silent in the locked bathroom. Sam reported that during one such "fit" his mother had held him down and spat into his mouth in retaliation for Sam's having spat at her. It is of interest that when Sam later reminded his mother of these "fits" she insisted that they had never occurred, to the dismay of both Sam and his father.

In the three years prior to his seeking help at the Centre, Sam was already deeply disturbed in his sexual development. He was frankly paranoid about girls, who he claimed mocked or ridiculed him for his impotence, a matter that was confirmed dramatically in his first sexual encounter. However, a private sexual life found expression during this time in his tendency to run naked through the streets after dark, both wishing and fearing to be seen. He also entered women's lavatories, where he masturbated, leaving his semen on the floor. Furthermore, he wandered unclothed through neighbors' gardens at night, peeping through their curtains. He related these matters to me with a mixture of excitement and self-disgust.

Although he had done reasonably well at school, Sam felt at a disadvantage when comparing himself with those of his contemporaries who had succeeded in gaining university places. In this regard he was narcissistically wounded. At another level, however, he was deeply tied to his parents, and after some months of analysis I was rather convinced that his nonnegotiation of a university place was in the service of his need to remain at home.

When Sam began his analysis he had few friends. There had been one brief friendship with a boy of his own age when he was fifteen. The two had indulged in mutual masturbation, something Sam was deeply ashamed of and wanted to forget. It was apparent he had only superficial friendships with his peers, always feeling that he was "odd" or "different," invariably expecting to be rejected or ridiculed, but at the same time anxious to prove himself sexually with a girl.

The Analysis

The analysis began on a quiet note. Sam, who was brought to each session by his father, used this to disown responsibility for both his attendance and his problems. After some three months of treatment, I interpreted Sam's collusion in the process of his being infantilized by his doting father. Although this was greeted with a burst of anger, the affect was not maintained, and Sam soon returned to his dull defensive posture. During this opening phase I recorded my own feelings of boredom in response to the low-key affects Sam revealed. This was in spite of a build-up of highly personalized and by no means uninteresting "material." In this phase Sam tried to give up treatment, often with the encouragement of his parents. He also monitored my affects very carefully to try to find something that he could then claim justified his wish to terminate—for example, evidence that I did not like him. After the first vacation break from treatment, however, Sam seemed suddenly to be "in analysis" with extreme involvement and immediate technical difficulties.

With the falling away of his initial resistance, Sam was enabled to share the details of his sexual life. More ominously, he began to reveal a catalog of sadistic interests and fantasies, to which he masturbated. Gruesome murders on television gratified him. Anything to do with death, dying, or the macabre thrilled him. Tales of torture, rape, concentration camps, and sexual murders filled him with excitement. He wished he could have found the corpse of one of the Yorkshire Ripper's victims so he could have sex with it. These statements were accompanied by a rich mixture of embarrassment and excitement, which began to pervade every moment of the treatment. Although the meaning of all this was not immediately clear, it was nevertheless now obvious that Sam depended on his object's suffering or death for his own feeling that his penis was alive (excited).

So emerged Sam's necrophilic fantasies, which at times related to his mother, whose breasts and "slit" (as he contemptuously called her genitals) fascinated him. He reported a dream in which she was dead on a mortuary slab and he was having intercourse with her. In another dream he was strangling her, a transparent bag over her head, with her teeth becoming a vampire's fangs as she died. In yet another dream she was dancing naked before him and she had a penis. Once he dreamed that she had two penises. In his everyday life, he savagely attacked her verbally at home, triumphantly ridiculing her, calling her a bitch, cow, cunt, shit, pig, and so on. This alarming behavior made me anxious that were he to suffer a sexual humiliation by a girl there was a distinct possibility of murder and the acting out of the necrophilic fantasy.

On one level this loathing of his mother's body covered his fear that he might be homosexual, but except for the episode of mutual masturbation with another boy when he was fifteen, he vehemently denied any such interest. Later, however, he revealed wishes to be tickled and hugged by his father (who had bathed him until he was thirteen), as well as curiosity about homosexuals and what they did. He had a compelling interest in a black man at work, whom he hated, yet envied for his supposed sexual potency. His masturbation fantasies were of dead girls over whom he was triumphing, denigrating the "slit" that disgusted him but also terrified him, as did his own feelings of impotence and castration. He had a vagina dentata fantasy of devastating intensity. He was confused, perhaps even deluded, about his sexual identity, at times being uncertain whether or not he had a penis.

His need for control and his tenuous hold on reality could be surmised from his relationship with his feces. He enjoyed treating his parents "like shit" and worried that other people might see him as "a shit." He manipulated his column of feces skillfully, giving himself masturbatory pleasure and a feeling of power, delaying defecation, and eventually passing a stool into a tissue, smelling it, feeling it, and wrapping it up before going to the lavatory with it. He volunteered, "I don't eat it, if that's what you're thinking." He expressed dismay and shame at the extent to which he was not in control of his own body and especially his compulsion to finger his anus. His anus seemed to him to control his finger, so that sometimes he awoke in the morning with his finger there. This is not to say, however, that he was attempting to disown the compulsion to masturbate anally; indeed, he had told his parents about it, hoping for reassurance that he was not abnormal. This curious sharing of intimate aspects of his personal and inner life was a recurring feature of his relationship with them. There is, however, ample evidence that both parents readily colluded in this and possibly even invited it. For instance, Sam was able more than once to get his mother to inspect his anus by complaining that it was itching. As a late adolescent he evoked cuddles from her when she came to comfort him in the privacy of his bedroom.

As noted earlier, I was initially bored by this dull, angry boy who talked "at" me and did not hear my interventions. This put me in touch, through my countertransference, with the part of Sam that felt dead to him. I could begin to appreciate Sam's inner feelings of deadness by seeing my own boredom as a way in which Sam could communicate this deadness to me.

Just before my first vacation of the analysis, Sam's violent feelings toward me surfaced. He had previously overcome some resistance, with my help, and had reported details of his private sexual world. I had indicated my awareness of how courageous he had been to risk this. He reacted with acute paranoia and contempt. He experienced me, quite concretely, as hating, mocking, laughing at, and ridiculing him, and was deeply distressed. This never abated over the five years of analysis that followed. I became the mother who humiliated him for his impotence, and no manner of interpretive intervention, transference or otherwise, could quell his resentment and rage. My boredom had passed—now I was frightened. His rage was explicit, and he threatened to "smash up" my consulting room. After some weeks I introduced a parameter: "If you smash up here, I will suspend the treatment." This remained a bone of contention as he bitterly complained, "My parents let me get away with it but you won't," with an incredulity reflecting his omnipotent feeling that he should be allowed to do whatever he wanted.

My anxiety about his aggression increased when murderous feelings emerged. In this context he referred angrily to "the other kids" I saw during the holidays, which I took to mean my own children. I was therefore relieved when I relocated my practice from an office in my own home to a private consulting room, where, for the first time, I could conduct the analysis with some small degree of comfort.

My reports of this period of treatment mention how Sam "snarled" and "growled" at me. Once I recorded that he "barked" something at me. Thus I became aware of having unconsciously identified the dog in him, and once again my countertransference had helped me locate what he felt he was being treated like in his inner world. In the transference, his cruel and relentless hatred, mocking, disgust with me, wish to shit on me, contempt, and denigration clearly represented his attack on his mother, aimed at triumphing over her, seeing her break down, go mad, feel castrated and helpless. And this corresponded clearly to his fantasy of the dead girl. Hoping to achieve fulfillment of the necrophilic fantasy, he came to sessions in a state of excited sexual expectation.

On the other hand his dependency on me deepened dramatically, forcing him painfully to realize that he needed me—also, of course, representing the mother. The end of sessions became unbearable, holidays catastrophic. He was palpably anguished when I indicated the end of a session, and frequently exquisite feelings of rejection and paranoid convictions of my hatred and contempt for him emerged. He also became increasingly dismayed by my putting him in touch with his underlying wishes to be loved, admired, and even held by me. Significantly, the analysis soon exposed his underlying terror that his mother might tumble to the needy feelings underlying his hatred—namely, his wish for permanent union with her, about which he felt deeply ashamed and humiliated, and which was undeniably echoed in the transference. Even more terrifying to him was the possibility that she might respond positively to his needs, thus re-creating the incestuous union that he so dreaded and that was so palpably present by implication in the transference. His struggle to maintain an incest barrier of sufficient strength to conceal from his mother his blatant sexual wishes toward her and, more important, his underlying wishes for a permanent merger with her became obvious. Were these to be revealed she would become aware of the meaning of his attempts to humiliate her—namely, that they were a cover for his dependence on her. All this was patently clear in the developing transference.

He began to see that he hated his mother for leaving him as a baby and recalled his screaming fits, which did not deter her. So too he could approach the deeper feeling that she had hated him—represented by her leaving him. At such times he experienced himself as dead, repeated with me now in the transference through provocations to get me to talk, to attack him, to react, responses that he hoped would make him feel "alive," particularly sexually alive. This is less of a paradox than it at first appears, since if he could leave a session feeling "aroused" or "alive," the object at risk outside—that is, the girl representing his mother whom he might murder—was temporarily protected.

This was exemplified in Sam's own description of the analysis: "You suck me in here like a piece of shit, then you push me out and I feel flushed away, got rid of, hated like a dead shit." Here we can see the relationship between his anus and the column of feces and how it was enacted in the transference, especially his attempt to assume control over the abandoning analyst who makes him feel dead by attempting a reversal of roles.

Sam would have dearly loved to realize his wish for gratification— namely, to leave me knowing that I felt dead, useless, a shit, so that he could remain unaware of his underlying feelings of envy and admiration, which filled him with despair and self-hatred. Thus, despite his endless resolve,

"I'm going to make you suffer," a distinct pattern was established and clarified—namely, that when he left the session frustrated by not having succeeded in making me "dead," he acted out by metaphorically murdering his mother at home.

Throughout the analysis Sam was obsessed by thoughts that I was interested in his bottom and penis, so much so that he avoided arriving on time for sessions and thus obviated having to walk ahead of me to the consulting room. He had to check his fly repeatedly, and he kept his coat buttoned up when he was on the couch, so that I could not see his chest. In time, this delusional projection of his sexual preoccupations began to wear thin, and for the first time he assumed a grudging ownership and understanding of them. Technically, this posed a considerable problem since, on the one hand, if he saw me as accepting him, I was a receptacle for his projections and therefore disgusting, whereas if, on the other hand, he felt rejected by me, this surely meant that I hated him, was disgusted by him, and so on. The notion of me as a professional person trying to help him was not one he could integrate; thus, a treatment alliance of any real moment was conspicuously absent.

There were, however, slight shifts. He was eventually able to acknowledge positive feelings toward me, particularly wishes to be kissed, hugged, touched, and so on, in response to which he was consumed with self-loathing. Apropos of this, his anal masturbation was interpreted as reflecting his wish to merge with me, representing the parental couple and Sam in a state of permanent nonseparation. This found unexpected confirmation when he revealed his virtually full-time, compulsive anal masturbation between sessions, on weekends, and especially during breaks. Even within the sessions he experienced me as a fecal penis in his anus, with which he felt merged and comfortable—but when the session ended he experienced me as having withdrawn from him, and his only recourse was to use his finger as a substitute.

As the foregoing description suggests, Sam was not easy to like. He experienced my sympathetic responses as a threat, and he reacted in a deeply paranoid way to anything that suggested my interest in him. It was always essential for me to monitor my countertransference very closely. Early in the treatment, I needed to remind myself continually of how ill he was. Eventually my heightened awareness of the malignant and devious ways in which he attempted to enlist my collusion in his destructive attacks on the treatment, and of myself as representing his mother, to whom he was so deeply and primitively attached, served me well in helping me to survive these attacks.

With regard to his sexual relationships with girls, he was impotent and deeply fearful of their genitals. He often attempted sexual relationships, however, although he always failed. He could be mildly excited while the girl remained clothed and did not experience the vagina dentata fantasy, but when the girl's clothes were removed he was paralyzed with anxiety. Once he skillfully persuaded a girl to suck his penis, and she did so until she was exhausted while he remained without an erection. He felt triumphant over her, contemptuous of what she had done, and yet dismayed by his impotence. His image of her genitals was clearly verbalized as an anus, and as he fingered her he had experienced himself as being "in her shit." Paradoxically, he also used his tongue to explore her vagina. He volunteered his terror that he would lose his penis and she would gain it. He was also fully convinced that his sexual exploration of her would result in his discovery of her penis. Ominously, at the back of his mind remained the most worrying fear that a girl would humiliate him for being impotent and that in an out-of-control rage he would murder her.

A Clinical Session

Some clinical material from a session is now presented to substantiate the foregoing generally descriptive account and, particularly, to follow some of the transference manifestations in detail. For this purpose I have chosen a session that is fairly typical in the sense that it is the sort of session to which I had become accustomed. I have deliberately attempted to preserve the repetitive quality of Sam's remorselessly attacking pressure on me, so that the reader can share my feeling of being "hammered" by this.

The central feature of the analysis at this juncture was Sam's relentless obsession with wishes to destroy the hated analyst. This was expressed openly and consistently with associated excitement and anticipated triumph. The possibility that he might achieve such a "victory" was sufficient to consume him with denigratory attacking impulses and provocative utterances. Interpretations of these observations seemed to fall on deaf ears, as if he could not bear to be touched by the analyst's endeavor to work with him. In time, however, he experienced his failure to drive the analyst mad as a further humiliation; he saw this as the analyst's being stronger and having succeeded over him, with consequential fears that he would be overwhelmed by dependent feelings. The notion that his derision and contempt for the analyst, representing a caring or surviving mother, were based on envious feelings was interpreted as a defense against feelings of emptiness and loss. He provided some acknowledgment of the correctness of this interpretation but without an enduring response or evidence of working through.

So far as being able to ally himself with what might be termed the constructive aims of analysis, Sam was singularly unable to cooperate. To him this would have meant surrender, with all its implications. Thus, his conscientiousness in attending did not, in my view, reflect the existence of a treatment alliance. On the contrary, it had a clear addictive quality, much more akin to a transference perversion.

The session reported below occurred in a week leading up to a long holiday weekend. It was preceded by a session in which he had reported that he had seen me in the street the previous day and reacted with "shock." He said, "It's as if you are alive; it's unbearable for me to have such a thought. I want you to be dead. I'm only safe when you are dead; that's why when I leave here I have to stick my finger up my arse and imagine that you are trapped up there, like a piece of shit, so that I can be in complete control of you. Ugh." This was followed by mounting and murderous rage, which was interpreted as his attempt to reverse his own feelings of deadness on seeing me alive after a session; that is, my being alive impinged on his fantasy that he had left a session with me "dead" inside his anus, and he now had to reestablish his aliveness by trying to make me feel that I was dead. This linked with times when he experienced his screams as not being heard by his mother when she left him to go out, times when he experienced himself and indeed his mother as dead. The reconstruction was that at the time he was enabled to experience a triumphant sense of aliveness through manipulation of his column of feces, into which he could project his feelings of deadness and so overcome them. This was reenacted in the necrophilic fantasy in which the dead girl was identified with the feces and which in turn confirmed his aliveness and enabled him to feel safe and intact.

In making this level of interpretation it is necessary, indeed vital, to be in touch with one's own countertransference. The feeling of emptiness, uselessness, and deadness in the face of such a battering is perceived by the analyst not simply as an attack but as the patient's only means of communicating what it feels like to be him (Sam). When presenting material such as this to colleagues the analyst is frequently asked, "How can you stand it?" The answer is that one must be on very good terms with one's own unconscious and countertransference. That is not to say that this is a certain recipe for success; however, it does help both patient and analyst. The reader should be mindful here that the analyst's response is to tell the patient that *he* hears his screams, whereas the patient insists that his mother did not. I would stress here that such patients invite the analyst to provide empathic failures, and the foregoing remarks aim at showing how *not* to oblige the patient by colluding in the process of destroying the analysis.

There is, however, another factor, perhaps a crucial one, which is that

Sam's case was seen in the context of a group support system. The analyst who has the opportunity to share such material with his colleagues has, in my view, a distinct advantage over those who work more or less in isolation with these difficult patients. In the private sector there is some evidence that analysts who work under such duress for one or another reason lose or drop patients when the countertransference becomes unmanageable. The presence of a support group potentially militates against countertransference and transference acting out. It is also of interest to observe this support group and their own individual propensities for transference and countertransference identifications, normal and pathological, with analyst and patient, which fluctuate quite remarkably at different times. This whole area is worthy of a publication in its own right. But it can justly be said that there are moments in the analysis of patients like Sam when the hope, spirit, and enthusiasm for continuing reside solely in the support group. At those times the analyst has to be grateful for their presence. Yet at the end of the day it is the analyst himself who has to have the basic resources if such a treatment is to go forward.

For some time I had taken this hammering from Sam for being alive, and now he continued his attack with snorts of self-disgust for needing me, charges that I was useless and contemptible, wishes to make me suffer, growls and open hatred, empty threats to stop treatment, and above all hopelessness at his "addiction" to me, by now linked by him to his compulsive anal masturbation. For my part I was in some personal difficulties, often feeling distressed and uncomfortable and having to watch my self-protective mechanisms very carefully so as to obviate the possibility of a countertransference acting out. With this background I now report the session.

He growls as he enters the room and makes noises of disgust when he lies on the couch. "Ugh. Hmmmph." He expresses his hatred of me for making him need me and snarls bitterly at me because he feels "dependent": "I keep my job just so that I can come here. Ugh. You disgust me, just sitting there. What bloody use is this? Aren't you going to speak? No answer. How long is this treatment going to last? Why don't you say something? I suppose you just think that I'm trying to get you to talk." Then, after a moment of silence, "I'm just talking to the fucking wall and I can't get up and leave. Ugh. I can make my parents suffer and I bait them all the time but it doesn't work with you. They react. You refuse to. You say that I get sexually excited if I can get you to talk. Ugh. You're not going to give in, like them. I want to make her suffer. You should hear her calling after me, 'Sam, Sam.'" He is now silent for a few minutes.

I interpret his anguish at the forthcoming long weekend break, his pain, his sense of loss, his feeling that I am leaving him alone with his madness and his murderousness. He interrupts me with a snarl of contempt. I go on to tell him that, despite the snarl, we both know that behind it there is a longing for closeness, a wish to possess me, share my life, and especially a wish that I would never leave him, that like his mother I would call him back or run after him when he leaves.

This is based on our mutual awareness of how threatening it is for him to be put in touch with me as an empathic mother who knows he is in pain, but it is par for the course that his initial reaction is to defend himself against integrating it.

He again responds with a snarl and a derisory "ugh." Then, "Why do I listen to such rubbish about the break? You and your weekends. You have a cheek, always taking breaks and not asking me. I have to just take what you give me. Yes, it disgusts me that I want you to consult me first." I now interpret how frightened he is that were I to know the feelings he has for me I will hate him, in the same way that he hates himself for having them. Again a snort in reply. However, in referring to my autonomy and his "needs," he betrays the defensive quality of his attacks on me.

Toward the end of the session I show him the terrible nastiness that consumes him and with which he is compelled to attack me. I suggest that were he to show me other than the nastiness, he would be frightened of how vulnerable he would be, and I put it to him that he is terrified that I will mock him, just as he mocks me when he feels my goodness in looking after him despite his hatefulness. Once again he responds with a shower of derision. "What goodness, what are you talking about, this is bloody ridiculous, coming here for four years like an addict, I just want to shit on you. That's all I want, to make you suffer, like her. I do it at home and get away with it; what drives me mad is that I can't get away with it here.[1] I want to bait you and provoke you. I want you to be dead. Dead. I don't think of you as alive. It disgusts me to see the others [patients]—ugh, and to think of your wife and kids."

I interpret that it is clear that he wants not only to treat me like shit but for me to feel that I am a shit; he also wants me to be a *dead* piece of shit that

---

1. What he "can't get away with" is a reference to the time when he smashed my lavatory bowl by letting the seat fall free into it ("an accident," he pleaded), for which I insisted he take full responsibility and pay, as he grudgingly did. This was also a technical parameter which gave him the opportunity to make reparation, and it was one for which he was able later to express some gratitude. Similarly, I insisted that he make a contribution to his fee commensurate with his income. In this way he was put into the situation of having to acknowledge me as a "new" object and not simply a replica of his parents, a development that contributed to the expansion of his reality testing.

he can possess and control, trapped in his anus, manipulated by him, doing to me what *he* wants, having no autonomy or freedom, like the corpse, the dead girl, and without the possibility of retaliation. He agrees grudgingly with this. "Yes, it disturbs me no end that you are alive. I could murder you. It frightens me to think of it. I'm getting close to smashing up here."

Here I interpret that the problem seems to be that he has gotten to love and need me too much, that this has made him feel vulnerable, like a baby who needs his mother's breast but expects to be rejected and to have his cries unheard by her, simply to be abandoned and left, just as he now feels as we approach the weekend break. It is the end of the session, and he leaves with a sneer of derision and contemptuous denigration.

This session is a good example of the attacks I had to withstand daily. He simply brushed aside my interventions, showing no interest in the genetic roots of his problems, effectively deadening me, my spirit, my enthusiasm. He openly wanted to murder me, so that I could serve his need as a dead object over which he would have complete possession and control and in comparison with whom he would feel alive. It was also evident from this that his provocations were aimed at getting me to behave disgracefully toward him, which would enable him to see me as worthless, in order that he could deal with the envious feelings he experienced acutely when he saw me as having a supply of goodness that he needed. This was amply interpreted, too, with little but derision and denigration in response.

This material illustrates how the denigrated analyst can represent a corpse, which, being both castrated and dead, cannot offer resistance, opposition, or retaliation. This made Sam feel alive by contrast, and it was how the perversion was lived out in the transference.

Concluding Comments

In the foregoing account of an aspect of a very difficult analysis, I have tried to bring the reader into the consulting room. The emphasis of the description was on the transference and countertransference manifestations and the special treatment difficulties that had to be negotiated in order to keep the analysis viable.

In my view these special treatment difficulties were primarily in relation to Sam's virtual incapacity to use his analyst as a "new" object. Thus, what was enacted in the transference echoed his previous experiences with his parents. His typical response was to oppose the analyst's efforts to modify the quality of these feelings as they emerged in the transference, and to this end he fought against accepting and integrating transference interpretations. In short, Sam insisted that the analyst *was* his mother or father, and he suffered major anxieties when his capacity to maintain this notion was threatened— for example, when he was required to make reparation for damage to my offices. The countertransference problems to which this gave rise are amply reported in the clinical material.

The reader is reminded that Sam showed evidence of deep disturbance at various stages of development. For instance, his reactions to separations in infancy and childhood are abundantly clear in the history and were repeated dramatically in the transference. His sadism was manifest even in latency— for example, his methodical pulling out of the fur of a cat and later cruelly tormenting the dog; this, again, found expression in the transference. Then, his sexuality and the wide range of its disturbances at both a fantasy and a reality level—for example, masturbating in women's lavatories, running naked through neighbors' gardens, homosexual conflicts—once again found ways to manifest and express themselves in the relationship with the analyst. Through the psychoanalytic understanding of his compulsive anal masturbation, which subsumed and reflected these various pathological manifestations, it became clear that his central masturbation fantasy contained ingredients that came to the surface in successive stages of development, right up to late adolescence and young adulthood.

It would appear that the big achievement of the analysis was the communication and unmasking of the necrophilic fantasy. In turn this led to uncovering and focusing on the deeper problem of his obsession with anal masturbation. Thus the central masturbation fantasy became and remained a live issue in the transference. The further achievement of the analysis was the analyst's survival in the wake of massive provocation by the patient. I was enabled to do this not least through vigorous monitoring of my countertransference, obviating gross countertransference acting out. With regard to this, it was clear at certain times that Sam actually sought a countertransference acting out by his analyst and consciously strove to evoke it, since this would have meant that the analyst had joined him in and gratified the perverse fantasy.[2]

2. The general subject of necrophilia and necrophilic fantasies is considered comprehensively in Baker (1984), together with a somewhat different version of the clinical material and substantial theoretical and clinical conceptualization.

Marion Burgner

4.

Cara: The Destruction of an Analysis—Treatment of an Adolescent with Bulimic and Vomiting Symptoms

This analysis, which ended prematurely after one year, was of an adolescent girl with incapacitating symptoms of bulimia and vomiting. Cara, aged seventeen years, telephoned the Centre saying she had heard we offered intensive treatment. She expected, in fact demanded, that analysis be offered for her immediately, and such an omnipotent expectation was characteristic of Cara's approach to the world. Instant gratification of wishes was paramount, and it was unthinkable for her to envisage delay, whether imposed by others or by herself. Perhaps the main reasons for the persistence of such peremptory, internal demands for immediate satisfaction lay in her inability to tolerate anxiety or, indeed, any other affect, as well as a hopeless conviction that she was beyond help. Certainly the emotional climate, as it emerged in the transference, was undeniable: within this adolescent there was a clamoring, needy infant who despaired of my capacity to sustain and help her; but there was also a triumphantly sadistic child who felt compelled to destroy what was offered her.

Cara was seen for six assessment interviews by a colleague at the Centre, Dr. A., before she was referred to me for analysis. A slight, extremely thin girl, with frizzy hair and carefully applied layers of makeup, she was provocative and seductive in her dress and dramatic, histrionic, and demanding in the presentation of herself and her problems. Dr. A. found her both irritating and likable and was left feeling very worried—responses that I also experienced during the analysis. Tears rolling down her face, Cara said that she wanted to die and could not rid herself of this idea; the year before, when she was sixteen, she had taken thirty-eight Dramamine tablets. Earlier suicide attempts from latency on were revealed during the analysis. During the assessment, she underplayed the centrality of the addictive binging/vomiting cycle in her life. She and her parents had tried family therapy for some months and dismissed it as useless, as they did her brief treatment by a psychiatrist.

At the time she came to the Centre she was studying for university entrance examinations and had been offered a place at a prestigious art college. During the analysis, she postponed entry to college and held down a boring office job which she aggrandized beyond recognition. She had few friends, and boyfriends usually took her out no more than once; her social life was sterile and repetitive, without enjoyment.

Cara's parents, who had come to England separately from South America in their late teens, met and married when they were both young. She was born some years after the marriage and was their only child. Mother had suffered from depression, probably since Cara's birth if not before, and had become dependent on alcohol and other substances from Cara's eighth year. The mother was an intrusive presence from the time of Cara's first contact with the Centre; father was initially less overtly involved, but later his interference was more subtle and destructive. The parents endeavored to deal with their acute ambivalence toward their daughter by uniting in their attacks on the analyst and on the process of analysis.

Cara adulated her mother, seeing her as attractive and flamboyant, whereas father was viewed as just the opposite—tatty and insignificant. In the interview I had with the parents, I was struck by the discrepancy between them and by their shared acrimony and destructiveness. The mother came in dressed as if for a party, with false hair piled high, long false eyelashes, and heavy makeup, while father, soberly clad, looked thin and careworn. The battle between the parents crackled sporadically in my presence, and it seemed that, in their continuing sadomasochistic onslaught on each other, honors were evenly divided. It also gradually became clear that there were situations of a personal and financial nature in this family that Cara was specifically forbidden to disclose to me. The event the parents seemed to fear most was that their daughter would be seduced away from them by the analyst and that the three of them would no longer be able to share the destructive and incestuous excitement contained in Cara's disturbance. The parents monitored their daughter's every move, forced her on the scales, locked the kitchen so that she could not get at the food, and locked the lavatory to prevent her from vomiting (though then she would vomit secretly into plastic bags). She would flaunt her thin body at them, and they would grab at her protruding bones beseeching her to eat so that menstruation would return. The shared excitement among the three of them was maintained in consistent attack and counterattack.

In my first brief meeting with Cara to discuss practical arrangements about starting analysis she was reasonable, placatingly charming, and careful not to show me the extent of her problems. At the beginning of the analysis, I found her pseudosophistication, her triteness of phrase, and her conventional cleverness rather irritating, although she was nevertheless likable. In fact I do not think I ever quite stopped liking her, although I felt sorely tested as the analysis proceeded. She seemed often to be echoing the way her mother might think and speak rather than have thoughts and feelings of her own, and the mother's presence in the consulting room was palpable right from the start. Cara demurred about using the couch since she wished to see my face and monitor my responses, although she eventually agreed to lie down.

Cara was a very lonely, isolated girl, and it is relevant that the first incident of binging and vomiting occurred when, at the age of sixteen, she felt utterly alone and abandoned by her parents and acquaintances. In the first week of the analysis she said it was predictable that her friends would abandon her because she had nothing to offer them; she spoke of their becoming bored with her as, of course, she feared I would as well. She felt there was no fun in her, and I silently thought that she was right about this—that beneath her dramatic, hysterical façade she was a pathetically bleak and joyless girl. She said she had once had sexual feelings for a boy when she was drunk at a party, and she described how she could have transitory and excited feelings with a boy she might encounter on holiday in the sun. In fact, she was unable to have feelings for a boy, concentrating solely on her own effect on men: "My interest is only in their interest in me," she said.

I shared with Cara my impression that she was so terrified that fun feelings, sexual feelings, and indeed any other feelings might get out of control that she had to curtail *all* feelings; it was only her binging that was allowed free expression, and then she immediately reestablished control by vomiting. This binging/vomiting pattern was an excited focus for her, and it took on a life of its own with the beginning of analysis, seeming to increase in frequency and intensity. Undoubtedly, she hoped to replicate with me the repetitive, annihilating scenes between herself and her parents and to involve me in their shared, mostly unspoken panic that she would eventually kill herself. She was able to talk of how her parents were terrified for her but could not accept my interpretation that the three of them shared a terror of her death. She described how she would greedily eat for an hour until she was full to the top and then, once her parents had left the house, make herself vomit for a further hour. She added that she would continue eating and not bother to vomit were it not for the fact that she would grow very fat.

The binging and vomiting certainly had a number of important psychic meanings for her, however, as we came to understand during the analysis. One such meaning was the concrete way in which Cara experienced her quarreling parents as fixed characters in her internal world whom she continuously tried to attack with her massive intake of food and subsequent expulsive vomiting. Of importance too was Cara's narcissistic conviction that the binging and vomiting were her very own possession, done for herself and on herself. A further psychic determinant was concerned with the feelings of panic and rage she experienced when she felt unwanted and abandoned, whether by the analyst, parents, or acquaintances. When I interpreted, after one weekend break, the rage she expressed with the binge and the ensuing internal calm she sought with the vomiting, Cara responded: "When I am hollow and empty, then I am alone and sometimes quite calm." I could then link this illusory calmness with her extreme vulnerability, her feeling that to accept me as part of her internal world was dangerous since she then exposed herself to abandonment, whereas, if she destroyed me, there was no further loss to be feared, and she would maintain her omnipotence. After the first six weeks of analysis, there was a long weekend break of four days. She talked of "needing my parents to be with me because of their vigilance; otherwise I would stuff and vomit every two hours. It is like bacteria inside me which I cannot control." Plainly, the internalized parents were experienced as consuming her. Equally plainly, she was frightened about the first distinct break and about her capacity to internalize and retain the analyst as a benign object or as somebody to be destroyed.

Cara described herself as always having been given absolutely everything she wanted, but she was unhappy at school, adding that the girls ganged up on her. She volunteered that she had begun to steal when she was about ten. Her stealing was a distinct precursor of the bulimia and vomiting and probably expressed much of her disturbance in prepuberty and early adolescence. She stole consistently from the age of ten until sixteen—possessions from other girls at school, stationery from school, and money from mother. She would amass the articles and buy quantities of makeup with the money; she used little of this but threw it all together in carrier bags in a useless mess. The analogy was plain to see: her envy of what other girls and mother had was enormous, but everything she stole from them was useless; it gave her no pleasure whatsoever. Similarly the food she crammed into herself, whether of gourmet quality or junk food, was equally valueless and was made into a vomited mess. Similarly, too, what I gave her in sessions was experienced as useless and was messed up by her and her parents. But the stealing had another dimension: falsehood and double-dealing were familiar to Cara in terms of family behavior, and any superego introjection that had taken place was of a delinquent parental morality. The entire analysis carried the hallmarks of secrecy and deceit. But the ultimate and pervasive deceit was the parents' omnipotent conviction that, if only their daughter were restored to them from the analyst, they would make her well.

For Cara and her father I was not only invested with the power "to take their baby away," as father phrased it; I was also, in their paranoid world, a powerful analyst who threatened the sexualized relationship compulsively shared by the three of them, and whom they felt compelled to destroy. When she began analysis, Cara was sometimes still bathing with her father, occasionally also with her mother; sometimes she crept into bed between them to watch a late-night film. She remained adamant that this was perfectly natural behavior for a seventeen-year-old, although, describing her father's passionate embraces after she had attempted suicide, she did observe, "I could have been his wife, not his daughter." Cara and her parents were determined to perpetuate the erotic, incestuous ties between them, and they were equally determined that I should not interfere. But there was never really an oedipal rival in Cara's world, only the effect of triangulation; she was sexually number one for father *and* for mother. She characterized herself as "a pawn, as glue between my parents; without me they would fall apart." I added that they were glued together in a closed system where they had no need of others and certainly felt they had no need of me. In effect, for all three of them I came to stand for the external superego who threatened to interfere with their perverse, gratifying relationship.

We came to understand during the analysis that Cara felt able to experience herself as separate from her internalized objects only by destroying them in the compulsive cycle of binging and vomiting. But with her retreat to this polymorphously perverse state, not only were internalized relationships annihilated but her adolescent body was also destroyed. Just as Cara felt herself "addicted" to the binging and vomiting, characterizing it as a "yearning" not to be denied, she often expressed the fear that she would "become addicted" to me, "dependent and never wanting to leave." Similarly, with mother, she often had no sense of separateness—she felt that they lived inside each other's skins, sharing their craziness, addictiveness, and spurious sexuality. When I interpreted her anxiety about being engulfed and swallowed up by her mother, Cara vehemently contradicted me, assuring me that that was what she really wanted—to be engulfed; indeed, this issue of being engulfed or separate was absolutely essential to her disturbance and to the transference. I was experienced both as the desired occupant inside her body as well as its constant persecutor who had robbed her of her sexuality and greedily taken it over for myself. In her quarrels with her mother, the latter would scream at her that she (Cara) would get better only when mother and father were dead. In talking about the possibility of her parents' deaths, Cara said she would never accept it; she felt so close to them that she would simply go on pretending it hadn't happened.

As the first summer break approached, Cara expressed her oppressive fear that she would become so much worse that committal to a psychiatric hospital would be inevitable. Her veiled threat to kill herself became linked with the whole issue of control over me—of her overwhelming feelings of rage that she could not stop me from taking a holiday, from giving up my control of her. She described a book written by a "hippy girl who had to tear herself away from her father," and we talked about the tearing that continually occurred inside and outside herself—her vomiting, whereby she attempted to tear her father out of her and herself away from father, and the excitement of her parents tearing her away from me and each other. She complained that her parents kept constant surveillance over her, both in her flat, where her father was doing repairs at each of the windows in turn so that he constantly looked in on her, and in the local food shops, where she felt that mother, by following her around, had made a public exhibition of her daughter's craziness, drawing attention to all the food she bought. I interpreted how she seemed to have three parts to herself at present: the caring part, the wish to feed and look after herself and everyone inside her; the destructive, murderous part that stuffed herself and everyone inside her; and the controlling part that vomited everything and everybody out but had nonetheless failed to control me. I enlarged on these aspects of herself in terms of the feelings of triumph, envy, rage, and, finally, utter despair.

Cara then spoke of her feeling that I was leaving her to do everything on her own and that she did not trust me to return to her. I interpreted her anxiety about acknowledging her dependence on and need for me, and her response was that this was really the trouble—weekends were very bad; she could not rely on me too much because separations increased her bad feelings and her symptoms. We could then explore her anger as well as her desolation and despair about weekends and holidays. One of the problems, as Cara saw it, was that she would never be able to "wean" herself from me, that she would be dependent on me and addicted to me forever.

The next period of eight months was to see her gradual and systematic destruction of the analysis. In retrospect, I think she could not begin to tolerate having to postpone immediate gratification of her need for me. When we resumed after the summer break, Cara quickly gave me to understand that she was torn between going home and "relaxing" (binging and vomiting) and coming for her session first. She became more overtly denigrating and tormenting, triumphantly seeking to replicate the sadomasochistic battle with her parents, wanting me to be as "servile as mother, obeying my every whim." In the final weeks of the analysis, when she was constantly missing sessions, I understood that Cara was driving past the top of the street, omnipotently looking down the hill at the consulting room where I was available to her for her session, and then continuing on to her flat for her triumphant binge and vomit. Then I could interpret her panic about being lovingly and angrily involved with me and how she had to rush home instead to a passionate involvement with herself and a displaced, destructive onslaught on me. To this Cara brought the fantasy that I sat in my consulting room during her nonattendance, "crying your eyes out," as distraught and terrified for her as her parents were. As I explored this and also mildly disclaimed any such feelings, Cara angrily and crisply retorted that she refused to accept what I was saying: "It can't be so because if it were, there would be no point in my staying away."

There were moments earlier, however, when she could acknowledge her emptiness and desolation. As she said: "The trouble is you are only available for fifty minutes a day, and I need somebody inside me all the time; therefore it has to be myself." The paradox was plain to see: object constancy, in the sense of maintaining an affective relationship with the specific internalized object, was impaired; essentially she could relate to objects only in a functional part-object way. When they were physically present, they satisfied her needs and wishes; when they were no longer there, she was compulsively forced to fall back on her self as the narcissistic object.

As her paranoid feelings in relation to her body and to her internalized objects gained in momentum, the binging and vomiting became even more compulsive, as did the taking of quantities of laxatives, forty tablets at a time. Cara focused on her physical complaints—sweating, hair loss, stomach cramps, swollen legs, fatigue. In our analytic work the focus was on Cara's triumphant collusion with her parents against the analyst and how I had become the main internalized and external object in their shared destructiveness. They fought together as a parental twosome and as a family threesome to bring about the end of analysis and her consequent return to the family.

For the first time since she had begun analysis some six months before, Cara missed a session. The next day she woefully told me that, on the way to a meeting of Anorexics Anonymous, a meeting she had intended to substitute for her analytic session at her parents' suggestion and her own agreement, she had crashed her car into an oncoming car. Cara had often talked in a taunting way about the effectiveness of other treatments, but this was the first time, as least as far as I knew, that she had tried to seek an alternative to analysis. My endeavors to explore the crashing of the car as an anniversary enactment of her previous suicide attempt as well as an expression of her despairing conflict over whom she would destroy and whom she could allow to survive may have helped her temporarily, but she was quick to come back and tell me her father thought I was talking crazy rubbish. She missed another session the next week and returned to tell me analysis was making her worse and she was going to stop. My response was directed to the two occasions when she had missed sessions and had taken drastic action—crashed her car and decided to stop her analysis. Perhaps these two actions were related to her dilemma over whether to keep us intact and working together or to destroy us.

The content of some sessions highlighted not only the denigrating attacks upon the analyst but also the ways in which Cara successfully kept herself from understanding what was happening in her internal world. When I suggested that fantasy and reality sometimes confusingly overlapped, Cara recounted what had happened that day at work when she had told another girl about the scintillating weekend she was going to have, even believing this account herself—about the planned visit of many friends, the fun they would have together, and the mess they would leave behind. I interpreted the sadness and loneliness contained in this fabrication and in her losing me over the weekend, and I took her back to the mess she experienced inside and outside herself. She complained that the men at work treated her like a child despite the enormous effort she made to wear the dressy clothes of a career woman in her thirties and that, notwithstanding these clothes, she failed to feel grown-up. I suggested that she was trying very hard to keep her body like a child's and that the discrepancy between her body and her adult fantasies made her very confused and unhappy. So far so good, but she became angry when I went on to point to the excited sexuality that was palpable in the binging, vomiting, taking laxatives, and defecating—her sexuality was not hidden, only disguised. She attacked me for not making her better, not providing her with somebody special who would love her; instead, she said she simply felt crazy inside her head and grotesque on the outside of her body. Indeed she often felt she was her "parents' crazy baby."

The external situation worsened concurrently with the internal one. She gleefully contributed to horrifying, hysterical scenes between herself and her parents, ensuring that they visited her flat and saw the chaos she created and the bowl containing the vomit from the previous twenty-four hours. She disclosed that the binging and vomiting, occurring two or three times daily, had a sexualized vitality of its own. She would weigh herself before the hour-long binge and afterwards vomit for a similar time into a large bowl, carefully judging whether the amount vomited corresponded to the amount eaten; weighing herself several times during the vomiting, she could stop only when her weight was the same as before the binge. Cara elaborated that when she was at her ideal weight (eighty-four pounds), she felt "fragile and helpless," a person everyone was concerned and caring about, whereas with an extra kilo she felt—delusionally—"oafish and clumsy." She indignantly refuted my comment about her confusion as to whether her body felt masculine or feminine. There was confusion too in the speed with which her feeding switched from pleasure to attack; she aggressively stuffed the food into herself and then scratched and damaged her mouth and the back of her throat in her frenzied efforts to vomit up the food and the objects inside her. While she attacked her body mercilessly, it continued to be experienced as persecutory. Gratification was transitory; the addictive abuse of her body in an attempt to substitute for a relationship invariably failed.

Cara's provocative style of dress was remarked upon at the diagnostic stage. There were occasions when she came to sessions looking like a high-class prostitute. Female attributes (breasts and hips) were an abomination for her; and although she claimed that she wanted "a penis right in there," she could also acknowledge that she was "absolutely terrified of it." She reflected that sex repelled her although in fantasy she yearned for it; and the fantasy was enacted with an amorphous object with which she danced in a light-headed haze after binging and vomiting. Cara herself made the link between giving up masturbating and her binging—"when I stuff, my whole body shakes with excitement." We came to understand that her illusory, though transitory, moment of calm was just after the vomit, when her parents were experienced as outside her and she belonged only to herself—that is, until she allowed their next invasion. And, in vomiting me out, she conducted her analysis outside the sessions; in subjecting me to a relentless discarding, she protected herself against awareness of trust and attachment.

She became increasingly frightened about the damage she was doing to her body, fearing that "my sexual organs will atrophy." But any satisfaction she might have felt in the analysis palled when juxtaposed to "the excitement of my feast"; she left carrier bags full of food in the waiting room, knowing throughout the session that she could mastermind the overwhelmingly superior excitement afterward and that our analytic interaction was a pale shadow of what was to follow when she was alone. She reflected that the trouble was she could not find in herself "a yearning from" the food; she brought herself up short to say she had not meant "yearning" but another word she could not now remember. I interpreted her confusion between *yearning* and *weaning* and how she yearned to be continually at the breast with the accompanying unseparated relationship with the analyst/mother. Her intolerable loneliness and despair, her feeling that it was impossible to share with me what was happening in her inner world, were all consistently explored, but I felt that her closed repetitive system of autoerotic gratification might well prove too powerful an adversary to the analysis.

As the analysis slowly but inexorably ground to a halt with a pattern of increasing nonattendance, she became more frightened at the extent of her involvement with me. She feared she was "falling apart," becoming like a crazy drug addict she had seen begging in a New York street some years before. She was also terrified that her badness would run amok and cause me to disintegrate. At times she barely differentiated herself from me in the possibility of our joint disintegration, which she characterized as tantamount to going crazy. She brought a theme from a futuristic space film in which there was a female monster who beguiled people by allowing them the wish-fulfillment of turning her into whomever they most desired, whereupon the monster retaliated, extracting all the salt from their bodies and turning them into a heap of nothing. This Cara felt she did to me when she stayed away from sessions; she felt that her power and control over me were at stake. As we explored this, I could interpret that something else was also at stake—namely, her terror and envy of my monsterlike power over her—and this brought us to her pervasive wish to be totally dependent on and unseparated from me.

Cara now experienced me as the firmly lodged, persecuting, internalized object, and she could barely bring herself to attend sessions. Finally, when she came for one session in response to yet another letter from me, I told her we had to terminate. I explained that I could not continue on her terms of an illusory analysis characterized by her elective absence from it, although I emphasized my willingness to continue if she came regularly. I carefully interpreted her excited destruction of the analyst during her absences, either in collusion with her parents or in the binging and vomiting sequence, and her excited, fantasied triumphing over me that continued internally. I suggested to Cara that a major characteristic of her analysis and indeed of her relationships was this sadomasochistic emphasis on "beat or be beaten." Although I felt that Cara had been put somewhat in touch with her excited destructiveness in our work together, she had also managed to keep this characteristic split off and encapsulated in her binging/vomiting symptom. Thrice-daily enactments of these primitive fantasies were—at that time, at any rate—far too gratifying in an autoerotic context; the dyadic relationship of analysis was intolerable for her.

It is important to emphasize my countertransference responses during the analysis. In my work with Cara, I was frequently aware of feelings of anger, rage, impotence, guilt, disappointment, responsibility for her disturbance, to name but a few; I was also experiencing some of what she could not and dared not allow herself to feel. If such adolescents remain in analysis long enough, however, it is sometimes possible to continue working with them within the transference so as to facilitate a measure of psychological separateness and, in effect, to repair some of the developmental distortions that have occurred from infancy onward and have culminated in adolescent breakdown. I must also emphasize the recurring doubt I felt about the possibility of successfully treating this adolescent, entrenched as she was in the family environment; it had become clear to me that analysis did not stand much of a chance unless Cara was able to continue to live apart from her parents.

Cara did, however, leave analysis with some awareness that she had not annihilated me, and she accepted inpatient referral to an anorexic unit. After discharging herself from the hospital and taking a holiday, she wrote asking whether she could resume analysis. I was prepared to take her back, but it was decided at the Centre that, given the six months' break, Dr. A. should see her first to explore her current life situation as well as to consider with her the feasibility of further analysis. Cara did not keep the appointment with Dr. A., nor did she respond to the offer of another interview.

She contacted me again nearly two years later, demanding to be seen immediately. She had moved away from her parents and had a boyfriend but wanted inpatient admission at a different hospital to deal with her "habit," which was as strong as ever. Her refrain throughout this interview was on the uselessness of the treatments offered to her so far. She seemed in touch with her own destructiveness toward all therapy but ineluctably compelled to put such destruction into operation. She also struck me then as quite inaccessible to therapeutic help.

Some two years after that, she got in touch with me again and came to see me. Now aged twenty-two, she looked very different from our last meeting. Her weight and appearance were normal, and I learned that menstruation had returned. She was neither attacking nor provocative and stressed that she had specifically returned to see me and that she was no longer suicidal. I had learned at our previous interview that her university studies had failed. She was now working in a responsible job, and her success pleased her a great deal. She had bought her own flat and was living quite apart from her parents. From her account, her mother seemed increasingly disturbed and dependent on alcohol, and the parents were still locked together in their sadistic quarreling. Cara herself, however, seemed somewhat more separate from them; she supposed that the more she stayed out of their lives, "the more they would just have to get on with it and with each other." She spoke of a relationship lasting two years with a young man. They had been good for each other, supplementing each other in many ways, and she was very distressed when this ended. She had recently started a new relationship with a man to whom she felt attached. She had come back to see me and to ask me to resume therapy (not analysis) with her since she still felt compelled to binge and vomit *once* daily. She was now really frightened of how "addicted" she was and worried that her addiction might interfere with this current relationship. I referred her to a colleague for further help, and she started therapy with him.

I have now known Cara over a five-year period, although she was in analysis for only the first year. The central issue in the analysis was the achievement of psychological separateness from the parents, particularly from the mother, and from the analyst in the transference. The pervasive anxiety she experienced at the prospect of becoming separate was dealt with by repetitive attacks upon the internalized objects and upon the body/self. In this perverse solution, the fantasied destruction and revitalization of the object constantly recurred, and she continued to keep the object available as part of her internal world and as an unseparated part of the self. When the analysis ended, the central dilemma—how she was to become psychologically separate from her parents without destroying them and herself as well—appeared unsolved. In her most recent contact with me, it seemed as if she had achieved some measure of separateness from her parents but had remained "addicted" to the binging and vomiting, albeit in a somewhat modified form. It remains to be seen whether she will now allow further treatment to help her.

Donald Campbell

5.

Charles: A Fetishistic Solution

When Charles first came to the Centre at age sixteen, his sexual life reflected his confusion about his gender role identity, his fragmented body image, and his failure to come to grips with the developmental tasks of adolescence. He was either impotent or ejaculated prematurely. Charles's penis, a split-off object that he referred to as "Fred," was experienced primarily as "anesthetized" and occasionally as a weapon that he used to "bang into" a woman or to tease her by withdrawing it when she wanted it. He consciously envied the woman's passive receptive mode, which was linked in his mind to his mother's physical and emotional withdrawal.

Charles, however, came seeking help not because of his precarious masculine identity but because he was acutely aware of himself in groups and felt deeply rejected if he was not always included.

History

Charles was the youngest of four children. By the time he was born, two sisters, eighteen and nineteen years older, had already left home. His youngest sister, Miranda, was seven. After Charles's birth his mother became very depressed and paranoid and has been treated pharmacologically by a psychiatrist ever since. Charles was placed in a day nursery, and Miranda, who was beyond mother's control, was sent to a boarding school for maladjusted children.

His mother's response to what she considered to be masculine in her son was limited and inconsistent; at times she was violent and rejecting and at other times seductive. Charles shared with his mother the belief that his father, who had been repeatedly unfaithful and violent, had left the family during Charles's first year because he was envious of the attention his wife gave their son. Charles rarely saw his father thereafter. Instead of supporting Charles's identification with his father, his mother put Charles in her own place vis-à-vis his father. During father's occasional visits she would tell him of Charles's various misdeeds and father would beat him. The boy always felt that his father wasn't really interested in him and came to see only his mother even after they were divorced. Although frightened and hateful, Charles did not reject his father entirely. He continued to look for a "better father" and recalled repeatedly standing outside the house of a man his mother had been seeing, much to the puzzlement and annoyance of the man's wife.

Mother worked full time and was under a psychiatrist's care throughout Charles's preschool years. Meanwhile, Charles came to rely on friends in his neighborhood. After nursery day care and, later, infant school, Charles would go to a friend's house or to one of the local shops. Although she was able to provide a home, his mother had difficulty perceiving the realities of her son's development. Charles recalled that after mother gave him the front-door key he discovered that he was too short to reach the lock and so waited on the front doorstep until she came home. She was also unpredictably violent, and there appears to have been a sadomasochistic component in their relationship. He remembered how, as a small boy, he would often run out of the house at bedtime, with his mother in apparently good-natured pursuit as he dodged between parked cars. But suddenly she would lose her temper and beat him viciously.

Charles shared a bed with his mother until he went to boarding school and when he came back on holiday until he was fourteen. Although he consistently denied that there was ever any sexual contact, Charles remembered staring at his mother's breasts through her nightdress and feeling teased that he was not allowed to touch them. He felt triumphant over Dad and his peers while at the same time sensing that this wasn't right. Nocturnal enuresis appears to have been the first sign of disturbance in Charles's body image. He wet the bed every night, and mother, who slept with her back to him, woke every morning soaking wet.

Charles developed into a charming, defiant lad who lied, ran away from home, and stole from his mother. By the time he was seven, the local authorities had responded to his frequent shoplifting and breaking-and-entry offenses by placing him under a supervision order and sending him to a long-term boarding school for maladjusted children. At this point his sister, Miranda, returned home.

Charles was miserable at boarding school and tried to run away. The school emphasized discipline, and he found the staff cold, mechanical, and uncaring, except for a female teacher who seemed to like him and talked with him. She was the one from whom he stole. Further signs of disturbance in Charles's body image occurred at boarding school. Feeling helpless and depressed in his new environment, he talked of having engaged in fellatio and mutual masturbation with another boy in the dormitory, who was also a bed wetter. By ten years of age, Charles himself was no longer enuretic.

Although Charles's mother had visited Miranda frequently when she was away, he could recall her coming to see him only once in the seven years he spent at boarding school. And she never remembered his birthday. He felt that she had deserted him and always believed that she preferred his sister.

Charles was lonely and frightened during his holidays at home. As he was still under a supervision order, he paid regular visits to the psychiatrist at the local child guidance clinic each holiday. Charles became so frightened of what he described as his mother's "bizarre" behavior when she returned home from work that he threatened to run away. In fact, he rarely left home, preferring to stay in the living room alone, next to the gas fire, endlessly watching television. He became afraid of going to the lavatory because he thought there were biting monsters in the toilet. This paranoid fantasy, which he reported as occurring only at home, may have been the first sign of a vulnerability to psychotic functioning related to the use and experience of his body. At night he again slept with his mother, while his sister occupied the spare room.

As he entered puberty Charles began showing more serious signs of disturbance in his body image. He became interested in girls and picked them up and dropped them with arrogant indifference. Eventually one of his girlfriends rejected him first and Charles became depressed. He carved her initials on his arm.

Later, at age fourteen, he achieved a certain renown at school by stealing a set of keys which gave him access to a television set and drugs from the nurse's office for after-curfew parties. Eventually the headmaster came to suspect Charles of theft, followed him, and searched him. The following day Charles made his first suicide attempt by taking five Nembutal. He slept deeply for twenty-four hours.

A week later, Charles's mother was admitted to hospital in an acute paranoid schizophrenic state, according to reports. Charles made two more serious suicide attempts in the next six weeks and each time was admitted to hospital in an unconscious or hallucinated state after taking a smorgasbord of tablets, LSD, and alcohol. Expelled from boarding school, he returned home depressed. During the next year at the local high school he was isolated and acutely anxious in any social context. Now living at home, he insisted on, and got, his own room. Probably influenced by his regular contact with a child psychiatrist during holidays from boarding school, Charles told his GP that he wanted to talk to somebody about his problems and was advised to come to the Brent Consultation Centre.

The Centre was impressed by Charles's deep object hunger, the narcissistic orientation of his relationships, and his persecuting superego, as well as his determined motivation and access to affects and internal conflicts. When Charles's defenses of denial, splitting, and projection were interpreted, his arrogant, false-self veneer cracked and he wept. He was referred to a local clinic for analysis when he was seventeen.[1]

Charles's first analysis was interrupted by the unexpected departure of his male analyst, to whom he had become very attached. During the ten months of this analysis Charles made seven suicide attempts and was hospitalized five times. Six weeks into his second analysis, this time with a female analyst, Charles broke off his treatment to visit a former girlfriend in France for a week. He was taken back into analysis but broke off again a month later to visit the same girlfriend for two weeks. Upon his return he was outraged that his analytic place had not been kept. He was referred back to the Brent Consultation Centre and came in a panic about being without an analyst, preferring to see himself as a helpless victim rather than as the one who had terminated his second analysis.

When Charles was nineteen years old, nine months after returning to the Centre, he was offered five-times-weekly analysis with me, his third analyst. The following clinical material is taken from the first three years of an ongoing analysis to show how aspects of Charles's struggle during adolescence to disidentify from his mother and identify with his father appeared in the transference and affected his body image and the use of his penis.

Use of Fantasy

From the beginning Charles talked readily and brought dreams and associations, but his fantasy life had the polymorphous-perverse character of a child's, and it was difficult for me to understand these fantasies in the transference.

During the second week of his analysis Charles reported feeling angry

---

1. When Charles first came to the Centre, the research study had not been organized. Therefore, psychoanalytic treatment could not be offered.

the previous day when he saw another patient come into the waiting room as he was leaving. He then drove over to his sister's, but she was preoccupied with a visiting friend. Charles therefore left and went back to his mother's, where he was living with his girlfriend, Emma. When he arrived, however, Emma's parents were in the living room, and Emma asked if he would mind leaving them alone. Charles went to bed, and Emma and her parents talked until five o'clock in the morning. He thought that Emma lacked warmth and sincerity and that their relationship ought to end. He should be angry, but he couldn't feel any anger.

I pointed out that he had begun by telling me how annoyed he was on finding that someone else had come to see me, that someone else was with his sister, and that Emma's parents were with her. He thought he needed to have somebody just for himself but instead felt that other people were excluding him. Although I did not say so at the time I wondered if seeing the other patient had increased his anxiety about being displaced by someone else— something he felt had happened when his first analyst left, and something he had then done to his second analyst who, in his view, had retaliated in kind. I said that when he felt excluded, as he did after the previous day's session, he saw me as ruthless and wanted to get rid of me and any feelings he had for me.

Charles associated to being inside a beer keg which is rolling down a hill, begins to leak, and explodes. He said, "There is a fist hitting, I put a face to it, it is my father's face. I want to kill him. I take his penis and twist it round. I pull the penis off and eat it, then shit it out, then eat it again, then shit it out. The penis grows and gets bigger and bigger; it becomes two penises and turns me on. I run to hide inside the barrel. The penis looks inside at me as I cower in a corner. Emma . . . wanting to get inside Emma. My tongue inside her vagina goes up till I touch the bones of her nose. I stop her breathing. My tongue comes out in front of her and says, 'Will you?' She says she will, so I let her breathe again. I discover she has the penis inside. I eat the penis again but shit it out and she eats it and now she has it inside again. I often think about wanting to be inside Emma, putting my fingers into her nipples and going inside. Getting inside her belly. Biting her. I would get great pleasure in just biting her."

My first reaction was of feeling overstimulated. Then I wondered if I was being provoked into an exciting, intrusive game, and I felt distinctly wary. I said that he was quite anxious about being supported by me, contained by me, as though I was the leaking beer barrel which he then exploded from inside with his anger. Charles associated to wanting to take something in but not being able to hold it. I said that when he becomes desperate about wanting to get something from me he becomes more aggressive and attacking, but then ends up losing what he has bitten off and swallowed and feels empty again.

Charles immediately remembered visiting his father in Brighton when he was twelve and having an argument that escalated into a fight. His father broke Charles's arm with a blow. "It was something silly; I don't even remember why he was asking me. He just kept asking me if we had an orchestra at my school. I said we didn't have one, but we could get one together because there were enough kids in school who could play musical instruments. He countered by saying that was not what he had asked me. He wanted to know if we had an orchestra. I told him again that we could have one if we wanted to. It went on like this with him asking and me answering. He became furious. Then he hit me and my arm hurt. I ran out of the house and started to hitchhike back to London. I was twelve years old and didn't have any money. On the way I was picked up by a chap in a Rolls-Royce. I didn't know it at first, but he was homosexual. He said he would give me a pound if I masturbated him. Then he said he would give me another pound if I let him masturbate me." Charles went on to say how disgusted and sick he was about this experience at the time but how much he needed the money in order to get back home. He still felt some revulsion in talking about this experience.

I began to make some sense within the transference of his first fantasy. The most persistent image was that of a woman who possessed an anal penis. Charles's search for a penis inside his girlfriend led to his wish to get inside her. There were two aspects of the transference. My reaction of being overstimulated reflected the excitement he felt in thinking about me as the mother with an anal penis. Charles, however, also anticipated my retaliation as his violent father in the transference and associated to a memory of provoking his father's attack and, in this way, identifying with his mother while turning passive into active. I said that I thought he was trying to tell me about being excited during a row with his father, which he had provoked, and then feeling helpless to do anything about his father's attack. This was followed by exciting another man, being able to control that man, and then getting something from him, but only after giving him his penis. I linked this to Charles's fear that he would have to give me his penis if his dependency needs were going to be met. Instead he tried to excite and stimulate me with his fantasies in order to reestablish some control over me. Charles was quiet at this point and then said, almost to himself, "So that's what I was doing. I had no idea." He appeared relieved when he got off the couch to leave.

This material reflects the multilayered transference that was difficult to follow in Charles's analysis. At the conscious level, the father appeared as a violent figure who could be provoked and then controlled, like the man in the Rolls-Royce, by Charles's passive, submissive behavior. This session was typical of Charles's almost daily attempts to seduce me into taking him over or penetrating him with my interpretations, which he tried to stimulate with bizarre fantasies that he referred to as his "free associations." This was understood by me as his attempts to "pervert" the analytic relationship. Responding to the content of his fantasies would have gratified his perverse fantasies. Instead my interpretations focused on the process and the use he was making of his "free associations"; in this way his attempts at pre-oedipal wish fulfillment were kept at the center of the analysis.

I thought Charles's fantasy and memory about provoking his father's attack had been triggered by thoughts about the unhappy departure of his first male analyst as he was beginning again with another male analyst. I did not understand at the time the extent of Charles's fear of being abandoned by me (his mother in the transference), which triggered primitive regressive wishes to get into me and resulted in confusion about his masculine body image and self/object boundaries. This was apparent in the fantasy of the fecal penis and the phallic woman.

Gradually over the months and years that followed, however, the transference experience in the session and the content of his fantasy became clearer. The fantasy represented a displacement of his feeling of being rejected by his mother and uncontained. Charles was plagued by pre-oedipal anxieties of abandonment and lack of containment, whch he defended against with fantasies of getting inside the woman. As a consequence, he was unable to turn away from mother and identify with father, who was seen as threatening violent retaliation.

Later in the transference, Charles attempted to re-create the provocation of his father's retaliation. His violent father's penis was not an object to be internalized but one to which he homosexually submitted (as he did to the man in the Rolls-Royce). Charles, however, did not develop his gender role identity in this direction.

Although there is evidence of homosexual anxiety and castration fears related to a retaliatory oedipal father in the following material, Charles did not search for a penis in a man or surrender his penis to a man. In fact, the incident with the man in the Rolls-Royce was the only homosexual experience of his adolescence. Men were too dangerous to use as objects upon whom he could displace his intrusive wishes. Consequently, Charles's projected oral sadism (the fantasy of eating penises and biting Emma) was directed toward females and triggered his castration anxiety at the hands of a woman. It is to the woman that he submits.

The Motorcycle, Suicide, and Nonpayment of Agreed-upon Contributions

During the first three years of his analysis Charles defended against his castration anxiety by displacing his penis onto his highly valued motorcycle, which was an indispensable extension of his body image. Charles felt "at one with the power" of his motorcycle and loved the "buzz" he got from racing dangerously at high speeds. But the castration threat was enacted during a number of motorcycle accidents. A pattern emerged from these accidents. First, they occurred when Charles was faced with a loss or separation. Second, all of them could have been avoided if he had slowed down and driven with a normal degree of anticipation. Instead, he ignored perceptual warnings and was oblivious to traffic and road conditions. He assumed that others should look out for him. Our analytic work uncovered the excitement he felt when flirting with death by driving at a speed or in a manner that was unsafe. This manic, omnipotent state was sexualized by identifying with a deanimated penis throbbing between his legs. Masturbatory excitement defended against depression and anxiety associated with feelings of being abandoned after sessions, over weekends, or during holidays.

Charles's self-defeating and potentially self-destructive behavior, which was linked to underlying suicidal fantasies and previous suicide attempts, was a central feature of his analysis. The theme of dicing with death dominated his suicide fantasies, which were now unconscious and displaced from overdosing on drugs to pushing at the limits of reality with his motorcycle. The accidents were interpreted as unconscious attempts to kill himself. Charles's suicide fantasies were directly associated with intrusion, and he acknowledged the pleasure he achieved in hitting into things with his motorcycle.

Throughout his analysis there was a repetition of his twisting off my interpretations (his father's penis), swallowing them in apparent agreement, and then shitting them out, thereby showing me that they were dead and useless while he had something better with an idealized woman. Nevertheless, a more positive father emerged in the transference when he brought material that contained his wish to be rescued by me from a phallic woman.

On a Monday six months into his analysis, Charles announced that he wanted to cancel his Friday morning session because of Emma's insistence on driving his motorcycle all night to a holiday resort, without a license and without experience in handling a heavy bike or driving at high speed. Charles planned to sit behind her as the passenger. He coolly dismissed as alarmist my observations of his anxiety about disappointing Emma. Analysis of several previous "accidents" made it clear that he had used his motorcycle as a suicide weapon. I became increasingly alarmed about the danger in this trip and angry that he would put himself in jeopardy again after all the work we had done on his suicidal fantasies. My countertransference feeling was of helplessness to do anything about a woman who had taken him over. I based my interpretation of his anxiety on this feeling, and Charles agreed.

On Tuesday Charles told me that he might be in danger of losing his part-time job. In fact, William, who supervised him and had got him the job in the first place, had been sacked. He associated to his mother's attempt to use him to get social security benefits. Although he had a job and lived in a hostel, she reported that he lived at home and was totally dependent upon her. He remembered tearing up the social security form in a rage, but then said triumphantly, "That's where I get my craftiness." Charles usually supported his mother's attempts to defy authority. In this instance, however, he identified with authority—the sacked father—and tore up his mother's deceitful social security form. But this momentary separation from her appeared to arouse too much anxiety and he again identified with her. Until the defensive use of this wish to identify with his mother and the sexual excitement associated with it was interpreted, I would not be able to contact his anxiety about separation from mother.

At this point I was aware of Charles's identification with a mother who secretly defied authority. I began by interpreting the wish which I felt underlay the anger—the wish to give up responsibility for himself in order to be looked after and cared for by mother, but to achieve this he had to get rid of father. I thought about the way he had "sacked" William when Charles took Emma away from him six months before. Now William was no longer his boss. It was as though he had also sacked me on Monday by brushing aside my interpretations and concern. Charles's symbolic oedipal victory in the transference left him with the excitement that Emma would take over and mother him. It became clear in the next session that this wish formed the basis of his suicide fantasy.

On Wednesday he returned to his dependency on Emma and his anxiety about disappointing her by not meeting her demands. He eventually associated to risk taking as a constant part of his life and recalled being excited by diving because of the risk involved. He then associated having once hit his head on the diving board, which left a scar. When he was able to see that this motorcycle trip was meant to fulfill a suicide fantasy, Charles decided not to drive all night Thursday but to leave after our Friday morning session. Then, on Friday, Charles was able to talk much more directly about his past suicidal wishes: "The important thing about suicide was wanting to be saved, have someone take me in, comfort me, cuddle me, and say it was going to be all right. I knew they were taking me seriously when I woke up with all those machines plugged into me. Then I knew they cared."

From what we knew about the meaning his motorcycle had for Charles, however, it was clear that the price he had to pay for being "taken in" by a woman was to give up his penis to her. Charles's association to his mother's corrupt use of him also reflected his perverse excitement in identifying with an object who delinquently triumphs over a superego authority figure, which I represented in the transference. This defended against his anxiety about being abandoned to a ruthless woman who used him and did not protect him. In the absence of his father (who had been sacked by his mother), Charles was left dependent upon and identified with his mother. This identification with his mother's delinquency was enacted in the transference via his wish to cancel Friday's session and, later, in his refusal to contribute financially to his analysis.

As his dependency upon me increased, so did his anxiety about his motorcycle. Whenever the motorcycle was damaged or malfunctioning, even slightly, he repaired it immediately or borrowed money from his mother to buy a new, more powerful machine. As he said, "I can't stand the feeling of not having something reliable between my legs. And you can take that in more than one way." The cost of repair or repayment of his mother's loan came out of that part of his wages from a nighttime job as a security guard that he normally set aside to contribute to the analysis.

The anger at his father for the pain he had inflicted by rejecting and abandoning him dominated the second and third years of analysis, which were characterized by Charles's bouts of denigration and abusive shouts at me and threats of terminating analysis for my not giving him permission not to pay his contributions. As he often said, "I'll invest in Mother rather than with you where I have nothing to show for it." He was even more furious that I did not argue with him. This was interpreted as frustration of his sadistic attempt to get inside me, to get under my skin, in order to defend against the sense of separateness that was associated with paying me a contribution. When this failed he attempted masochistically to provoke an attack from me (his father in the transference) as he had done with his father in Brighton. Charles's excitement was in the *risk* of castration. Therefore, he needed me to react to his triumph over me and so flaunted his choice of his mother and what she concretely gave him. He saw me as retaliating by threatening his motorcycle, a fetishisticlike object which he could control, which gave him feelings of potency and narcissistic gratification and was, above all, a phallic object provided by his mother.

Charles's giving his mother money he had earmarked for me was multi-determined and was interpreted at a number of levels. Here I will focus only on the withholding of contributions as an identification with a phallic woman who satisfied herself. By not paying his contribution, Charles maintained the fantasy that he didn't need me because he could do the analysis himself. His nonpayment of contributions enacted an aspect of his fetishistic use of me as a part-object that made no demands on him and could be dropped at his convenience.

The analysis proceeded precariously along a thin line between surviving as a transference relationship within which he could remember past depriva-tion of a father with whom he had wanted to identify and being destroyed by his suicidal rage at what he perceived as my real deprivation—my obstinate refusal to orally satisfy his hunger for a reliable penis. Hardly a week went by during the first three years of his analysis in which Charles did not threaten to terminate because I did not tell him how he was doing or what he had achieved. His threats were accompanied by abusive shouting, attempts to bait me with questions, or mocking denigration of my analytic role. There were no con-scious attempts to kill himself during this analysis, but many "accidents" occurred while he was driving his motorcycle, usually in a manic, omnipo-tent state. He narrowly escaped serious injury several times.

Gradually Charles was able to grieve for some of his early deprivation, especially the absence of his father. His stealing, which had defended, in part, against his helplessness and acceptance of his father's limitations, de-creased, reducing his guilt and some of his self-defeating behavior. Charles also began to think about aspects of his father with which he might identify and so, gradually, lessen his identification with his mother. He agreed to meet with his father for the first time since boarding school. As a result of this tentative shift in the balance of his identifications during the third year of analysis, Charles was able to sustain a stable relationship with a woman for the first time, his new girlfriend, Charlotte.

When Charles moved away from his mother, however, his earlier anxie-ties about being abandoned by her were revived and countered by wishes to get inside a woman. As a consequence, he became frightened, unconsciously, of being trapped inside her and losing his separate male identity. His anxiety about castration by a woman increased his desire for me to be a real father to him, not the "as if" father of the transference.

Given the developmental tasks of adolescence, it is not surprising that the transference with an adolescent at times lacks an "as if" quality. The normal adolescent needs and uses real relationships with adults and peers to experiment with. Consequently, he will want to live out earlier conflicts directly with the analyst as a real person, not only as a transference object. Charles regularly complained, "You don't give me anything. You don't tell me you care. You expect me to miss you, feel like your son, but you won't be my father."

Hiding behind a Woman

Three weeks before a Christmas holiday Charles began the Monday session with a dream fragment in which he is in an underground tunnel. The underground train has broken down. Then a girl child star, someone from a television show with a camera crew, is having a birthday, but no one likes her. Charles goes down a hill with Georgian houses on either side to see this girl, but it turns out that she is a boy. She is given a dresser that she has always wanted, with two arms holding a mirror. He sees himself in the mirror and says, "It must be me." He then associates to his mother's dresser, which has a similar mirror, and remembers hiding behind it as a boy.

Charles next said that the previous week, while sitting on his motorcycle near my house after his session, he had seen me with my son. I live on a street with Georgian houses. I first took up his conscious longing to be with me as a son with a father, especially when he felt there was something wrong with his penis (the underground train which has broken down in the tunnel). Then he felt excluded by me. I next linked the unconscious wish to hide his gender identity behind a female (the girl in the dream who hides the fact that she is a boy and his association to hiding behind his mother's dresser) to his disappointment in me, the father, who was never available as a mirror for him. This acting out of his bisexual conflicts appeared as a repetition of his waiting, as a boy, outside his mother's boyfriend's house. Later, Charles waited outside my house after his session, and I linked his looking at my home to his fantasies of intruding into my life. In this way his voyeurism could be analyzed in the transference.

When Charles was faced with a particularly painful separation he often found a woman with whom he could enact his central masturbation fantasy (Laufer, 1976) by presenting himself as a curious but naive boy who was yearning to touch the woman's breasts. As he said, "I seduce the woman to seduce me." Once the woman was stimulated, Charles became passive and aroused by her excitement and activity. This central masturbation fantasy manifested itself in the transference via dreams, free associations, and veiled suicide threats in which damaged, starving, or at-risk aspects of himself were presented in an effort to seduce me into penetrating him with my breast/penis–like interpretations.

First I and then Charles would be identified in the transference with the mother of whom he said, "I wanted her to come alive but she never did." Charles's dilemma was how to stimulate mother's admiration of his penis and, at a deeper level, to get her to respond to his pregenital needs without also arousing her sadism. He compromised by identifying with his image of her as a woman with a penis while hiding his own penis and thus protecting it from mother and father.

Voyeurism and Fear of Engulfment

Before an Easter holiday break, during his third year of analysis, Charles described the elements of his recurrent central masturbation fantasy. "I am in heat at the sight of large breasts changing shape, the nipple sticking out, sticking up. Sexuality has to flow from the woman to me for me to be excited." His castration anxiety then reemerged as he associated to blood on his mother's sheets. He immediately dismissed this image by saying, "The vagina's never been exciting to me, it's smelly. It's like being attracted to a stripper. I like *watching,* but I'm not really excited when I have it. It's the sight of the big breasts that turns me on. It is emblazoned across my face. I feel like a child, a hungry child who wants to be satisified. I have this fantasy now of a woman on top, her big breasts hanging down, and I'm sucking at the nipple, happy. I don't feel like I'm a person. I lick the woman's breasts and put my penis between them. I'm only interested in parts of a woman; she's really irrelevant, like a wooden dolly I can throw away when I'm finished. I might let her masturbate me but that's all. When I leave she's in heat for my penis."

Charles's sexuality revolved around voyeuristic excitement achieved in seeing or fantasizing about large breasts. As he said, "I like watching, but I'm not really excited when I have it." Charles's voyeurism enabled him to defend against his anxiety about being abandoned by getting inside his mother, as we can see in his earlier fantasy of getting in a beer keg. But merging with a woman can be achieved only with the extinction of his separate masculine identity. In fact, Charles imagined himself looking up inside his mother, lighting a match, and "bang." Voyeurism as psychic intrusion reflects his wish to be taken in and the threat of oblivion. He frequently fantasized about his penis being "engulfed by a woman's breasts."

Fetishistic Use of the Object and the Self

How was Charles able to use his penis, and how was this understood in the transference? Charles did not make a homosexual adaptation. Instead he continued to seek out a woman for sexual gratification, but his castration anxiety could not tolerate the sight of a penisless woman. In order to maintain his disavowal of the fact that his mother did not possess a penis, a substitute was created—a fetish.

The fetishist still believes that the woman has a phallus but it is no longer the same as before. The fetish "remains a token of triumph over the threat of castration and a protection against it. It also saves the fetishist from becoming a homosexual, by endowing women with the characteristic which makes them tolerable as sexual objects" (Freud, 1927, p. 154). For Charles, the breast was a visible sign of the woman's hidden penis.[2] He was unaware of the symbolism and the denial of the woman's penisless state when he described one big-breasted girl as being "built like a centurian tank."

Charles's wish to be "engulfed by a woman's breasts" defended against primitive anxieties about abandonment by mother, but put his masculine identity at risk in the enactment of the fantasy.[3] Charles's reliance upon splitting to defend against this conflict was observed in the transference. On the one hand, his affectionate feelings for me were defensively sexualized in order to defend against his anxiety that closeness would lead to engulfment. On the other hand, he often experienced my attention and interpretive work as confirmation of his capacity to excite me, the phallic mother, into gratifying his passive receptive wishes.

2. Freud (1927) maintained that the object chosen as a fetish is associated to the last moment during which the inquisitive boy could still regard the woman as phallic. In this regard I am indebted to my colleague Ronald Baker, who suggested that Charles's choice of large breasts as his fetishistic object may have represented a displacement from the shape of his mother's buttocks, which were turned toward him as they lay in bed together. In any case, the breast was a suitable object for Charles because of his insatiable hunger. The acceptance of the breast in foreplay makes it a convenient disguise for the phallus—an essential requirement for a fetish.

3. The fantasy of his penis "being engulfed by a woman's breasts" was also central to his conscious and unconscious suicide attempts and illustrates the convergence of his pregenital wishes with castration anxieties.

Outside the session, Charles had to maintain a split between his sexual relationships and his libidinal investments. Sex with small-breasted Charlotte, the girl he cared about, was "unexciting" and unfulfilling, whereas he found excitement in a "one-night stand" or a "hit and run" with big-breasted girls. The girls he fancied with big breasts were unsuitable as partners and were immediately rejected after sexual intercourse.

It emerged in the analysis that Charles protected his penis by first converting the woman's engulfing breasts into a fetishistic object which he controlled. Charles always maintained that he was dependent upon the "sexual electricity" of the woman's breasts in order to be sexually excited. A woman's breasts—only those of a woman he did not care about—were experienced as the source of his genital potency. Charles excited the woman until her nipples were erect, and then he withdrew. As she took over the active role in seduction, Charles identified with the fetishistic object and experienced himself as the source of sexual and narcissistic gratification for the woman. After ejaculation Charles was reassured that his penis had survived. The fetish had served its function, and the now denigrated breast/penis could be discarded "like a wooden dolly." In this way Charles compulsively attempted to master the excitement, frustration, and castration anxiety he experienced in his mother's bed.

The exciting and rejecting duality of a fetishistic interaction gradually emerged in the transference. There had been clues in the content and use of his fantasies in sessions, his fetishisticlike use of the motorcycle, and his dismissal of me by refusing to pay his contributions. I was also struck by the contrast between Charles's apparently thinking about my interpretations and his denial that he had any feelings about me or ever thought about me. As far as he was concerned, I was simply dismissed after a session. He had clearly split me off from my words. It was not until Charles reported during a session that he was fantasizing himself masturbating that I could take up his fetishistic use of my words. I was, in the heat of the transference at that moment, the deanimated fetishistic object which was powerful and exciting.

The projected sadistic, depersonalizing aspect of the fetish, also represented by my words, was a source of identification as well, however. I was often flooded with dreams and free associations, as in the first session I reported, which were intended to excite me when Charles reversed the fetishistic roles. After stimulating my interest, he could use my interpretations in a masturbatory way and then drop me "like a wooden dolly."

Occasionally Charles could see that he himself was the rejected wooden dolly—an object that had been viewed as exciting and then attacked and discarded. But when he was feeling abandoned by me or anxious about wanting to get inside me, he again identified with the exciting fetish and turned me into the rejected wooden dolly.

Vicissitudes of the Transference

Charles's fears of being abandoned by his depressed and, at times, schizophrenic mother motivated a fantasy of getting inside her. This fantasy, however, could be fulfilled only at the cost of his survival as a separate masculine self. This intrapsychic conflict combined with the rejection and absence of his father undermined the normal development of identification with father and disidentification from mother.

As I described earlier, Charles broke down as he entered adolescence. He made his first suicide attempt at fourteen, and had made nine more attempts on his life before beginning his analysis with me. His suicide fantasy was then enacted in numerous motorcycle accidents which occurred during manic omnipotent states and were motivated by his wish to be taken over by a woman.

Following interpretive work on Charles's suicide fantasies, a new wish emerged in the transference: the wish to be rescued by father from mother, who was experienced as abandoning and castrating. This wish was made conscious through interpretation of his plans to cancel a Friday session and allow his inexperienced girlfriend to drive him on his motorcycle through the night at high speed.

The positive father transference, however, was tenuous for two reasons: his wish to be rescued from mother jeopardized his dependent tie to her; and the rescuing father was also violent, unreliable, and mostly absent.[4] Charles's disappointment and despair that I would not be a real father to him led him back again and again to his mother and to threaten to terminate his analysis.

The shift in his identification from mother to father seesawed over a period of more than two years. Charles's effort to separate from his mother and to take over responsibility for his penis competed with contradictory wishes that were evident in the use he made of his motorcycle and in his decision to repay his mother rather than contribute to the cost of his sessions. This was reflected in the transference, where he experienced me at various times as the

---

4. See Burgner (1983) for a report of her study of children and analyses of adults who grew up without fathers. Her finding—there is a "protraction of the original narcissistic interference both in their self-investment and in their sexual identity; they are adhesively and ambivalently tied to the remaining primary object" (p. 19)—is confirmed in Charles's analysis.

impotent, "castrated" boy, the useless and rejected father, or the defeated oedipal rival.

Gradually, the pre-oedipal fears of abandonment that fueled his suicidal fantasies and sadomasochistic bond to mother subsided. A growing investment in treatment, manifested in his contributing financially to his analysis, enabled Charles to achieve enough separation from his mother to maintain a consistent relationship with his girlfriend, Charlotte. The phallic-oedipal castration anxieties that remained were defended against via his identification with a fetish. The transference, at this stage in his analysis, was often characterized by his attempts to stimulate me into becoming an exciting fetish, the phallic mother, with whom he wished to identify. This use of the transference for perverse gratification was a fundamental resistance to insight in the analysis.

By becoming the fetishistic object, Charles disavowed his dependency needs and experienced himself as a self-sufficient, self-contained, and exciting object that was sought after and not abandoned. He saw himself as the fetish for the woman. By reversing roles Charles put the woman in the position of being in heat for his penis, just as he had been in heat for mother's breast. In this way, Charles incorporated this removable penis with which he had endowed the woman, bolstered his fragile genitality (Greenacre, 1960), and renewed his depleted narcissistic reserves. While the creation of a fetish defended against his castration anxiety, Charles's identification with his omnipotent mother's "penis" defended against pregenital anxieties associated with abandonment and engulfment by her.

Postscript

Charles made considerable progress in resolving phallic-oedipal conflicts, anxieties associated with competing with his father, and rage at father for leaving his son with mother. Although Charles does not consciously wish to die, the unresolved pre-oedipal conflicts have left him vulnerable to unconscious suicidal fantasies which could become activated by a crisis that renders his fetishistic solution ineffective. Charles could be at risk in the future if he is unable to find libidinal gratification in his fetish, especially during a crisis, and regresses to enact a suicidal fantasy. At that time Charles's defensive organization, built around his fetishistic orientation, would be insufficient, as it was in the past, to protect him from his suicidal impulses.

Charles cut short further understanding of his fetish by terminating his analysis prematurely and unilaterally after seven years. From the many factors that contributed to his termination, I will consider briefly two interrelated ones that have a bearing on the themes of this chapter: (1) his wish to feel "normal" through an external achievement, and (2) his resistance to working through his ambivalence toward his fetish.

Like many ill adolescents, Charles hoped that the achievement of a culturally recognized milestone would constitute proof that he was, finally, normal. Although he had been underachieving academically and left school at sixteen, he was obviously bright and never abandoned the hope that he could succeed academically. By his third year of analysis, Charles understood more about his need to defensively denigrate academic achievements as hollow and useless, his frustration and rage when encountering a question he could not answer, and the deprivation he felt when he had to postpone gratification. He then decided to take an A-level course in sociology with a view to going on for a degree.[5] His subsequent academic effort was supported by a positive identification with me, a growing sense of his own potency, and increased capacity to tolerate frustration and anxiety. Charles earned a good grade in his A-level exam and was accepted at the college of his choice in a B.A. course in sociology.

Charles fashioned a "solution" to his self-destructive tendency and perverse fantasies based on the newfound prospect of attaining a B.A. degree. He saw the achievement of a college degree, more than anything, as proof that he had overcome his problems and was normal. From the time he started college, Charles used his analysis to clear away whatever undermined his capacity to achieve academic success, but his motivation in other aspects of his life waned. At this time he unilaterally set his analytic termination date to coincide with getting his degree and starting a new job. With the attainment of these goals, he believed he would no longer need analysis.

The adolescent's wish to achieve an external milestone that will be seen as evidence of normality, a phenomenon not uncommon in analytic work with adolescents, poses a technical dilemma for the analyst: how can he support the adolescent's wish for success in the real world and help him, analytically, to achieve it while not colluding with the patient's resistance to analysis or destruction of it? This dilemma can be resolved only in the interpretive work with the adolescent.

Charles's preoccupation with getting a degree was used in the service of resistance to understanding more about his confused sexual identity and his relationships with women. The outcome of his analysis represented a success insofar as he was able to make internal changes sufficient to achieve aca-

5. An A-level course is a pre-university attainment and is a requirement for university entrance.

demic success and quickly find a satisfying job. Without these successes, his future would be bleak. Nevertheless, Charles made use of his academic achievement and the accompanying feelings of normality, as well as positive changes in his relationship with Charlotte, to defend against the analysis of pre-oedipal wishes gratified by his use of a fetish.

As Charles's castration anxiety diminished, his use of big-breasted women as fetishistic objects decreased, and he began to think about Charlotte as a whole person with distinctive needs and interests. He set up a home with her. His central masturbation fantasy of being excited by the sight of big breasts continued, however, as did his denigration of Charlotte for her penis-less state (represented by her small breasts).

These internal shifts coincided with the cessation of Charles's "suicidal" motorcycle accidents. The analysis of Charles's self-destructive impulses by his two previous analysts and myself led to his eventually giving up suicide attempts and accidents as a means of gratifying pre-oedipal wishes to be taken over by mother and exacting revenge against her for frustrating these wishes. However, the libidinal impulses that fueled his suicidal fantasies and attempts now found gratification in the fetish. The residue of pre-oedipal longings and anxieties contributed to the persistence of his fetishistic orientation.

It is not uncommon for a young adolescent to use girls in a fetishistic manner as he experiments with his penis. Charles and his peers had related to girls at his boarding school in this way. There may also be a fetishistic orientation in foreplay among adults which becomes pathological only when a man is unable to restore his partner to a whole object. Charles's inability to shift from a part-object to a whole-object relationship reflects the danger that his fetishistic orientation may become organized and fixed as a perversion to protect his vulnerable gender identity.

Janet Humphrey

6.

Bill: Severe Breakdown and Attempted Suicide

Bill was eighteen when he suffered a severe breakdown that culminated in a serious suicide attempt. His psychoanalytic treatment commenced about nine months after the suicide attempt.

Bill, the third child of professional parents, had two sisters, three and six years older, respectively. His mother had had several miscarriages before his birth. When Bill was born, mother was staying with her parents in Manchester, but when he was a few months old they went to join his father, then agricultural consultant in a remote district of South America.

For his first two years, Bill thrived in the care of a nanny. At age two and a half or so he appears to have been a happy child who fit well into a play group that had been started by a few European families living in the district. But then his father had to move, followed thereafter by frequent changes (at least every two years) of place, country, and school. Bill's nanny left, and from that time on he was cared for mostly by his mother. She was described as physically undemonstrative and rigid in her attitudes, and she appears to have been overly ambitious in promoting her son's earliest education, for she regarded him as special and clever, in contrast to his two sisters.

The frequent moves, determined by father's work, meant that the family was often separated from him, and during these disrupted times Bill seems to have become a solitary, difficult, rather unhappy child, liable to tantrums and often withdrawn and talking to himself. A pattern of his unpredictably wandering off alone with a few possessions is noted as having started when he was six. He is said to have resisted his second nursery school, while at home he paid little attention to his sisters and showed no interest in toys, except for a teddy bear which he finally discarded only at the time of his breakdown, when he was eighteen.

Bill's younger sister followed the elder to boarding school in England when Bill was eight years old, but he did not recall consciously missing her at the time. He did remember that his parents, now with only one child at home, concentrated on encouraging him to achieve at school. As he had no companions, they provided him with numerous pets, which, of course, had to be abandoned when he, in turn, left for boarding school in England at ten years of age.

It seems to have been father more than mother who openly regretted sending all the children so far away to school; yet father idealized the expensive modern boarding school as an institution which offered a contrast to his own school days in a northern industrial city during the Great Depression. He often explained to Bill that a boarding school education in England for his children was a prerequisite of his job and an opportunity they should not miss. In school, Bill at first found it very hard to adjust to group living and had to be moved into a room of his own, as his mother had predicted. But eventually he seemed to settle down and accept the sitution. From this time on, Bill and his sisters took long tiring journeys to spend holidays with their parents in distant countries and always-changing homes, although for short breaks they went to the warm and settled family home of an uncle and aunt in a small country town near London.

When he was thirteen Bill's parents briefly returned to England, and grand preparations were made for his bar mitzvah. Unfortunately, the day arrived just after two family bereavements; although he had looked forward to the event with pleasurable anticipation of personal recognition, Bill felt when it came that the occasion was not for him but that he had been required to perform for his parents and the mourning relatives. After the ceremony he immediately dissociated himself from the clothes and trappings of the occasion and abandoned the vague hope for a change in his image of himself.

During his fourteenth year Bill's isolation, self-doubts, and unhappiness continued. He said that the desperate letters he sent home went unanswered, although his father later recalled feeling worried but having sent "sensible replies." This period culminated in Bill's taking an overdose of aspirin at school. He recalled a wish to die but, in retrospect, was unsure whether his intention in taking the overdose had been to kill himself. He never spoke of his despair at the time, he said. It seems, however, to have been around now that important changes began. In contrast to his own small size, he became an admirer and follower of Donald, a heavily built, somewhat older boy notable for his bullying demeanor and delinquent feats. Donald was also the main purveyor of drugs in the school. The relationship with this boy apparently fulfilled some aspect of Bill's sadistic fantasy and also revived and provided some longed-for perverse kind of gratification linked at least in fantasy with his father. In Donald, Bill had found a corrupt model to reinforce certain identifications based on his perception of his father as a feared but despised object who had enjoyed little success in life.

Through his association with Donald, Bill achieved a new status among his peers and the self-assurance provided by the pseudomasculinity he assumed by adopting or sharing Donald's reputation for daring, disruptive, and abusive behavior. Never before having properly belonged anywhere, he now felt accepted in the group, which experimented with drugs. Under these new auspices, he became a leader in the local disco and an active member of the football team. Bill's first sexual relation with a girl, when he was sixteen, was within the group and drug ethos of this period at school. He felt it to be a nonthreatening but unreal experience because it was achieved only in line with group expectations.

Meanwhile, he had not been working up to his potential in school, and at eighteen he passed his exams but failed to achieve the grades required for university entrance. So he left school not knowing what to do next and went to stay with his parents, then temporarily settled in London.

At first he worked at whatever temporary or mundane job he could find, but he was isolated and living under great tension. Although staying in the same house with his parents, he felt estranged from them. He did maintain some links with past school friends, but became increasingly depressed and withdrawn. After some months of this miserable existence, Bill decided to leave home and, together with a friend who shared his interests, he went off to pursue the idea of becoming a free-lance photographer. Despite their brave hopes, events not surprisingly did not unfold as planned, and hardship and disappointment were inevitable. He soon had no work and very little money to live on.

But now his despair turned to euphoria as he became compulsively preoccupied with strict dieting, bodybuilding, and yoga exercises. He began to experience what he later described as transient feelings of detached lightness and elation—a short-lived state which he called a "high" and which frightened him whenever he remembered it.

He decided to go away and, with no particular goal, set off for Greece. But whatever hope of independence he may have had soon collapsed, and after some weeks he reappeared at home, evidently ill and in a depressed and agitated state. It was at this time that he thought clearly of suicide, and he later said that with this thought he immediately felt relaxed and calm.[1]

Although his parents were worried by Bill's appearance and his very disturbed behavior, they nevertheless left him alone in their London house a few days after his homecoming while they went to Birmingham to attend a funeral. Bill had been invited to go too but had refused. On the day his parents departed, he took a train to the country in order to carry out the suicide he had planned. He swallowed tablets he had previously collected and cut his wrists, and then became frightened and sought help, a course that took him to a hospital. Within a short time, however, and against the advice of the doctors he discharged himself. But through his own volition, he came a few days later to the Brent Consultation Centre, which he had heard about from a social worker.

When he was first seen at the Centre his interviewer found him to be in a gravely disturbed and confused state. He showed frequent lapses of attention and moments of apparent detachment. Surprisingly, however, he seemed to form an immediate positive, though passively dependent, relationship with the interviewing analyst and accepted the recommendation that he return to the hospital from which he had discharged himself only a few days before.

Through the following nine months, Bill remained in the hospital. His brief attempts to stay with his parents always broke down in violent scenes and arguments. But throughout this period he maintained a continuing, though irregular, contact with the interviewing analyst at the Centre, always phoning when he wanted another appointment. Gradually the possibility of psychoanalysis was explored and decided upon. Bill was reluctant to remain in the hospital, but he accepted his interviewer's advice that he should do so while his antidepressant drug was gradually withdrawn. The hospital staff agreed with these arrangements.

The Analysis

Bill's subsequent analysis lasted for twenty months, until he himself imposed a termination. His refusal to continue the analysis was the outcome of his awareness of his failure in the protracted struggle he had set up to control and

1. A description of similar feelings is given by many of those who later actually attempt suicide.

modify the analyst's stance and independence. In an effort to ensure the containment of his sadistic and destructive urges, which were constantly projected, he went to extremes of persuasion and maneuver to force me to comply with his wish for a different approach and for less frequent sessions. Interpretation of the frustration of his primitive transference wish to gain a kind of safety by enviously possessing me did not suffice, and he was left with an awareness of his intensely destructive wishes toward me as a real person. It was at this point that his anxieties became intolerable to him, and he felt impelled to leave the analysis.

At the diagnostic stage there had been some hesitation in recommending analysis for this young man because of his primitive and unstable ego structure, and when psychoanalytic treatment was eventually offered, a limited objective was envisaged. Now, in retrospect, it can be said that at the time of his premature termination there were some general signs of improvement in his life-style and potential for relationships, and his increased self-awareness in some areas represented some limited permanent achievement. Nevertheless, his extreme vulnerability remained unchanged.

During the analysis Bill's moods and behavior were changeable and unreliable, and he was likely to experience the breakthrough of unmodified destructive impulses with the threat of ego disintegration. At times there was severe risk to himself in his pattern of acting out. In attempting to maintain himself, he made much use of splitting and idealization as defensive maneuvers. He tended to facilitate his ego-splitting mechanisms and boost his sado-masochistic/perverse fantasies of destructiveness by the frequent though intermittent use of drugs—mainly marijuana and amphetamines, although he would occasionally sniff heroin—with the aim, he said, of "killing psychic pain." His up-and-down pattern of drug use was essentially defensive, intended both to dull affect and to facilitate either a compulsive exhibiting of the grandiosity of his overaggressivized self-image or an equally compulsive obliterating from awareness of other idealized self- or part-objects. These defensive maneuvers did not, however, suffice. There were frequent moments of breakdown, and at times in the analysis, a psychotic transference predominated, which I had to learn to contain and cope with in various ways.

Nevertheless, it was the reliable continuity of the analysis and the unchanging analytic situation itself, insofar as they represented inescapable aspects of reality, that had to be maintained as the important pillars of the treatment alliance. Naturally, providing a sense of continuity was complicated by the holiday breaks and also by Bill's hospitalization for a month. During the period of hospital detention he was started on a fairly high dose of a major tranquilizer. Bill felt this medication to be powerful and controlling, partly because for a time he experienced unpleasant physical side effects which altered his sense of his body. His dependence on the tranquilizer gradually became a major factor in the development of his resistance to psychoanalysis.

Clinical Material

In the following account of Bill and his analysis, I will focus on areas of particular technical strain and those that illustrate the pattern of breakdown as it reoccurred in the analysis. I will describe three phases of about six months each:

1. During the first months, Bill experienced acute regression in the transference, with feelings of extreme dependency toward the analyst and an incorporative, part-object mode of relating. During this time transient loss of boundaries and fragmentation of his sense of self occurred as well as brief episodes of clearly psychotic functioning.
2. Following the second holiday break there was a period of acute breakdown and "withdrawal" during which time Bill's only sense of continuity and his only hold on reality was the analysis. This phase culminated in his readmission and detention in the hospital and a start on fairly heavy medication. This was an approach to Bill's treatment determined by the hospital psychiatrist, but it was in part a response to anxiety and management problems in the hospital nursing staff.
3. There followed a phase of "recovery," as measured by improved functioning in a general way, with Bill living at home and working part time. But it was now that he was attempting to be controlling within the analysis and sadistically intrusive toward the analyst. He took to using marijuana and amphetamines frequently, particularly before coming to his sessions, and a split between home, hospital, and analyst became a strong source of resistance in the analysis. During this phase, the continuing high dose of the tranquilizer helped Bill to avoid psychic integration of the knowledge of his recent acute breakdown, and little capacity for insight developed.

Phase One. Bill had been living in the hospital for several months before starting the analysis in September. He continued to live there during the first three months, traveling to his sessions about one hour each way by bus.

Although Bill was at first always doubting and testing the analyst's reliability and tolerance in comparison to the hospital's, which he had come to accept, his dependence on the regularity and safety of the analytic session, which also fostered his regression, was very marked. Once on the couch, he would lie motionless, usually with his eyes closed, and would speak in a rather abrupt, affectless, and monotonous way with long pauses. The controllingness implicit in his immobility and tortuous speech was manifest, and often he reacted to an interruption with immediate anger, followed rapidly by blank withdrawal.

At the first weekend break in the analysis, rather than return home or to the hospital, he went off without telling anyone to stay with his old school friends, to play music and smoke pot. This way he sought to deny the loss of the analyst and to ensure the continuity of his supplies, although he clearly experienced the abrupt change and accompanying sense of triumph as both mentally and physically disagreeable, since they brought frightening recollections of his acute breakdown and suicide attempt. The primitive destructive orality of his feeling at this time was evident in that a good session, valued by him, would be followed, on his return to the hospital, by compulsive overeating of junk food, which he both disliked and considered to be harmful. Similarly, at the end of a "good week" in analysis and back in the hospital, he would resort to self-indulgence by smoking marijuana, although he could not easily cope with the effects, which he described in terms of a strange bodily sense of derealization.

In the first month or two of the analysis, it became increasingly clear that it was his intolerance for frustration or delayed gratification (within the transference) that tended to bring about inner panic or outwardly directed rage—often manifest only in moments of detached blankness. He recalled how his solitary play and isolation when he was a child had then served to cut him off from disappointing objects. In these early sessions, the moments of blanking out and detachment could be linked to his sense of my failure to meet his intense and primitive dependency needs. Although he made conscious efforts in learned ways—such as discussing his feelings in the hospital group—to try to control and contain what he described as his feelings of extreme dependency and his thought that he "lived only to come to analysis" (an idea that also contained fantasies of envious destructiveness), he was not always successful.

I will give an example of the overwhelming and primitive quality of his affect and regression. Because of an unexpected event, I had to cancel a session ten days ahead. On the day I told Bill of this, he showed no reaction to the news at first, hardly appearing to take in what I said, but then he himself stayed away the following day. In the next session, confronted with the fact of the missed day, he became very distressed but then blanked out. Later he told me of his conviction that my forthcoming absence must mean either that

I was going to a funeral or that I was seriously ill myself; we recognized his fears of his own impulses and the urgency of his need to control his fears by anticipating the danger. He remained very shaken, however, and in the week following this, he experienced an episode of transient psychotic confusion in the bus on the way to his session. He reported that he had been reading Conrad's *The Nigger of the Narcissus* but had moved his seat because he felt conspicuous. Not conscious of any motive in doing so, he had then placed himself next to a large black man, another passenger, and his transfixed staring had provoked this man to attack him. As he told this story, Bill emphasized the man's large size and noted that he himself was always thought to be small and unaggressive. He was frightened by awareness of the inappropriateness of his behavior and his partial awareness of the acting out and projection of his own sadistic impulses.

Later in the week, following the day when I was away, he developed a state of detachment with diffuse tension and agitation of psychotic intensity in the course of a session. When this happened, I, in turn, became fearful of his potential for violent action. Feeling a need to interrupt the acute regression in the transference, I suggested that he sit up and talk—as he eventually did, with relief to us both. In the following days he was in a calmer mood, and some minimal insight into the mode of triggering and releasing primitive functioning, which tended to lead to the now familiar and oft-repeated pattern of near breakdown, seemed possible.

As time went on, Bill appeared to be more involved in activities in the hospital and, in a more hopeful mood, was looking ahead and making plans. He began to speak, however, of his lack of trust in "the possibility of a shared emotional experience"; he complained that closeness to another person was inevitably experienced in bodily ways, as excitingly erotic or deadeningly dull, and that his intense fear of the uncertainty of his emotions made him favor such "extremes of reaction." At the same time he also began to make frequent, rather ambiguous references to his preoccupying thoughts about girls, which were paralleled by self-conscious doubt and concern about his appearance and physical condition. He said he felt a need to drain off his dependent feelings before coming to a session. He was also aware of wishing to intrude into whatever I might be doing when he was not with me. Along with these intrusive wishes, which were interpreted in the transference, were fears that success in work or in achieving physical fitness might make him feel "high" so that he would "crack up" again. It was difficult, however, for him to recognize how close he was to enactment of his exhibitionistic impulses within the analysis because such interpretations tended to make his fears escalate. At this time also his experience of himself in a session might vary from detachment and derealization to a sense of a concrete body image. Once he described crossing Vauxhall Bridge on the way to a session, feeling good about being part of the world; but he then identified himself with some "splendid glass tower blocks" he could see. At first he felt marvelous, but then he was terrified by the unreality of the accompanying sense of elation. A state of breakdown within the transference seemed to be taking place.

Now, after some months of analysis, his anxieties increased as we approached the Christmas break. They were expressed as fear of emptiness or loss and as hostility toward me connected with the frustration of his overwhelming needs and anticipated losses. We continually reviewed his ways of dealing with himself by projection and by splitting the transference between the analyst and the hospital; but resistance to the analysis developed more strongly as involvement with a girl patient at the hospital took precedence over all else. This girl had been a heroin addict, had lesbian tendencies, and had attempted suicide. Initially Bill had realistic doubts about the validity of the relationship, which he described as a mutually feeding and sexually very tentative affair between "two miserable people who had just been thrown together." He also had some recognition of the affair as an acting out of his dependency and neediness toward me.

But now a setback occurred. He had gone with his cousin on a long train journey to look into the possibility of some photographic work. Beforehand he had been worked up, irritable, and excited about the event, but once on the train he became panic-stricken, realizing the "enormity" of what he was doing in going for interviews. Before reaching their destination he sought to allay his fears by swallowing a large lump of cannabis, which he had been carrying in his pocket. This had the disastrous and not unexpected effect of making him feel hopelessly confused, unable to speak, and fearful of going insane. Although his cousin helped him get through the day without total collapse, he was unable to communicate or achieve anything. Later his cousin chided him severely for his stupid behavior, and he felt very ashamed. As we worked on all this in the next few sessions, this episode seemed to confirm a now familiar pattern of disintegrative anxiety likely to occur at a point of actual personal achievement. In this instance the impulse to incorporate the lump of cannabis had been an attempt both to control the anxiety and to dissociate himself from the chance of success.

It was at this time that Bill himself spoke about the split as well as the connection between his acute fears of rejection, manifest in his "paranoid feelings," and that "private, powerful inner feeling" that sometimes made him feel mad with racing thoughts. He felt he could hold onto this state through an attitude of withholding and withdrawal, thereby resisting total depletion. At such a time, when his bodily and emotional experiences of himself were so close to each other, he was very resistant to any intervention in the form of interpretation.

It was planned in advance that Bill could be discharged from the hospital as soon as the analysis resumed following the first holiday break. In the month preceding the holiday, he was much preoccupied with the pressing need to find a flat, but there was a lot of anxiety in anticipation of the break as well as fears related to the prospect of actually having to cope with his hospital girlfriend in a flat of his own. These anxieties were interwoven. The girl was then in a suicidal condition and detained in the hospital; Bill both envied and identified with her in pressing his need that I should stay and look after him. He feared that away from the hospital in a flat of his own there would no longer be any barrier to risking physical sexual intimacy with the girl, and he was aware that preoccupation with his physical health and body had successfully diverted him from thoughts of sex with a girl ever since the brief affair he had at school had ended. But despite all his doubts, he pursued the search for a flat with a sense of great urgency that also had a quality of manic denial. Eventually he found a place to share with a friend where he could spend some of his time, although he was not actually to be discharged from the hospital until I returned from holiday.

With the start of the analysis again in January, all his realistic plans for the flat and the girlfriend rapidly collapsed and he became very depressed, confused, and quite hostile toward me. His state of regression was accelerated by his getting flu. Unable to manage, he resorted to going home to his mother, who was by chance once more alone at this time, his father having gone abroad. But the paranoid fears of his father's reaction to finding Bill at home on his return and his fantasized revenge now assailed Bill, and he became increasingly agitated and confused. In the analysis he seemed very tense, often speaking in a rambling, fragmentary, and resentful way. At times the transference seemed to have a delusionary quality as he spoke angrily of his refusal to collude with "food being rammed down," and he warned me of the violence inside himself. Such sessions are hard to describe, but I will here give some material from a fairly typical hour of this disturbing period.

Bill came punctually, as usual, and as if continuing from the previous day, spoke of his anger and distrust of everything. He said he had been crying on the bus, had a feeling that he wanted to do everything on his own, and didn't trust coming here. I interpreted that he did not trust that I could tolerate and help him contain his anger, which led him to speak of his feeling that he needed the support of the hospital and that I was preventing him from returning there. He talked at some length about his father's lack of understanding of his situation which, he said, his mother understood only too well. He complained that his father expected all three of them to eat together but that he himself could not stand it.

He then berated me for giving him the chance to come here and attack the "happy family." I said I wondered if it was *my* "happy family" from which he felt excluded and which he felt he might attack, and I pointed to the projection and the many contradictions in what he was saying. Bill replied that he didn't see how things could be otherwise and that the only way to get anything clear was to be in the hospital. I interpreted that he saw the hospital as a neutral place of safety where he could stop himself from destructively pushing his wish to be in my house. He replied that he was scared of how resentful he felt toward me and said he was feeling as if he could be a danger to some other person. I was very much aware of the tension mounting in him and was feeling slightly apprehensive myself. I felt that it was important not to let the silence develop but to continue talking, and I reminded him that when he had felt like this before, it had helped when he let himself sit up and look at the reality of the room. He did not move or speak, but eventually, as I went on talking, he heaved himself up on one elbow on the couch, and after a while, seeming calmer, he murmured that he wasn't going to move and he did not want any advice. I pointed out how necessary it had been for him to recognize his separateness from me.

The following day he was much calmer. He felt that the previous session had somehow been an important one and had meaning for him. At the same time he feared losing the insight and brief glimpse of self-confidence he had had, and he was becoming increasingly anxious in anticipation of his reaction to any change or break in the analysis.

At this time, in view of his very disturbed state, he was persuaded to return to the hospital during the day while living at home and coming to analysis in the evening. He was frightened by some awareness of his inability to think straight and by the intensity of his insatiable, angry, and demanding feelings both toward me and toward his parents. But there was also a part of him still strongly sustaining the treatment alliance with me as well as striving to use the support of the hospital discussion group. What was worrying, however, was his repeatedly expressed persecutory fear regarding future deprivation of the analysis. This fear kept erupting in moments of acute hostility and resentment toward me for my planned holiday break. He envisaged himself greedily possessing my empty room in the future, but then, being unable to continue with this thought, turned to self-damaging and suicidal thoughts. It was during this period that Bill began to reveal glimpses of the sadomasochistic content of his private fantasy life and his autoerotic preoccupations, centering on ideas of withholding and deadness.

Just prior to my departure on holiday at Easter, he seemed to be coping more adequately with his life; his anxiety lessened and he entertained only passing thoughts of suicide. But at the same time, I was concerned about an unusually clear primary process and concrete quality in his references both to his own body and to his anticipated loss of me (and the analysis). He recalled "a nice teddy" he had kept until he threw it away at the onset of his acute breakdown. Responding to my interpretation of his need to find a substitute for me when I was away, he warned me that he knew someone from whom he could buy heroin and that he imagined buying some and taking too much. In retrospect I can recognize that the coolness of his statements in these sessions before the analytic break were linked with a defined suicide plan in his mind.

Phase Two. I was away for two weeks during April, and when Bill returned to analysis afterward, I was at once aware of a marked change and general deterioration in his appearance and demeanor. For many weeks his only sense of continuity and hold on reality appeared to derive from the analytic situation and from his knowledge of me as a real person. At the first session after the break, for which he came thirty-five minutes early, he looked like a dirty and neglected tramp and he had the staring gaze of a drug addict. He said that from the beginning of the holiday he had been trying to destroy himself but couldn't actually do it. He said that he had tried to lie in bed, to stay in empty rooms alone, to sleep with people he did not love, and to hitch around aimlessly, but he could not finally settle to die. He admitted to having taken dope, sleeping pills, speed, and on that day an injection of what he called "slug poison" (sometime later in the hospital he was found to have a very high blood level of marijuana, and there was evidence that he had been sniffing heroin). At the end of this session, when he left my room, he remained holding onto the edge of the door, with his fingers inside, for what seemed like two or three minutes before he slowly moved off.

On the following day I arrived home almost an hour before Bill was due and found him already standing on the doorstep, white and staring, with a dazed look on his face. I remained on the step outside the front door talking to him for some minutes until gradually his color came back and he began to respond. I said I was talking to him outside on the steps because I thought he needed to be as much as possible in touch with the reality that he and I were two separate people standing there. Eventually I said that we would go into the house and talk but that he must sit up and that we would be talking in a different way than usual. He told me he had taken some heroin because he had heard it was the best "killer of pain," but it had not worked. I tried to explain that the pain he wanted to dull was connected with primitive, compulsively tormenting fears of loss experienced toward me in the transference but that I was also a real, helping, analyst-person. I said I could not help him understand his pain if he could not keep himself safe, and to be safe he needed to be in the hospital that night. As we continued talking he said he wanted the heroin to be the cause as well as the control of the threat to himself . . . he muttered about the family being lost in a car in Cairo and father losing his temper and wandering away so he was separated from his family in a crowd . . . and so on. (Bill had spent one school holiday when he was twelve with his parents, who were briefly living in Egypt, and there had been previous reference to some frightening experience and delay on the journey there with his sister.)

Eventually, having calmed down greatly, Bill accepted my suggestion that he telephone the hospital ward from my office and tell them that he would be coming to stay there. He agreed to wait while a taxi was called to take him.

During the following two or three months he never missed a session except for a four-week period when he was detained in the hospital for his safety. Through these months he was exceedingly disturbed, appearing to live mainly in a world of psychotic fantasy and often acting at great risk to himself. Sometimes he would return to sleep in the hospital, but often he spent the night hitching rides on the highways or sleeping rough and picking up food wherever he could get it. But always he returned for his analytic session, although he was usually neglected and dirty in appearance. He was often incoherent and confusing in his talk, and death or suicide was a recurring theme.

There was a sadistically intrusive quality in Bill's extreme dependence on me during this period, and my countertransference anxieties were considerable. I frequently emphasized to him that there would be no progress in the analysis unless he could be responsible for himself and return to live in the hospital on a regular basis for the time being. But for some days he was unable to decide to give up his restless and hazardous wandering. As he became somewhat aware of his closeness to total breakdown, he grew frightened and agreed at one session that I should telephone for a relative to take him to the hospital. The decision to detain him on an order in the hospital for a month for his safety was taken after consultation between myself and the hospital psychiatrist, and met more or less with Bill's cooperation. The subsequent decision to start him on medication was the psychiatrist's response to Bill's demand and to the nursing staff's anxiety over management problems with him.

I visited him once in the hospital during the time he was detained there, and Bill phoned me once or twice. I also kept in telephone contact with the psychiatrist. Eventually, it was clear that considerable difference of opinion among the ward staff had developed regarding whether further psychoanalytic treatment would be beneficial and whether he should be allowed to return, as Bill himself was pressing to do. Eventually I received a telephone message from him expressing his intention to come back to the analysis as he was no longer compulsorily detained in the hospital. I told him that I intended to seek agreement for this from his ward staff and doctor. But given the conflicting opinion among the ward staff, my request met with contradictory responses and pessimistic views regarding his prognosis. Meanwhile Bill, who felt he had made his own decision, arrived punctually for a session at his familiar time.

In his first session back, his behavior contrasted strongly with the incoherent, fragmentary, and often delusionary presentation I had come to know. He was clearly anxious but also greatly relieved at having made it back; he described with tears of relief the nostalgic and circuitous route he had taken as he pursued the landmarks of previous journeys to my house. Recall of lost homes and old feelings of self-reproach were there alongside the familiar urge to discard and spoil anything good. But for the moment he felt protected by an unusual degree of self-observation, which had also enabled him to make his own decision about returning to analysis.

During the following week he was anxiously reviewing his position. He wished to sleep as if to hold onto it, but no longer, he said, did he wish to kill himself. At times he would revert from musing on the past—particularly past holidays marked by acute tension and parental strife—to expressing bitterness and resentment toward me for controlling him. When I interpreted the projection and the painfulness of holding and owning all these feelings within himself, he acknowledged how irritable and restless he was feeling. During these sessions I insisted that he sit upright as he needed all his awareness to maintain his assurance of separateness from me.

On the last day of his first week back in analysis, Bill was very tense and anxious. He had thoughts of not returning to sleep at the hospital and considered ways of stealing vicarious gratification by, for example, taking and reading his cousin's letters to his girlfriend. Bill acknowledged that, by his restlessness and his stirring up of reciprocal anxiety in others, he was expressing envious destructiveness, and he recognized the old wish to come between his parents. But attempts to bring his feelings directly back into the transference by interpreting his reaction to the forthcoming weekend separation from analysis made his anxiety escalate. At moments in the session his usually pale face would flush, and he would edge forward on his chair; his urge to leave rather than face the immediacy of his violent feelings was evident to us both. In the course of this session he referred to the desperate loneliness he had felt when he was first sent away to boarding school, and he spoke of possessing a kind of totem, a carved wooden object that had been a source of comfort at this time and possibly served a fetishistic function.

Bill had been aware when he returned to the analysis that there would be only a month left before my summer holiday. But his reaction to this ceased to be characterized by envious demandingness, and he became more preoccupied with fantasies of passive submission. During these few weeks he spent "too much money"; for example, he used up a legacy from a dead uncle by coming to his sessions by taxicab all the way from the hospital. Sometimes he would arrive several hours early. He had fantasies of being bound up and being a dead thing which I would be forced to take with me when I went away.

During the last week or so before the summer break Bill was realistically engaged in trying to work out ways of helping himself to cope. He was much less attacking and anxious, although he often seemed sad and listless and would think longingly about being in his bed in the hospital. To help him deal with my four weeks' absence I proposed that while I was away he should telephone me in the country at a fixed time once each week. While he was considering this idea, exciting thoughts of resuming his wandering and hitching rides began to creep in. He observed that he himself could not drive and that when he hitched rides he never knew what he might be letting himself in for, although he knew "the excitement of the open motorway." I interpreted that my offer had felt like a seduction, which was exciting his greedy, sexual curiosity, and I commented that the dangerous hitching facilitated his sadomasochistic fantasies. Bill responded to these interpretations with an urgent impulse to telephone his parents to reassure himself they were safe, and I linked these thoughts to the plan to telephone me.

At the beginning of the last session before the break, when I handed him written directions about dates and phoning, his first response was a wish to leave me and the analysis at once. This was accompanied by thoughts about ways of flirting with danger, drugs, and suicide, but for the moment he seemed able to contain these ideas. The thought of a safe return to the hospital seemed the most attractive.

Bill succeeded in maintaining himself in the hospital during my holiday, and he phoned once a week at the agreed-upon hour. He spoke for only a few minutes, telling me what he had been doing and, I think, reassuring himself that I was still there.

Phase Three. At the resumption of the analysis after the holiday, there were new sources of resistance. He had been sitting in a chair rather than using the couch for the past two or three months, and now, while lying back in the chair, he would often slowly and elaborately roll thin cigarettes, which he would smoke in slow puffs. When he had no tobacco, he would ostentatiously pick wax from his ears with a matchstick. At times he would drum rhythmically with his fingers on the arm of the chair for five minutes at a time or, in a ritualistic way, snap his fingers or his knuckles. Throughout he would watch me closely, and I interpreted the provocation and the substitute gratifications in these activities, which were helping him split off his potential dependency on me.

During this time he was also concentrating upon his physical condition and appearance. He acquired new clothes and odd hats, which he would wear continuously for two or three weeks at a time. He also spent much money taking cabs and buying food on his journeys to and from analysis. Sometimes he came on his bike and parked it in my front yard for a couple of hours while he went off to get food after the session.

At first there was an aspect of secrecy and stealing from me in these activities, but a provocative flaunting of his behavior, which clearly had a manic quality, took over. This became more evident as his involvement with another ex-fellow patient who had been a heroin addict led to frequent heavy use of marijuana and amphetamines. On occasion Bill would come to a session clearly affected by the drugs—provocative, teasing, and triumphantly hostile and unreceptive to or uncomprehending of any interpretation I might make.

He had been warned in the hospital and was well aware that heavy use of drugs was likely to potentiate his prescribed medication and increase unpleasant side effects, including loss of erectile potency. Thus his indulging in these drugs could be seen, in part, as an unconscious masochistic submission to the regressive pull of dependency. This was in keeping with his felt need, at this time, to satisfy his parents and stay with them at home—a situation that was currently idealized while the analysis and I were degraded and made worthless. By resorting to extreme splitting, facilitated by the drugs that fueled primitive, persecutory fantasy, he avoided the complete psychotic break or confusional state that had happened on other occasions.

It was from this position that Bill's intractable efforts to sadistically control his analyst and demolish the analysis began, which eventually led to the premature termination. This could perhaps be regarded as a suicide equivalent.

Postscript

After Bill terminated his analysis, I heard nothing of him for more than a year. Then he wrote to the Centre asking to come in to talk things over, and eventually I saw him. He had managed to continue living at home, briefly holding occasional jobs.

He was still taking a fairly large dose of the prescribed medication, having become increasingly phobic about relinquishing it, but he seemed to be more or less managing to avoid serious dependency on amphetamines or marijuana. He had not, however, been successful in achieving any lasting relationship and was feeling increasingly isolated and lonely, especially as his parents had plans to close the house and leave London—thus once more confronting Bill with the loss of a stable home. By the time I saw him he no longer had much in the way of work to do and little other aim or purpose in life. He persistently requested that we consider resuming his analysis, while at the same time he felt drawn to becoming once more a hospital inpatient. There was no indication that he could maintain himself independently, and his return to analysis under the auspices of the Centre was not considered feasible, at least for the time being.

Anne Hurry

7.

Kevin: Self-Destructive Action and Suicidal Wishes

Kevin was nineteen when he began cutting his face and was referred to the Centre, but his tendency to damage himself had been lifelong. As a child he had had frequent accidents, some serious—he had fallen from a shed roof onto his head and had been knocked off his bicycle by a car. As an adolescent he would bang his head against the wall, hit himself in the face, and burn his hands with lighted cigarettes. Shortly before coming to the Centre he had begun cutting his abdomen, and the cuts on his face were moving down toward his throat. He had made one suicide attempt by throwing himself down the subway stairs. He also provoked others to attack him; at school he had been a persistent victim of bullying, and after leaving school he was often attacked by other men in the street or in pubs. He was a heavy drinker.

Kevin arrived at the Centre like a frightened child asking to be protected, pitied, and made better. The idea that feelings or actions could be understood was foreign to him, and he was quite out of touch with his inner world. Unaware of his motivation or of conflict, he acted directly on impulse, and he experienced and expressed feelings via his body rather than his mind—in pains, dizzy spells, and epileptic fits. Only two feeling states—anxiety and excitement—seemed directly accessible to him.

After some months of preparatory interviews Kevin began his analysis at the age of twenty.[1] At this writing he has been in analysis for nine months. He made an immediate and intense attachment not so much to his analyst as

1. Although Kevin was beyond the upper age limit when he began his analysis, he was within the age limit when he first came to the Centre.

to his treatment, to "having someone to talk to." He found weekend and holiday separations unbearable, and at such times he was at considerable risk of self-damage or suicide. Of necessity, analytic work within the relationship to me focused upon his reaction to separation and his need to act out. Gradually it became apparent that his fear of separation was accompanied by an equal fear of closeness, which implied to him the danger of being engulfed or taken over by the other. His need to escape the danger of closeness, his wish to be separate and to take independent action, further powered his self-destructiveness.

Reactions to separation and to closeness were by no means the sole determinants of Kevin's enactments. His conflicting sexual identifications and his anxiety and guilt in regard to his sexual fantasies also played an important part. His sexuality was intolerable to him in any form. He was terrified that he might be homosexual and longed for a girlfriend to prove that he was not. At sixteen he had been involved in homosexual activity in a public lavatory. Apart from this episode—of which he was intensely ashamed—he had allowed himself no sexual gratification with another person. He was unable to accept a masculine role, feeling that women must reject him or that he would damage them. He was horrified by his fantasies of raping women and especially by the possibility that he might enact his fantasies of sexual activity with little girls. Unable to find any acceptable sexual identity, Kevin longed to remain a dependent child.

The origins of Kevin's difficulties around separation and closeness and of his conflicting sexual identifications are gradually becoming clearer as his history emerges in the course of his analysis. Kevin was brought up in an almost suffocating, often sexualized closeness to his mother, yet was always threatened by the possibility of losing her. His father had left home shortly after the boy's birth. Kevin has two sisters, six and eight years older than he, and a brother four years older. For his first three years Kevin slept in a cot in his mother's room, allegedly because she did not like being alone. She is a depressed and anxious woman, blind in one eye, and suffers frequent attacks of dizziness. Kevin remembers feeling worried about her during his latency years, when the family lived in public housing in a slum area. Mother felt very threatened by the neighborhood children, who would throw stones at the windows. She would sit at the kitchen table, shaking and smoking, her head in her hands. She found it hard to bring up four children on her own and made her difficulties clear to the children. She often thought of suicide, saying she was going to put her head in the gas oven and wishing she had killed herself while she was pregnant with Kevin. When he was eleven, the family moved to a quieter neighborhood on the advice of the mother's doctor, and she became somewhat calmer.

Kevin did have some escape from the home; he used to visit the family of his only friend and sometimes go on holiday with them. We can infer some anxiety on these holidays from the fact that until he was fourteen he wet the bed nightly when away from home. In the company of his friend Kevin took part in some delinquent activities, such as fire setting and break-ins. Apart from this friend he appears always to have been a solitary child, anxious, bullied, and doing poorly at school.

When he was eight, his fourteen-year-old sister became epileptic, and he remembers how horrible he thought she looked. And then at fourteen his own fits began. On leaving school he was not able to join the navy because of his epilepsy. This was a disappointment, for the only photographs he had of his father showed him in uniform. Kevin took a job as a clerk instead.

Fear of Separation

Kevin's fear of separation was evident from the beginning of his analysis. The end of sessions felt like an interruption, and weekends brought thoughts of self-damage. He was able not to endanger himself seriously, however, except during weekends that led up to holiday breaks. (There have been two breaks, at Christmas and Easter.)

Kevin came to his sessions by subway, and he would often begin by describing the torments he had suffered on the train, where he felt persecuted by feelings of being looked at and inevitably condemned and rejected: "People must see how horrible I am." His "horribleness" consisted of any sexual wishes or aggressive impulses. He was terrified of losing control on the train—by touching someone sexually, as he had done in the pub, or attacking someone, as he had done at work.

He also felt certain that I would see how horrible he was and reject him. He indicated that the alternative of rejecting me was open to him, describing how he had rejected a girlfriend the moment he felt unsure of her. He had told her he did not want to go out with her any more, with tears running down his face, although he did not know why he said this to her. Later in his analysis he would come late to most Monday sessions, rejecting me and keeping me waiting as he had felt rejected and excluded over the weekend. He saw suicide as the ultimate way of abandoning me rather than being abandoned.

Weekends brought thoughts of cutting himself, although he has not in fact cut himself since treatment began. I learned that his cutting had taken place in a dissociated state much as does the act of suicide. Kevin said it was "like I am looking at a piece of glass and I hardly know any more about it till I wake up next morning." The cutting itself had never hurt, although he would begin to feel the pain when he looked in the mirror or saw his mother's reaction. At first Kevin tried to attribute his weekend cutting wishes to rejection or humiliation by others. But eventually he was able to tell me that on weekends he was constantly aware of not having "someone to talk to" and would watch television films about psychiatric help, in a rage that he was not at that moment "getting the treatment." After a while he could see how his wishes to attack me for abandoning him were turned back upon himself. The cutting also satisfied his need to punish himself for being "bad" and contained a further punishment and humiliation because his cut face showed others how bad he was.

Suicidal wishes were indicated from the start in connection with the cutting, but it was in relation to holiday breaks that they came to the fore. When I told Kevin the dates of the coming Christmas holidays, he indicated the extent of the rejection he felt by speaking of them as "three months" rather than "three weeks" and telling me of his belief that his mother had once tried to kill him. When he was two or three he had been crying because of toothache and his mother did not know what was wrong; she had "gone mad" and kept giving him more and more pills until he had to be taken to a hospital. Recently, when his sister had been speaking of this, he had said to his mother, "Oh, so you tried to kill me then." He showed how unprotected he felt by telling me that he had once nearly been run over when crossing the road in his sister's care; a neighbor had said that his mother had no right to leave him in the care of a child. But he also tried to reassure me—not "burden" me—by telling me that he would cope. Although he was at times aware of his rage and murderous wishes toward me, he could not speak of them in any detail: "There are some things you ought not to feel." He felt intensely guilty and was often tempted to cut or kill himself in order to punish himself, to protect me, and to make me feel sorry for him.

Feeling so abandoned, Kevin longed for his father as controller, protector, and punisher. But father was not there, and Kevin's rage toward him was equally guilt-provoking: "It would be dreadful to hate your father." This guilt reinforced his wish to kill himself. Terrified of losing control, Kevin found others who would provide what he felt he needed: the police. In the penultimate weekend before the holiday, drunk on a Friday night, he simultaneously made an attempt to identify with his ideal of the strong controlling father and risked being beaten up by trying to break up a fight through holding back one of the combatants. When the police arrived he invited punishment by being "cheeky" to them and then wandered off down the middle of the road, drunk and clearly in danger. The police arrested him, telling him it was for his own protection, and shut him in a cell for the night. There Kevin felt safe, protected from the violence outside and, more important, from his own violence, knowing that he could not hurt anyone.

Over the last weekend before the holiday he again found a means of enacting his conflicts around attack and punishment. At the train station a man kicked and swore at him. He wanted to attack the man and hurt him as he had been hurt, but he felt this was "very bad"; it would be better to be locked in a police cell where he could not hurt anyone. When I linked his fear of loss of control with a desperate attempt to keep away the anger he felt toward me lest he *really* hurt me, Kevin said, "I try not to feel that way, but I can't help feeling that if I did hurt anyone it would be you."

When Kevin returned from the holiday, he told me he had not cut himself, although he had been tempted to because he had felt lost and excluded. His anger toward me was now less alarming, and as weekends approached he could talk of how he felt I should suffer and be miserable. He was able not to attack himself or to invite attack again until he had to book his summer holidays at work; he was then forced to the awareness that there would be other separations. At this point he got himself beaten up by two men from the pub who accused Kevin of looking at them. He was knocked down, kicked, and badly bruised in the body and face. This time he could see more quickly how he induced others to take the role of the aggressor and to provide the punishment for his attacking wishes toward me. Since then he has been able to retain this hard-won insight and has managed not to invite any further attacks, even though he continues to feel that his wish to attack me is fraught with danger.

Later he spoke of how the invitation to attack that he offered others was also an invitation for them to murder him, to beat him to death. In that way he could die with no conscious feeling of guilt—it would be someone else's fault, and he would not be attacking his mother or me. He sought an alternative way of avoiding guilt over suicide—by finding someone else to blame. He had recently joined a dating agency in the hopes of finding a girlfriend but (because he had given them a description of himself that was guaranteed to ensure rejection) had received no replies. He said he wanted the dating agency to fail, because then his last hope would be gone and he could kill himself. Alternatively he displaced blame onto his doctor. He carried heavy packages at work, hoping to injure himself so as to get back at the doctor who he felt had not given him enough time. He added that he often thought he had cancer inside him. If he had, he could *really* go to a hospital, get some attention, get revenge on his doctor, and die.

These wishes paralleled his wishes toward me, who had not cured him and did not give him the time or attention he felt he needed. If he could make his analysis fail, then he would have lost what he felt was his last hope and could die blaming me. At the same time he could get revenge on me, show me what he felt, and show me up as a bad analyst: "I ought not to think like that, but I do want revenge on you."

Kevin's feelings of abandonment and rage at being left, and his consequent guilt and fear of loss of control, could at first be seen to relate primarily to feelings in regard to his absent father. But it is increasingly apparent that they are rooted in Kevin's relationship to his mother and his ongoing fear that she will leave him either by walking out, as his father had done, or by killing herself. This fear is now clearly reflected in the relationship to me. For instance, when I gave Kevin real cause for reproach by keeping him waiting for fifteen minutes, he was unable to express any protest. Instead he raged about his boss. Only when I had taken up his need for this displacement could he tell me that he had thought I must be dead. And afterward he was unable to tell me how angry he had felt in case I said I had had enough of him. His mother did not like anger; if he ever protested to her she would go off upstairs. And while she was there he was always afraid that she might be dead, and he would walk round the house calling to her to make sure she was still alive: "Mum . . . Mum . . . Mum . . . "

Kevin longs to be at one with his mother; he feels that she and he are "part of one another," that he will never be able to separate from her, and that he would not be able to go on living if she were to die. He feels that they are alike in their need for each other, in their constantly thinking of or worrying about each other, and that they share many unspoken thoughts. For a long time he was prepared to sacrifice any life of his own in order to be with her. Prior to his analysis, he had assured her that he would never marry and leave her.

The fact that mother was reassured by this promise and repeatedly demanded that Kevin confirm it was but one indication of her narcissistic use of him. From the time she kept Kevin in her room to assuage her loneliness, she appears to have used him to satisfy her own needs while failing to recognize his emotional needs, even directly denying that he had any feelings contrary to those she wished him to have. I have come to see this as an important reason for Kevin's difficulty in experiencing emotions and his inability to experience and express his feelings other than via his body.

Fear of Closeness and Union

Kevin's experience of himself as never having been able fully to differentiate himself from his mother was based on his defensive need to deny his fear of separation and the extent of his rage. If he and she were united or remained as they were, he could not lose her and he would not destroy her. But this defensive stance left him a prey to the fear of being taken over and losing his separate existence, even though a part of him longed to be separate and independent. He did go out on his own, jogging or to the pub, in spite of his mother's demands that he stay home or take her with him. But even while away he would experience his bond with her. Any separation was felt as a hostile attack, and in the pub he would be miserably ashamed, thinking other people would see that he had left his mother alone.

He longed for a father who could satisfy mother's needs and rescue him from his close bond with her, and with whom he could identify and so develop a separate and masculine self. But he felt that any such identification was forbidden by mother. If he came home hot and sweaty after running, she would say, "You look just like your father"; if he went off to the pub, she would tell him of his father's drinking and her fear of father's violence. Kevin longed to know the reality of his father so as to have the hope of another way of being. He said of father's loss, "It's as though he had taken my image as well as his own." Without such an image, he was left with the double despair of his own depression and of the depression he carried in identification with his mother. Shortly before the Easter holiday he said that he saw no point in living, going on until sixty (his mother's age), always as miserable and afraid and lonely as he was now.

At this stage I was experienced, like father, as someone who might help him be able to separate, become himself. My leaving him was experienced as leaving him a prey to his despair and his close bond with his mother. Damaging himself, being damaged, and killing himself were seen as ways of becoming separate and alone, of taking independent action. Although in the transference Kevin's greatest fear has always been of being abandoned, he is also beginning to bring the accompanying fear that I will not allow his separateness or any independent action when he speaks of his various plans for self-destruction. For instance, he tells me about his heavy smoking, and how others have said it will kill him. He denies any danger and insists on his right to decide for himself, vividly conveying both his longing to be protected and his fear of being taken over and controlled.

But Kevin's fear of losing his separate identity is still experienced primarily in relation to his mother. In a bid for privacy, he attempts to destroy his very thoughts. Since he believes that she knows everything in his mind he tries not to think things of which she might not approve; in particular he tries to blot out any sexual or aggressive thoughts. He is also prepared to damage or destroy his physical body in his bid to achieve separateness. Just before

Easter, when he again felt I was leaving him to be swallowed up by his mother, Kevin spoke of how he wished to cut himself or to get beaten up: "Cutting makes me feel that I exist."[2] He wanted to go to a hospital where he could be "alone." Similarly, to end up in a police cell was seen not only as a protection from outer and inner violence but also as a means of being alone. When I noted the reality that neither in a hospital nor in prison would he be alone, Kevin responded, "But if I killed myself I would be."

It may well be that self-damage and suicide as means of becoming a separate and independent individual will remain a potential risk for Kevin until his fear of being taken over can be experienced and worked through more fully in the transference rather than in relation to the original object, the mother.

Conflicting Sexual Identifications and Wishes

An important factor in Kevin's self-destructive enactments and suicidal wishes was his inability to find any sexual identity he could accept. With the onset of puberty, when his body became fully masculine and his sexual needs urgent, his conflict around whether to be at one with or separate and different from his mother was greatly reinforced. Masculinity was felt as forbidden and as carrying the threat of the loss or destruction of mother. Homosexuality was seen as destructive to himself and to his masculinity and, again, as involving the loss of mother. Kevin longed to be a woman, but this was impossible, just as it was impossible for him to remain a small boy or to become the little girl he often wished to be or felt he was.

I do not wish to give the impression that this material unfolded in any orderly way. On the contrary, from one session to another, from one moment to the next, he would switch his stance defensively. His changing identifications and the extent of his need to disassociate, suppress, and deny gave the analysis a curiously discontinuous character. Rarely, if ever, would Kevin continue the work from one session to another; it was often as though the previous sessions had never occurred. It seemed that he had no sense of continuing selfhood. Things simply "happened" and Kevin would react to them each time as though they were new and surprising. For instance, on the train a man would put his hand into Kevin's pocket, and he would think, "That's

2. It has been described elsewhere (Hurry, 1977, 1978) how the struggle to become separate and independent may motivate the act of suicide. Haim (1969) has also pointed to the adolescent's need to confirm his independence from the object as a motivating factor in suicide. In Kevin's case it appears that actions that are "equivalents" of suicide, such as cutting, are motivated by the same need.

funny, what's going on then?" as though he had never been aware of homo-sexual fears or feelings. Technically, it was often necessary to focus on the fears that led him to move from one stance to another, and he does now seem to have gained some ongoing sense of self, although this brings the painful awareness that he is made up of many different aspects and does not know how to be. He is deeply depressed and, increasingly deprived of his various modes of enactment, at real risk of killing himself.

I believe that this risk would be less had he been able to find a solution to his sexual conflict—that is, to find a sexual role with which he could iden-tify, whether heterosexual or homosexual. In this sense, homosexuality can in some cases represent an *alternative* to suicide rather than an equivalent, as Joyce McDougall (1979) has suggested. Lacking any such alternative, Kevin has often felt that suicide was the only way out.

For the sake of clarity I shall give a picture of Kevin's conflicting sex-ual identifications and wishes before summarizing their part in his self-destructiveness.[3] Much of the content of sessions was rooted in Kevin's anxi-ety with regard to his feelings about men and, to a lesser extent, about little girls. This anxiety was presented somewhat floridly, in part because the mas-ochistic demonstration of his misery was very gratifying to him and in part because he sought a state of sexual excitement as a means of avoiding his depression and deeper fears. It was often necessary to focus on this defensive search rather than interpret the sexual content. In response, Kevin would de-scribe, for instance, how he felt interrupted at the end of every session and would set off down the road feeling abandoned until he could work up his excited fears and feelings. In sessions, where he felt I knew what he was feeling, he could experience himself as having an existence. Separated, it was as though he could no longer experience himself as having firm bound-aries, and he sought some sense of selfhood, however tenuous and tempo-rary, in the reality of physical excitement. He once said, "When I have an erection I know that I exist. . . . I know that my body exists."

Nevertheless, Kevin genuinely felt persecuted by his sexual fantasies, and his homosexual fears served in part as a defense against his highly guilt-provoking sexual wishes toward his mother. At first he told me that the idea of sex between a younger man and an older woman was "disgusting." But there were hints that it was just such a sexual partnering he longed for. He

3. The greater part of the analysis of Kevin's sexual conflicts has not been carried out within the transference, for so far within the relationship to me Kevin's search for recognition and control has been primary, of much greater affective importance to him than the sexual fears and fantasies he has experienced in relation to me. As he put it, "I do have thoughts, but I feel safe here."

spoke of childhood memories of his excitement in relation to older women. For instance, at about the age of eight he had gone on a train journey with a friend's family. He had been sitting on the auntie's knee and it felt good, exciting, but then she had put him off her knee, and he felt that everyone could see what he had been thinking. He and his friend were both interested in her, although that seemed "dreadful with her being his auntie and that." Once they stayed the night with the auntie, and Kevin had thought, "Now's me chance," but nothing happened. It seemed awful to think like that.

Kevin's inability to defend appropriately against sexual wishes during latency is evident. Also evident is what might be seen as a lack of distinction between fantasy and reality: he seemed to have been surprised that "nothing happened." The same lack of appreciation of reality prohibitions was evident in his more recent interactions with older women. When he danced with a friend of his mother's at a social event, he became highly excited, certain that she fancied him, and anxious about her husband. His apparent expectation that his sexual wishes might well be met led me to wonder not only how far his mother's attitude toward him might be seductive but also whether he might have encountered an actual seduction during the early years in her bedroom.

So far I have interpreted only his feeling that his mother does fancy him and his guilt over and fear of his wishes toward her. For instance, Kevin spoke of his mother's wanting him to dance with her. He had a strong feeling that this was wrong. When I related his feeling of wrongness to his own sexual excitement toward his mother, Kevin said that this was not so because he kept a space between them. He immediately displaced his fears, speaking of how other older women fancied him, and this was wrong. At this point, I felt his fear of inappropriate sexual demands might now be experienced in relation to me, but Kevin did not respond to interpretation along these lines. It was only when I took up his struggle to avoid such fears in relation to his mother that he told me he felt she wanted him to fill in as a husband, especially since he had left school. Later he was to describe how frequently she referred to him as if he were her boyfriend—for instance, saying in a café, "Those people are looking at us; they must think we are boy and girlfriend." This both gratified and shamed Kevin. Above all, it terrified him, for it carried the threat that his sexual wishes might actually be realized.

He has as yet by no means fully accepted his own wishes, but he has come somewhat closer. He told me that his own auntie fancied him, and that he thought, on a weekend visit, she might come into his room at night. Auntie's husband was dead, so she was "a woman on her own." When I asked

Kevin whom this reminded him of, he said "Mum . . . but you couldn't really fancy your mum. . . . It would be awkward-like." Just before Easter, however, Kevin was able to tell me that he believed both his mother and he had sexual thoughts about each other. This was "bad, but inevitable." He knew that when he was reading his sex magazines in his room he both wished and feared she would come in.

We cannot as yet be certain to what extent Kevin's view of his mother's sexual wishes toward him arose from the projection of his own wishes toward her and to what extent they are based upon reality. I think his perception of his mother's unconscious wishes is probably fairly accurate and goes some way toward explaining the extent of his need to retreat to homosexuality. If this view is correct, we have the picture of a mother who cannot allow her son to be separate, who uses him narcissistically, virtually as a part of herself, yet at the same time is highly seductive toward him.[4]

Although it is also possible that Kevin's view of the incest barrier as breachable is founded on events within his relationship with his sisters, we know that he was consciously terrified of the possibility of homosexual interaction with his brother with whom he shared a room. At first, he attempted to blot this from his mind and denied any such thoughts. When I mentioned the possibility that he might have fears about his brother similar to those about the men whom he saw as fancying him, he replied, "Oh, no, that would put the fear of God up me." It was not until after Easter that he could speak of lying awake at night, terrified that his brother might come in drunk and get into his (Kevin's) bed. Finally, he was able to speak of not only fearing such an event but wishing for it. So far, however, he has said that sexual play never took place between himself and his brother.

What he did remember was being attacked by his brother on a number of occasions. Again, he both feared and longed for such attacks. When feeling empty, humiliated, or depressed, he would turn to provoking his brother by interrupting his television viewing or speaking tactlessly to his girlfriend. During the period of Kevin's treatment, his brother has been able to control his violence, but he has made his rage toward Kevin very clear at times, once leaving him a note that stated, "If you value your life, don't speak to me." Kevin is both hopeful and afraid that his brother's attacks might end his (Kevin's) life.

Certainly in this relationship we can see one of the roots of Kevin's need

---

4. Glasser (1979) describes just such a mother in his account of the typical mother of sexually perverse patients.

to invite violence from others, of his sexualization of violence, and of his mode of inviting others to carry out his suicidal fantasy by killing him. We can also see one root of Kevin's view that to adopt a masculine role is so damaging and destructive that he dare not do so.

His picture of a "real man" was based on his image of his brother, reinforced by the image of his father as conveyed to him by his mother, and compounded by the need to defend against his own violent wishes. Throughout his life his mother has spoken of her fear of father, a drinker and an amateur boxer. She described him to Kevin as a rogue and a wanderer, who was off having sex with another woman even on the night Kevin was born. Kevin sees all sexual intercourse as violent, intrusive rape and feels that to get a woman pregnant is to damage her. It is also impossible for him fully to identify with the masculine role; he feels that his body is weak and inadequate and his penis is too small, so that his making love to a girl would certainly result in his humiliation and rejection.

Once, prior to treatment, he was invited into bed by a girl he met through a dating agency. But when he touched her he had an epileptic fit, after which she rejected him. One could understand this fit, whether or not it was hysterical, as a breakdown of ego functioning in the face of intolerable stress. And this very breakdown could be understood as an alternative or equivalent to suicide, a way of avoiding an impossibly conflictual sexual act. This is how Kevin sees it. He commented that it was as though, in bed with the girl, he had said to himself, "This won't do," and brought on the fit. The only other fit Kevin has had in the past several years was at the age of seventeen, when he was on holiday with his male friend. They were sharing a hotel room and both had been masturbating in a competitive way, comparing the size of their erections. Kevin became aware that he wanted them to masturbate each other. The next evening, as he turned out the light to get into bed, he had a fit. After this he broke off all contact with his friend.

He is now terrified of the intensity of his homosexual longings. Behind them lies the longing for his absent father. He searches for his father not only in other men but literally, by hoping to bump into him one day. But to be homosexual is intolerable to him. It means to be an emasculated man, "a sissy," and in the tough pub society in which he moves this would result in total isolation. Kevin believes that were he known to be "queer" no one would speak to him again, and his mother would tell him to get out. Women would reject him, and he would have no possibility of heterosexual relationships. Currently he believes that women do reject him because they are aware that he once "was" a homosexual.

This is how Kevin described the incident that took place in the lavatory when he was sixteen or seventeen. He accepted a homosexual pickup, but he also sought masculinity through it. In the lavatory the other man commented upon Kevin's small penis, saying "I can make it nice and big." It was partly because of this hope, both conscious and unconscious, that Kevin went into a cubicle and allowed the man to suck his penis. Later he felt persecuted by the frequent revival of the memory of this excitement when he was masturbating. But he also felt that the incident did not fully make him a homosexual since he had not taken the active part.

Kevin has suggested one solution to his conflicts: he longs to be a woman, a fully conscious desire. Indeed, he remembers having wanted this since puberty, but it conflicted sharply with his simultaneous wish to be a "normal male," which made him afraid to admit his feminine aspects and the extent of his wish to destroy his masculinity. What he brought first to his analysis was his fear that he was like a woman. People had commented on his appearance, someone once asking when he was out on a date, "Which one is the girl, then?" And people had often said he was just like his sister, a similarity strengthened in his mind when he developed epilepsy at puberty, as she had. This event confirmed his view of himself as a damaged female: Kevin said he had been frightened of being like a girl at that time. He had been very worried while waiting to develop, feeling that something was wrong, that "it" was too small. He was afraid, too, that he might lose "it." He had thought of going for some sort of checkup, but finally his penis had grown, he got pleasure from it, and that was a relief. But he had also thought it might be better to be a girl.

His wish to be a girl/woman was powered by both libidinal and defensive elements. Kevin felt that were he a girl he would be able to be with a girl and touch her as he liked. He could be a female united with a female. The strength of this wish was clearly conveyed in his fascination with lesbians and his guilty excitement when he watched two women performing a lesbian act in a pub. Further, Kevin felt that were he a woman he could be loved by a man and so could avoid the horror of homosexuality. Once, when he spoke of his likeness to his mother, I reflected on his need to be like her and commented on his wish to be loved as she had been, by men. Kevin responded, "Yes, when a man looks at me I feel I'm a woman—I think, 'I'm not queer because I'm a woman.'" This feeling of being a woman did not involve any change of his conscious body image; it was rather that, if a man looked at him on the train, he felt the man was looking at him as a woman and that his male body was "a disguise."

For a long time Kevin had also consciously believed that he would be "less evil" as a woman, that he would not hurt women as men did, as his father had hurt his mother. This emerged when Kevin was approached by a girl who offered him her phone number. Although excited, Kevin was also very alarmed. He said that there was something in him that did not want to accept any girl's approaches. "I might be old-fashioned, but I think you shouldn't go with a girl unless you are staying with her. You might get her pregnant or something." He felt that his father had endangered and harmed his mother in many ways. Just before Easter, when Kevin was beaten up and kicked, he told me he had lain in the road looking up at the other men as he was kicked, and then they kicked his eye. He had often thought that his father had damaged his mother's eye and was afraid his eye would be like his mother's. But the doctor had said his eye was all right. Kevin agreed when I took up his disappointment in not being *really* damaged and hurt like his mother, and he recognized that in his terror of being as violent as his father he preferred to be a hurt woman or girl.

His longing to be a woman had also played a part in his self-cutting. When he said he could not help thinking of men looking at his bum, of his feeling like a woman, and of his wish to be one, I wondered about a wish to cut off his penis when his abdomen cutting was moving downward. Kevin said yes, he had wanted to do it, but he knew that it would hurt. After the episode with the man in the lavatory Kevin had shaved his pubic hair: "Imagine if I had jerked!"

Thus Kevin could not accept the male or the female role. The possibility of undisguised gratification in either aroused intolerable guilt, fear, or shame. An alternative solution, and a preferred one, was to remain a child—but an idealized, nonsexual, nonaggressive child. Kevin often presented himself both within the analysis and to others as though he were a little boy. At the start of the analysis, if anyone asked his age, he would reply either "ten" or "fifteen." So convincing was his presentation that people often believed him to be much younger than he really was. But, of course, this solution was impossible, too. It has now become much more conflictual; although the longing to remain a child continues, Kevin is ashamed of looking like one and tries to appear grown-up.

Another fantasied solution is to be a little girl. Kevin's sexual fantasies about young girls have so far played a relatively small role in treatment. They have appeared largely in the context of his longing to be fathered and his adoption of a protective fathering role toward little girls. For instance, he met a little girl at seaside holidays who hero-worshiped him and whom he taught to swim. The last time he saw her he was horrified to find that, as he held her up in the sea, he had an erection. Thereafter, he no longer went on these outings. The fantasy that his father might care for little girls was related in part to his view of his father's relationship to his children by other women. (Father has had another family since leaving Kevin's mother.) Kevin received a great shock when he met his half sister at his aunt's. She had run away from home and appeared ragged and poorly looked after. Kevin could not understand how his father let her look like that. He longed to protect her and asked his mother whether one could marry one's half sister. When he told me this he also spoke of his hopes of getting married one day, so that he could have children and never leave them as his father had left him.

Kevin also believed that his father had wanted a daughter and rejected him because he was a boy. This belief emerged at a point where he felt there was a risk of his having heterosexual satisfaction. He was approached by prostitutes one evening and had said that he would "love" to go with them. Although he did not have enough money at the time, he knew he could go back. After telling me this, Kevin went on to say that recently he had felt he was "changing" when he looked in the mirror. He could not explain it, but somehow he seemed to be becoming ugly. I linked his feeling ugly with his reaction to his masculinity, remembered his wish to cut off his penis, and said that recently he had been making terrific efforts to get a girlfriend, trying to blot out his passionate longing to *be* a girl. Kevin then expanded on how both of his parents had wanted a girl and that his sister had said frequently that Kevin was supposed to be her sister. He had felt he had to be both boy and girl and to play with both his brother and his sister.

It appears that Kevin's later conflicts around sexual identification are based upon, and facilitated by, some confusion of gender identity (Stoller, 1975). I spoke earlier of Kevin's experiencing himself as a part of his mother and of his inability fully to differentiate from her. In addition, it now appears that his sexual identity was molded not only by his mother, who treated him as part of herself, but also by his sister (in whose care he was often left), who had wanted and expected a girl baby, and made her wishes very clear.

The role that Kevin's uncertainty as to his sexual identity and his conflicting sexual wishes plays in his self-destructive enactments is as important as that of his conflicts over separation and closeness. The onset of puberty was crucial to the intensification of his conflicts, and it was at puberty that he developed epilepsy. In late adolescence, following the failure of his tentative attempts to establish age-appropriate relationships with girls, his self-destructiveness took a more active form in his cutting and his suicide attempt. The relationship between his self-destructiveness and his sexuality is a complex one: his increasing awareness of his lack of a firm identity is exceedingly painful to him and has led to thoughts of suicide; his suicidal wishes and self-destructive behavior and thoughts in turn serve both to defend against and to gratify his sexual wishes.

Kevin's self-cutting, for instance, was aimed at avoiding any sexual gratification as a male or as a homosexual; through cutting he sought to disable himself as a man, and he believed he made himself unattractive to homosexuals. But his cutting was simultaneously unconsciously aimed at making himself into a woman and at gratification as a woman.

In eliciting attacks from others, Kevin avoids the gratification of, and is punished for, both homosexual and heterosexual wishes. But he also recreates the exciting and terrifying interactions with his brother, and so he enacts his fantasy of the primal scene, identifying with the hurt and beaten woman while externalizing the masculine, attacking parts of himself. All elements are present, whether directly or in identification. The child in Kevin is there, too. By the presentation of his attacked self, he hopes to win the pity, concern, and even admiration of the object. For instance, when he was beaten up and kicked, Kevin lay in the road, sure that someone would come along and be sorry for him. When passersby ignored him, he began to think of cutting or killing himself and sought pity from his mother, feeling the pain only when he saw her reaction. In the following session, too, he sought pity from me. Suicide itself was always seen as the ultimate way of achieving his various aims if he failed to achieve them by less final means.

Conclusion

Kevin's self-destructive acting out has occurred only in relation to holiday breaks. Thus, the analysis, apart from holidays, does provide him with some feeling of safety in the face of his impulses. But without the immediacy of analysis, he is lost.

Kevin's reaction to the Easter break indicates something of the nature of "holding" he experiences analysis as providing. He did not provoke attack from others, but he found a new way of acting out, although one based on old behaviors: he reverted to fire setting, endangering both himself and others. He told me about this as soon as he returned, saying that he had "done something silly" on the first day. He had been unhappy, had been missing his sessions, and went out and drank too much. He thought of cutting himself but did not do so. Then, on the way home, he started his old fire setting, lighting and dropping pieces of paper where the flames might catch and spread. He wanted to hurt others and not be in such pain himself. He had also thought of hurting himself, however, and held his hands above the paper before dropping it.

Analysis of this episode brought out the contribution of the various factors I have described in relation to his acting out. (In addition, the fire setting was seen in part as an attempt to avoid and control his excitement and rage through externalization.) Certainly the fire setting was a step on the path to suicide: Kevin said that he had wanted me to know what it was like for him, and I would have realized it if he had come heavily bandaged. To have burned himself to death, he said, would have been the most effective way of showing me what he was feeling.

I believed Kevin when he spoke of his hope that his action would convey his feelings to me. Although this statement conveyed in part his unwillingness to face the extent of his wish to hurt me (he had denied any wish to set fire to my house) and his hope that I would be hurt by the knowledge of how he felt, what he experienced as most important was the need to have his feelings recognized in an ongoing way. On several occasions he has told me that coming to his sessions is important to him because "you know how I feel . . . and when I am not here you do not know how I feel, and I have to save it all up . . . and . . . "

Whatever the content of the analysis, it seems that what Kevin experiences as its most important function is the recognition of how he feels. At this stage, I am in agreement with him. His feelings have never been recognized sufficiently—rather, they have been denied—nor has he been recognized as a separate being independent of his mother's needs. It remains to be seen how far the analysis will enable Kevin to recognize and own his own feelings and to contain his wishes in thought, rather than being driven to express his affects via his bodily states and his wishes in immediate, dissociated action.

Rosalie Joffe

8.

Mary: Attempted Suicide—A Search for Alternative Paths

Mary was first brought to the Centre by her mother when she was sixteen years old. She was anorexic and quite debilitated, and menstruation had ceased. It was learned that she had just obtained high grades in her examinations. She had been studying and dieting intensively and had withdrawn from everyone. She experienced a feeling of omnipotence, of being in control and needing no one.

The precipitating factor for her anorexia seemed to be the breakup of a close relationship with a school friend. This was a much admired girl with great social aplomb through whom Mary could lose her fear of being unacceptable. It was surmised that she had turned to this girl in her attempts to separate from her mother. Similarly, after she refused the offer of therapy, she turned to her younger sister, Doris, professed herself cured of her anorexic illness, and started eating again. She was, however, to return to the Centre three years later, when she was nineteen.

Family Background

Mary was the eldest, by two and four years, of three daughters of intelligent, well-educated, middle-class parents. Until Mary's adolescence the family was on the whole intact and caring. The father had always tended to be moody and withdrawn and was frequently absent on business. The mother appeared narcissistic and immature and described herself as not having felt ready for the responsibilities of motherhood when her daughters were born. During her husband's business trips she was withdrawn and depressed and spent much time in bed. Mary often experienced her mother as intrusive and felt narcissistically used by her. She maintained that "mother lived through her children—for example, dancing through them as she watched them dance." She had "fetched and carried" them to school and to a multitude of extra-school activities. All the girls had proved to be highly intelligent and talented, but Mary believed that the middle sister, Doris, was the prettiest and most gifted. Doris was said by the parents and Mary to have been clinging, demanding, and liable to temper tantrums while Mary was seen as compliant and trying hard to please.

The chronology of the changing family structure and alliances was not clear. If Mary is to be believed, there were always times when the four female members allied themselves against a denigrated father/husband. There is evidence of an early close and loving parental relationship. From the time Mary was eight years old the three daughters retaliated against the much resented exclusivity of the parents by ostentatiously excluding them from their secrets amidst much whispering and giggling. By Mary's seventeenth year, the girls had made the parents feel like intruders in the family home.

When Mary was ten, her mother had a miscarriage and, sometime later, banned her husband from the marital bedroom. By the time Mary was fourteen, family meals had become a thing of the past; everyone prepared his or her own food. Mary also dated her growing feelings of insecurity and distrust of her parents from the age of ten. Her parents came to be thought of as siblings—"as two more unreliable kids."

Alongside this picture of the parents was another one of strict, concerned parents who insisted on accompanying their daughters to and from parties. The parents seemed to Mary to confirm her own fears about sex. After Mary's anorexic illness she and her sisters became united against the parents. It is my belief that in this way they united their parents against them and kept the marriage intact.

The year before Mary's return to the Centre she and her sister Doris had left home after a violent row in which all five members of the family had ended up tussling on the floor. Mary and Doris lived in an abandoned house and received welfare payments. During this period Mary wrote and failed her school exams. Without informing Mary, Doris suddenly returned to the parents' home. Mary became frightened and followed soon afterward but continued to storm out of the parental home at times.

Return to the Centre at Nineteen

Mary told her second interviewer that her sister Doris was the most important person in her life. Doris, however, was working and spent every evening with a boyfriend. Mary was barely holding herself together by projecting her feelings of hate and madness. She insisted that her mother wished her dead and was "mad, bad, perverse, and paranoid." Mary was at times so out of touch with reality that she experienced herself as the "real and true mother" to her sisters. These projections allowed her to negate any parenting or loving function in her mother as well as her own role as a child. In the grip of this fantasy she saw herself as middle-aged, sexless, or, as she put it, "an aunt to her sisters' future children."

It seemed that incestuous fantasies were in danger of breaking through into consciousness. Violence toward both parents had already occurred when either of them threatened her fantasy and behaved like parents, assuming some control over her. For example, she had taken an axe to her father's study door to retrieve her paints and easel, which he had confiscated as a punishment.

Mary expressed no guilt about these attacks. She was completely caught up in a desperate battle to save herself from the madness she feared by projecting it onto her parents. It was not only Mary who was breaking down but the family structure as well. The father alone appeared able to keep a semblance of sanity and intactness. He continued to lead a successful life in the business world.

Mary almost refused treatment a second time when she understood that her parents would have to be seen. She insisted that this would contaminate her analysis and that her mother would take it over. She walked out on her second interviewer, but this time she returned to accept the offer of analysis under the Centre's research program. She came under our category of psychotic functioning. The behaviors that led us to this diagnosis were her use of splitting and paranoid projections, loss of the sense of reality (for example, the belief that her mother was usurping her role as true mother to her sisters), her use of statements that seemed to belong to primary process thinking, feelings of depersonalization, and acute confusion in relation to time and geographical place.

There were also indications that suicide was a possibility. Violence had broken through. There were massive distortions of the parental figures and hatred of her female body. She showed no guilt for her attacks on her parents and was intent on the search for revenge. She could not experience any good nurturing object inside or outside and felt herself as only hating and hated.

The First Five Weeks of Analysis

For Mary, to be in analysis was a confirmation of her fear that she was abnormal. In an effort to ward off this fear she bombarded me verbally with rapid nonstop attacks on her mother. From the beginning she found the end of sessions and the weekend breaks extremely difficult. Every Friday she felt I rejected her, which confirmed that she was unlovable and shamefully unacceptable. She tried to defend herself against these feelings and to maintain the longed-for relationship of the ideal patient/child to the ideal analyst/mother. Her unacknowledged anger with me was displaced on to her mother.

On the first Friday of her analysis Mary came late to her session. She was in a terrible state. She wept and raged violently and threatened never to see me again. She turned her anger onto the interviewer who had insisted on seeing her parents before treatment commenced. Just as Mary had predicted, her mother had messed up her analysis and was trying to take it over. Mary vitriolically recounted how her mother had taken over her menstruation, how she had searched for and found the first bloodstain on Mary's underpants. The present outburst was precipitated by the mother's asking whether Mary was going to her analytic session. Mary reported that she had hit her mother across the face, leaving a bruise. She was so enraged that she could have killed her without compunction, she said.

Mary's struggle to protect the analyst from her distrust and paranoia continued. By the end of the third week her defenses were crumbling; she could no longer maintain her manic verbal barrage. She often cried silently, lying curled up in a fetal position. My overriding impression was of the girl's tangible psychic breakdown and despair. She elicited great empathy and concern in me despite her powerful projections, which seemed to invade my mind. The struggle to keep Mary alive and the analysis intact was precarious. We both understood that I was powerless to prevent her from killing herself unless she allied herself with the wish to live. I made myself available to her by telephone over weekends and began the search for a hospital bed for her.

My aim in this phase of the analysis was to give Mary some insight into the defensive use she made of omnipotence and the compulsive and unconscious nature of her sense of doom and drive to kill herself. I put her in touch with her paradoxical triumphant determination to prove herself beyond help even in the midst of her desperate longing for help. In order to defuse the grandiose power she might feel in nursing a secret plan to kill herself, I shared my belief that she had such a plan and that this afforded her a sense of power over me and her own life in her attempts to counteract her unbearable feelings of vulnerability, helplessness, and lack of control. I acknowledged her need to reverse this state and prove me helpless to prevent her from killing herself. On the other hand, I undermined the rationale of her decision to kill herself. I firmly stressed that she was driven to enact an unconscious conflict or fantasy which, as yet, neither of us could understand.

Surely, death was too final and irrevocable a choice to make in ignorance of the true motive.

Like many suicidal adolescents, Mary was struggling to split off and deny the loving, caretaking qualities in her parents, her analyst, and herself so that her murderous impulses toward herself could remain unchecked and guilt-free. I understood the unspoken complaint, each time I ended a session or took a weekend break, that I, like her parents, would not care if she were dead. Mary felt deeply ashamed of dependency and struggled against it. In her mind it was linked with a longing for bodily care which in adolescence had become sexualized and incestuous. In this sense my concern for her was experienced by her as seductive. I stood in the way of the relief she sought from punishment in death.

In the fourth week, I noted: "Her defenses have cracked open. She cannot go on; suicide is an imminent possibility." That Friday Mary walked out of her session. I found her in the cloakroom, half lying on the floor, clinging to the wall, weeping. She would not talk to me and insisted on leaving, but she returned a few hours later. She had once more physically attacked her mother and then her father when he tried to restrain her. Mary then stayed with a girlfriend's family for a few days until she felt she was contaminating the friend's brother, who spoke of feeling suicidal about his exam results.

In the following week Mary went from friend to friend and ultimately to a hostel. She began to carry two plastic bags, one in each hand, everywhere she went. She took to wandering the streets like a homeless person with nowhere to go. She could hardly drag herself around. She again walked out of her session on Thursday of the fifth week. She made a suicide attempt the next Monday.

The Suicide Attempt

Mary sent a message to me from a general hospital, where she had taken herself. She said she had wandered around looking for a suitable place; when she found an empty church, she had entered and swallowed sleeping tablets. She described herself as having felt so dead the previous week that killing herself was just another kind of dead. She had experienced herself as split between "I" and "me." The "I" was going to do something to the "me," but the "me" suddenly didn't want to die. She seemed to hear my voice stating the case for the "me" who wished to live and who was being driven inexorably toward death. Mary changed her mind and managed to get to a hospital, where her stomach was washed out. The hospital refused to keep her more than one day, however, and she was admitted to a psychiatric hospital ten days later.

For about a month after the attempt the possibility of suicide was at its height. The mixture of deep despair and vulnerability, on the one hand, and omnipotence, hatred, and paranoia, on the other, was difficult to contain. She erected a defensive façade for the medical staff, insisting nothing was wrong with her. She expressed shame at having made the suicide attempt but even more shame at having changed her mind. She refused to cooperate, to bathe or change her clothes. She confided to me that the clothes protected her from the feeling of being "liquified." "Liquified" seemed to mean that there was no containing skin or structure to hold her together or to prevent leakage outward or others getting in. She further explained that after phone calls or letters from her parents she was filled with rage and revulsion at the thought that "my liquid and their liquid would become mingled."

Another time she said she felt as though she had just come round from her suicide attempt, yet she was in fact dead. This was hell! She believed that everyone on the ward and friends who visited were her own projections. This was the afterlife, with everything and everyone she was trying to escape from there with her. She knew, she said, that this was mad.

After a month Mary was transferred to an open therapeutic ward where I continued to see her three times a week for the next fourteen months. She could go out but had to negotiate with the staff the time she was to return. She also gradually began spending weekends at home with her parents. She was a very difficult patient on the ward. She fought against conforming to rules, refused to use facilities like occupational therapy, was provocative and highly manipulative, inviting expulsion. There was infinite scope for splitting the transference. Although Mary adamantly denied her dependence on the analysis and the importance of separations, there ensued a regular pattern to the week—each Monday she felt depersonalized and "cut off" (her words) from me; each Friday she was silent, unable to speak. She forgot impending holiday dates and extended her weekend and holiday visits away from the hospital by an extra day.

Early Object Relationships

I became aware of a special feature of this analysis: that a period of crisis would recur each year at the same time. She experienced a sense of impending doom as her birthday approached along with the anniversaries of her suicide attempt and hospitalization five and seven weeks later. This crisis period came to have a recognizable pattern and a double anniversary-type significance as well. As the transference unfolded it became possible to conceptualize a time of developmental traumas shortly after Mary's second birthday. It is my hypothesis that the ways in which Mary attempted to resolve the conflicts that then arose foreshadowed her later developmental distortions and breakdowns at sixteen and nineteen years and that they are being repeated in the analysis.

There were three major upheavals in Mary's second year of life. Seven weeks after her second birthday a sister was born. Shortly thereafter the family moved to a new house, which entailed the loss of their neighbors, an elderly couple who had been loving and supportive to both mother and child. In her second year Mary *seemed* to become the good, compliant "big" girl. But although she apparently identified with her mother's wishes for her to be clean, toilet-trained, and loving to her baby sister, there ensued a battle with the mother about food. This displacement from anal to oral rebellion can be regarded as a precursor to her anorexic symptoms at sixteen years of age. Both contained an indirect attack on the caretaking or feeding mother and the negation of the mother's parenting or feeding role.

Mary's seemingly adaptive compliance continued throughout childhood and appeared in the transference, where a covert battle was manifest in her difficulty in speaking or in beginning the sessions, in lateness, and in the difficulty she had taking in or remembering interpretations. Mary called this compliant behavior her "lovely-kiddy syndrome." It was this syndrome she tried angrily to dismantle at eighteen in the violent attacks on her parents. But without this mode of relating Mary was faced with a terrifying sense of nothingness and futility or a sense of unacceptability or abnormality. She had never come to terms with or taken responsibility for her feelings of envy, jealousy, and hatred, always tending instead to split and project.

Mary had little sense of self or of her own boundaries. Until adolescence everything she had achieved had been for her mother. She felt lost in her relationship to the analyst, who did not guide and direct. In the first years of her analysis she alternated between longing and searching for union or oneness with the analyst and terror of losing herself in such a union. Mary described a central fantasy in the first five weeks: she was caught in a bottomless cylinder in which, unable to reach the top, she was slipping down into nothingness. (In the fourth week of analysis, it will be recalled, Mary was found holding onto the wall in the cloakroom to keep from sliding to the floor.) The cylinder was understood as the body of the mother or the analyst or the total analytic holding situation, which had become so threatening. There was more to the fantasy, however. Mary sometimes could fly out of the

cylinder. I understood this to symbolize her defensive manic masculine identification and the unconscious fantasy that as a man she could safely enter the
mother cylinder and fly out again at will.

It could be said that the traumas at two years of age themselves had pre-
cursors in Mary's earliest relationship with a narcissistic mother who alternated between depression and withdrawal, on the one hand, and, on the
other, cathexis of infant and even intrusiveness. Without an experience of a
safe predictable relationship Mary as the infant was forced into early coping
and defensive modes of relating. This may result in disruption of the experience of "going on being" or "true self," and manifests itself later in feelings
of unreality and futility (Winnicott, 1960). In the transference Mary frequently exhibited a false lively excited manner as though she were trying to
elicit a response from a depressed analyst/mother. The reverse was also true
when I found myself working for both of us, aware of a heavy unalive patient. It was reported, for example, that in addition to her refusal to eat at two
and her anorexia at sixteen, Mary had weaned herself when the mother's milk
was failing.

It is my belief that such a need to adapt or "react" too early to a
mother's needs, which disrupts the early state of "going on being," is often a
precursor to later gender confusion. Mary believed her mother would have
preferred her to be a boy. She had no stable body image, a lack that was
reflected in the way she dressed. It may be recalled that she refused to remove
her clothes for the first week she was in the hospital. She wore men's boots, a
tattered pair of jeans, and a man's pajama jacket from under which peeped a
feminine lacy camisole and a delicate gold necklace. She also was subject to
frightening psychic experiences of body changes from female to male. She
negated the fact of her vagina and suffered from vaginismus.

She related to herself and to me as part-objects. When I visited her in
the hospital, I sometimes felt treated as a denigrated, useless appendage; at
times she did not bother to get out of bed for her session. She bought anti-
psychoanalytic books. At other times she related to me as an all-powerful
breast with whom she longed for the ideal union. Within this union we were
both asexual beings. Yet at the same time she began a sexual relationship
with a young male patient and suggested that she should find a sex therapist
for her sexual problems.

When Mary's fantasy of union with the ideal asexual analyst was disrupted by weekends and holidays, she experienced me as the one "who had it
all" and herself as the one who had not. She believed that only one of a twosome could have the breast or phallus. Her projected envy was experienced
as persecuting; for example, she described both mother and me at different

times as "protecting their territory." She felt she could complete herself only at the expense of the other. One or the other of us would die if she freed herself.[1]

Like McDougall's patients, who feel "they function to enhance the maternal ego," Mary was enraged that her very life bore testament to her mother's maternal ability. In the transference she nullified my interpretations and analytic nurturing. She could not bear to get better and thus prove me to be a potent analyst. Mary maintained that her mother seemed to take her over, to live through her daughters' achievements. She said that her mother knew even before she herself did when Mary began to menstruate. At times she experienced me as wanting to force her to be a patient and thus deny that she was also a woman. She complained that her mother and sisters in the past had forced her into being something other than a feminine child and robbed her of her feminine sexuality. She related, with much vehemence, how her sisters had always received the soft, cuddly, feminine toys while she received the hard ones. Her younger sister, Doris, always demanded and received "the rounded feminine" part of a slice of bread, while Mary received the lower straight part.

In early adolescence Mary had tried to separate from her mother and her "smothering" by forming a similar relationship to a girlfriend. When this girl disrupted their union by turning to boys, Mary withdrew into an omnipotent self-controlled regimen of study and starvation. The compulsion to need nothing and no one reached such proportions that she found herself unable to breathe or speak properly. When she rejected the offer of treatment from the first interviewer at our Centre she turned to Doris. This was to happen many times in the first three years of her analysis as she tried to escape union with and engulfment by me through relationships with Doris or young men.

She also came to detest her father as disgusting and ineffectual; he had failed in his parental role to her and had made unfair demands on her mother. But it was this humiliated, denigrated, anal-sadistic father with whom Mary identified. She saw her mother as beautiful and feminine with a lovely body, attributes her mother had passed on only to Mary's sisters. Mary found it impossible to identify with this mother representation. She looked like her father, she said.

In the third year of analysis, during a week's absence of both me and her father, Mary had looked forward to having her mother to herself. As in the past, however, when father was away, mother was sunk in depression. Mary

1. McDougall (1979) states that the homosexual woman experiences herself as an indispensable part of the mother, not only as the mother's phallus, but also as controlled by mother, like a fecal object.

said she wanted to stick a knife into her. She felt totally abandoned and un-safe in the house. We could begin to understand the double abandonment Mary had felt each time her father took a business trip. The father's real im-portance in the family began to emerge from the female members' denials and denigrations, and Mary's angry, violent identification with him became clear. He alone seemed able to arouse and excite the depressed mother. Mary recalled a time at age eight or nine, when her father was away; she had sneaked out of the house at night through the garage with her bike to join "the boys." She recalled that this was a time when her friends were mainly boys who rode around on bicycles. She used to experience herself as ac-cepted by them, not quite a boy but a special kind of girl. On her return the house was locked up, the lights were out, and mother had gone to bed. She had been devastated because mother had not realized that she was gone.

A Pattern of Crisis during Analysis

Although elements of Mary's breakdowns at sixteen and nineteen were re-peated at other times during the analysis, I shall describe only the repetitive nature of the crisis period that occurred each year during the anniversary of the first two months of the analysis.

The Pattern

1. A sense of impending doom would become focused on her forthcom-ing birthday.
2. A driven quality would emerge. Each year she would feel a compul-sion to change something such as the place where she lived or worked, accompanied by a flight into manic activity.
3. Ever-increasing feelings of rejection or the expectation of rejection by her objects would become more immediate, as did the tendency to provoke rejection or to use reversal by rejecting or leaving her objects.
4. A sense of her unacceptability and abnormality would mount.
5. The compulsion, in the first weeks of analysis, to force me to change her mother into a better/good mother was later concentrated on try-ing to change her own body or the framework of the analysis.
6. The flight from unconscious fantasies of an incestuous relationship with her mother or me to a girlfriend, her sister Doris, or heterosex-ual objects.
7. The need for violence to break the tension continued to mount de-spite her flights and maneuvers. At the time of the first anniversary,

instead of attempting suicide, she was beaten up. Later violence was contained only in fantasy.

The First Anniversary

Toward the end of the first year of Mary's treatment she began agitating to leave the hospital. She insisted that she had to leave before her birthday although the hospital staff and I felt this was decidedly premature. She now displayed the driven quality she had shown in the months leading up to her suicide attempt. She railed and raved with increasing desperation against me and the doctors. She felt for a while that she had to leave her boyfriend. She complained that I treated her only because of her interest in the research, so she might as well leave. Then, when all her efforts to arrange to live in a hostel failed, she withdrew into deep despair. She wept and said she could not try again. She was silent for a great part of the sessions. She sometimes could not bear the tussle in herself between reaching out to me and her boyfriend and living, on the one hand, and withdrawing, giving up, and dying, on the other. She recalled the "I/me" dichotomy of her suicide attempt. She wished that no one had emotional claims on her so that she could kill herself.

This despairing hopelessness would once more give way to frenetic activity to try to bring about changes in her external world. Steamroller-type speech again flooded the analytic sessions; I was unable to get a word in. It became imperative for Mary to force me to change the day or the hour of her sessions. She wished to have a break from her analysis. When she said she felt as though something awful was moving toward her, the link was made to the approaching anniversary of her suicide attempt, the memory of which she was trying to avoid by temporarily leaving analysis. I, like her mother previously, had become the repository for her feelings of abnormality.

Mary described herself as feeling ill in much the same way as when she was anorexic, although she was now overeating instead of starving. She recalled how "cut off" from everyone she was at sixteen. She had experienced almost a physical sense of not being able to speak or even breathe. She had a terrible sleeping problem. She described how sometimes she stuffed herself with food and then starved herself until she went down to ninety pounds and stopped menstruating. She described how anxious her mother became, forcing her to eat eggs and bread and butter—once at five o'clock in the morning. She acknowledged her mother's anxiety but felt it shouldn't have been directed to her eating. This seemed to be relevant in the transference, in the battle to keep her alive. She could begin to understand her gender conflict: in the past she had tried to rid herself of her pubertal sexual characteristics by dieting, whereas now she was overeating to hide them with layers of fat.

Her compulsion to bring forward and thus control the date of her transfer from the hospital to a hostel became paramount. The danger of her acting out was increased by my forthcoming holiday. She tried to deal with her feelings of abandonment by becoming protective of a fellow patient whose therapy had stopped and who was also preparing to leave the hospital—just as at sixteen she had tried to become mother/analyst to her sisters. She attacked analysis as futile as she had attacked her mother in the past. She forgot the last day we were to meet before the holiday. She had an impulse to break something, like hurling a bottle through the window.

In the first session after my return from holiday, I learned that she had also felt rejected by her boyfriend, whom she had verbally attacked in a provocative and destructive manner. She told me she had been letting herself get fat and uglier. The previous day she had gone to a hairdresser and had become terribly upset. Her hair was ruined, she said, and she wanted to put a paper bag on her head.

The following session her face was cut and swollen, and she was dizzy and clearly in a lot of pain. She led up to what had happened to her by first explaining her frame of mind before the event. She had phoned the local government department, demanding to know why the hostel was not yet ready, and had felt put down by the person on the telephone. Then her close friend in the hospital had returned from a visit to another prospective hostel but had shut herself away from Mary and refused to speak to her. Mary went to a pub as soon as it opened and apparently drank steadily for about five hours. Toward closing time a man Mary knew came in. She had had an argument with him previously, she said; she hated him, he was a "chauvinistic pig." She now had a shouting match with him which escalated into Mary's provoking him further by hitting him. He punched her on the forehead and she fell, striking the back of her head. She required stitches and was possibly slightly concussed.

Mary stayed in the hospital in all fifteen months, when she moved to a hostel. Her parents were allowed to help her settle in and were introduced to the hostel staff. She had not yet been able to resolve her splitting process and projections. Thus, she was unable to mourn the loss of the protection and caring of the hospital staff. Her behavior remained the same at the hostel, with the staff often being used as external persecutors. Once more she came to my consulting room five times a week, which meant that she could again use the couch instead of our sitting face to face, as had been the case in the hospital.

The same pattern has continued in subsequent years at anniversary time with gradual changes in the ways Mary finds to ease the tension.

Second Anniversary

On the occasion of the second anniversary Mary succeeded in provoking the hostel staff to expel her prematurely after eight months. She returned to her parents' home. She had begun to recognize her envy and jealousy, her splitting mechanisms and paranoid projections. She was at times able to express remorse for her attacks on me, her parents, and the hospital and hostel staffs. Despite reparative attempts and her desire to be a perfect daughter for a perfect, loving mother, she was nevertheless convinced that her mother wanted her dead.

At about this time a cat had a litter in the garage at Mary's home. The cat would leave the kittens at times but returned frequently to feed them. One day they disappeared, and the sisters believed their parents had had them removed and killed. When Mary asked her mother why she had not had abortions when she had not felt ready to have children, her mother had replied that she did not trust the doctors. Mary felt that it was awful to give birth to unwanted children. The absent kittens, believed to be dead, represented not only herself but her own unborn children, doomed never to live, and the hopelessness of her ever being able to identify with the loving mother cat.

Mary associated the material about the absent kittens to some long overdue library books her mother had recently returned. Mary had been carrying these books in one of her two plastic bags at the time of her suicide attempt. They were the books she needed for her examinations and symbolically represented her hope for a future, the part of her that wanted to go on living. Like the kittens who the mother cat thought were in a safe place, the books in the safe plastic bag had vanished. Mary could not trust her mother or me to want her to live and become a woman. She also at that time recalled her own guilt and her death wishes about the baby her mother had miscarried when Mary was ten years old. The link was made to her wish to kill herself—the mother's unwanted first-born baby.

Third Anniversary

Mary worked for a year in a residential home for old people and then for eighteen months with physically handicapped people. During this time she at last managed to study for and pass her examinations and eventually enrolled in a university.

As the third anniversary of her suicide attempt approached, Mary reported the familiar sense of impending doom and fear of breakdown, but she felt "real" as never before. It once more became imperative to change jobs, move out of her parents' home, change analytic times. But this time there was a flight into health. Her fears of an abnormal body were projected onto the crippled bodies of the people she now cared for. There were also flights into heterosexuality, but her affairs were on the whole short-lived, secret episodes with younger colleagues. I now became the "mad mother" who was standing in the way of Mary's normality. I refused to collude with her seeming health: she demanded that I should reduce her analytic times, to which I did not agree.

Subsequent Years and Bisexual Conflict

In the fourth year of Mary's analysis her concern about her body became so paramount that the anniversary date lost its significance. She now sported a conspicuous red streak in her hair. It seemed to proclaim to the world that she was a sexually available woman, yet like a man with a cockscomb! She continued to overeat and to diet. She became intensely preoccupied with her body and exercised rigorously. Tension often culminated in withdrawal into bodily ailments such as colds, a sore back, and a colon that gave trouble in reaction to her food abuse. She guarded against her tendency to seek a violent solution to her tension. She gave up riding her moped, for example, for fear that she would crash it in an effort to relieve her pervasive tension.

She became increasingly aware of herself as "bisexual." In her masturbation fantasies she sometimes identified with both the damsel in distress and the rescuing knight. The fantasies she hated most, which came into consciousness despite herself, were those of being a sadistic man. She became aware that she dealt with her jealousy and envy of beautiful women by looking at them as a man would. There were fleeting frightening experiences of actual body changes from female to male which she tried to control by intensified physical exercise, but the temptation to again lose touch with her body by confusion, denial, and the "floaty" feeling of having no body was now no longer open to her.

When she realized once that two boys were discussing her in a shop, she hoped they liked what they saw but feared they thought she was wearing drag, that the bright red streak in her hair was a wig, that she was a bit of a joke, a fat nothing with a man's body but with nothing of the man. She felt "butch." When she lost weight, she seemed to lose it all from her breasts so she felt even more "neither-nor." Instead of fat she felt herself as all muscle. After she had stopped taking contraceptive pills, she lost her periods for two months, which increased her sense of having a heavy neutered body.

At the height of her fears about sexual abnormality she was constantly afraid that others could see how crazy she felt and would recognize the bisexuality of her body. She overheard someone wondering if "that girl knows what a fright her hair looks!" Once more she went to the hairdresser and had a terrifying experience. In her words, she "freaked out." The male hairdresser had cut her very long hair too short at the back. She momentarily imagined that she saw a man's face in the mirror instead of her own. When she touched her hair she felt that something irreparable had been done, that it could never be changed back. Feeling powerless, she rushed out of the salon. She broke her hairbrush with the idea of attacking herself and had violent thoughts of jabbing her arm but was unable to do it. She remembered with horror a film she had seen in which a woman had cut herself by sticking glass into her vagina. The woman hated her husband and wished to rid herself of her sexuality. Mary had been aware of wanting to "let something out," to see blood, to stop the feelings with pain.

Mary told me the worst of it was that her father had not even noticed her hair. (In fact, it was only one inch shorter.) She related another recurring odd experience she had; when she looked at her sister Doris's face she experienced it as her own until reality reasserted itself. It had been that sister's hairstyle and face she had hoped to see reflected in the hairdresser's mirror, thereby becoming the ideal woman/daughter. But the too-short hair and irreparable damage actually had represented the unconscious fear of castration.

These hallucinatory experiences of change in the body seem to me to play a central role in such patients and to go some way toward explaining the compulsion to seek a violent "bodily" resolution—in Mary's case through anorexia, suicide, and, a year after her suicide attempt, provoking a beating after the first unsuccessful visit to the hairdresser. In the analysis she attacked its "body," or framework, by breaking appointments and being late. Mary turned from the female analyst to the male hairdresser for help, hoping he would give her the feminine attributes her mother and I seemed to withhold from her. She remained convinced that her mother wanted her to be a boy. In the transference I was experienced as one who rejected her, yet who jealously guarded against her becoming a proper woman whom men might love.

Mary broke her hairbrush because it was a symbol for the mother/analyst/hairdresser who should have made her beautiful. She fantasized attacking her arm with the brush, the arm with which she masturbated and autoerotically stroked her eyebrows, eyelashes, and hair. The arm was also symbolically understood as the arm of the mother/analyst, who in Mary's unconscious fantasy masturbated her with interpretations and yet constantly seemed to reject her. (Mary had had a disturbing dream in which her mother did masturbate her.) The film she recalled of the woman who hated her husband and

attacked her vagina represented the kind of fantasy Mary enacted in her suicide attempt as the attack on and hatred of the body her mother and analyst
failed to love.

In the subsequent period of Mary's analysis she remained uneasy during
the anniversary period, but it ceased to be a time of crisis or acting out. Her
ability to own and contain her feelings improved; her sense of self and her
own boundaries became well defined, and she no longer tried to resolve
her fear of rejection by a search for oneness with the object or by trying to
"get into" and become one with or take over her rival's attributes, as she had
done in the past with Doris. Rather, she now tried to hang onto the object and
to defend against rejection by means of sadomasochistic fantasies.

She doggedly attended her sessions, in this way demonstrating her apparent determination to work at her analysis. But she seemed to be compelled
to be late and unable to begin to speak, so there were long silences. At times
a potentially fruitful interchange between us would end in silence or disappear in subsequent sessions. There was a mutual sense of disappointment and
frustration. In Mary's experience I had failed to love her exclusively as she
was; nor, alternatively, had I provided her with my female attributes so that
men would love her. She became obsessed with ruminating fantasies in
which a boyfriend or I was rejecting and unfairly unkind to her. She indulged
in imaginary revengeful battles. This became the pattern for her masturbation
fantasies, which left her unsatisfied and in a state of tension.

The victimization quality in these fantasies was not new. It now became
clarified and was linked to sexual degradation. Mary recalled a childhood
game she had played at the age of nine. She and a girlfriend took turns verbally abusing the other, who pretended to be a beautiful woman tied up, helpless, and with her breasts exposed. Mary also recounted a "sadomasochistic" dream, which she said was "disgusting" and also exciting. She explained
first that she had the dream after a Friday session when she had experienced a
"terrible loneliness." She had engaged in a fantasy of recrimination toward a
rejecting ex-boyfriend prior to falling asleep.

The dream: A Victorian governor was punishing and humiliating some
women who were working in a kitchen. They seemed to have done something
wrong. They were beaten while naked, but the pain wasn't too bad. The governor seemed to be sniffing around and poking his nose up bums like a sup-
pository. He was revolting. It felt like being on show! It was pleasurable but
also unacceptable. It was like "a bawdy play."

It seemed that the dream was a send-up of my analytic role as the governor who searches out the insight by "sniffing" up her bum for the "filth" in
the secret, unconscious, exciting, beating fantasy of our analytic intercourse.

In the fifth year of her analysis Mary had developed an anal fissure for which suppositories were prescribed by her female doctor after anal examination.

The analysis continues. Mary is still much preoccupied with her body and the intake and output of food as related to the vicissitudes of her relationship to me. The conflicts and pain in the transference seem to be in essence not different from those she experienced when the distortions in development began, in her first and second years of life, and which became reformulated at puberty. She has achieved a great deal of insight, and many of her past defensive distortions have been undone. I do not know how much further she can develop or if she will ever be able to mourn what cannot be in her relationship with me.

Her achievements are many: outwardly she has been successful academically; she is an attractive young woman with good friends, a busy social life, and many interests, although as yet she has no permanent heterosexual relationship. She has refound the good as well as the bad in her parents and in herself. She can own her envy, jealousy, and hostility. She feels centered and has boundaries. Regression to merging and psychotic-type functioning and suicide are no longer options for Mary.

Roger Kennedy

9.

John: Starting Analysis of a Self-Mutilating Adolescent

John, aged eighteen, came to the Centre for help after he had attempted suicide several weeks earlier, when he was feeling very depressed. He had gone to a lonely part of a park and started to cut his wrist with a razor blade, with the intention of severing his artery. He reported that the pain of the cut stopped him. He then phoned the Samaritans several times before eventually being referred to the Centre.

He had tried to kill himself twice before: by cutting his artery at the age of seventeen and by suffocation with a plastic bag at thirteen. He had felt miserable and isolated, hating everything and wanting only to die. During the interviewing process, John cut his wrists on several occasions, particularly during a holiday break, and also cut himself superficially on his chest, upper abdomen, arms, and legs. He admitted similarly cutting himself several times before his serious suicide attempt. The episodes were related to a more general breakdown in several areas of his life, the details of which appeared only in the course of analysis.

John had been feeling depressed on and off for at least a year or so before reaching the Centre. He had felt sexually and physically inadequate, and his attendance at school had come to a virtual halt. His feelings of inadequacy had increased in intensity following his rejection by a girl he liked. He had suggested to her that she go to bed with him, and she had turned him down, not particularly aggressively. He felt sexually abnormal, however, as if he were the only one in the world who could not deal with girls. It was then that he began to cut himself. In these episodes he typically would bleed all over his room at home and then go downstairs naked to telephone for an ambulance. His mother would tend to his injuries. At the time, he felt little emotion about what he was doing, although during the first few months of his analysis he began to be aware of feelings of guilt and anger with himself and his body. Since his analysis started there have been no further incidents of self-mutilation.

Looking back at these episodes, he is aware of having felt excitement and pleasure, especially when he was wearing bandages, which made him look unusual and shocked people. John's cutting himself usually occurred when he was drinking heavily or abusing drugs, including hallucinogens of various kinds. John reported, after some three months of analysis, that he thought the alcohol released his inhibitions. He described a frightening incident from the period of his breakdown in which he had drunk a large quantity of alcohol and then climbed into his bathtub and cut his thigh with a razor blade. He then smeared the blood all over his body, associating the blood-letting with a kind of primitive ritual. He felt that what he was doing was aimed at getting rid of destructive feelings that had been overwhelming him as well as drawing attention to himself.

After about six months of analysis, John said that when he was cutting his body he was trying in a way to "merge" with his environment, losing his individuality as the blood flowed. He also described this activity as "symbolic of a spiritual suicide," in which he merged with his surroundings. I felt, as a result of reconstruction, that during the cutting he maintained a fantasy of a loss of self and a merging union with his mother; the act represented an identification with her and her menstrual flow. He has expressed in his analysis many times a fear of losing his masculinity, a feeling that was particularly acute during his breakdown. It may be significant that when I refer to his breakdown I mean only the more recent episodes. We have yet to deal with his first breakdown at puberty, when he tried to suffocate himself.

Other feelings John had, which I pieced together during the first year of analysis, included intense self-hatred, particularly of his body, which he wished to disown; it was too feminine, he felt, and not masculine enough. He had wished he could have another body, although such desires have never gone so far as to make him want a real sex change. He felt that the barrier between himself and the outside world was too thin, as if it would not hold, and that this was linked to his wish to cut his skin. He also outlined a number of homosexual experiences, especially during the breakdown, which included mutual and oral masturbation with other boys, although apparently not anal penetration.

After the first summer break, John said he was beginning to reexperience his breakdown during the weekends, although less intensely. He again took drugs and began to feel out of control. He said that during the weekend breaks, as before his analysis, he felt that the barriers between illusion and reality were disappearing. Everything was a fairyland: cars looked like fairyland cars, and the world was unreal; he felt himself to be inadequate and separated from other people, from normal sexuality and normal life, by a glass barrier. He also began to dress garishly and aggressively, with violent punk slogans daubed all over his clothes.

The analysis is beginning to clarify John's states of mind during the episodes of cutting. At these times there seems to be a breakthrough of psychotic or psychoticlike feelings or anxieties, in which he confuses illusion and reality. These anxieties are also related to his wish to remain merged with his mother in a childlike state so that he would not have to face sexual feelings or the reality of his male body, separate and different from his mother's. Thus, the act of cutting can be seen to represent in part an identification with the mother, an attempt to harm his masculine body, and an effort to rid himself of feelings of destructiveness, including those associated with castration anxiety, in a primitive letting of blood. He is also trying to deal with his psychotic feelings, however inappropriately, by discharging them through a bodily act.

One could say that so far the analysis has clarified and extended facts about John's breakdown that were presented in relatively crude and limited form during the interviewing process. This was partly because the interviewing was concerned mainly with the immediate issue of dealing with the acute suicidal crisis. By the time John was in analysis some months later, the crisis had settled down, to some extent at least; he showed much less acute anxiety about what was happening to him.

Background

John comes from a middle-class background. His father had severe alcohol problems when John was about eight to eleven years old, and he remains a somewhat ineffective and degraded figure in the family. Both parents suffered from depression in adolescence. The mother appears to be a much more forceful figure, to whom John has usually turned in anxiety states. Several members of the family have suffered from alcoholism, and there has also been some minor criminality. The maternal grandmother died when John's mother was an adolescent; she then had to look after her younger siblings. There is an interesting story about the mother's pregnancy with John, which he learned as a boy. It was said that his mother had an apparent miscarriage while pregnant with him; yet the pregnancy continued, so the doctors thought that a twin had been aborted. There was also a family fantasy about his birth—the umbilical cord was wrapped around his neck and supposedly indented an earlobe.

Neither parent has supported John's analysis. They attended one interview before the analysis began but have refused to attend again or to make any voluntary financial contribution to his treatment. His mother in particular put constant pressure on him, at least in the early stages, to give up his analysis and, like the father, constantly denigrates it. They both feel that John will "grow out" of his problems and does not need such intensive help; they have simply ignored the seriousness of the suicide attempts and the self-mutilation. Their lack of support posed a considerable technical difficulty in the first few months of the analysis. John would feel such conflict about being in analysis and "betraying" his parents that he felt he would have to stop. This made it difficult for me to deal with crucial issues since any meaningful interpretation might cause John to leave the analysis. Although there was no easy answer to this dilemma, I thought it important to try to be in touch with what it must be like for John to have parents who deny his problems, perhaps because they feel them too painful to bear. After a while we were able to leave the real parents, as it were, and focus more on his "internal" parents.

John is an intelligent boy deeply interested in politics; he dropped out of school during his breakdown, but is now attempting to pursue further education. He has a number of friends, mainly those with whom he has shared an interest in politics, drinking, or drug abuse. His first heterosexual experience occurred a few weeks after he began his analysis. Until then he had been excessively shy with girls unless they were "just friends." It is probably significant that his recent sexual experiences have been with girls who, like him, attack their bodies in one way or another—through abuse of drugs or repeated abortions, for example.

The Analytic Sessions

I will present some clinical material from John's analysis which seems to highlight a number of technical difficulties. This material is from the period leading up to the first summer holiday. First, however, I will outline some of the themes that have arisen so far during this early stage of the analysis.

The beginning went surprisingly smoothly. John was friendly and cooperative in our initial interview to arrange session times; he appeared to enter into the analytic situation with relatively little trouble. I was relieved but also uneasy in light of his history; I began to fear I might be missing something important, such as a suicide wish. This did not appear to be the case at that time; yet I have often been in doubt about how worried I should be with regard to his situation and mental state.

John very soon developed a fairly strong therapeutic alliance. He usually arrived on time for his sessions and was able to use them. After some months he began to feel that the analysis was the most crucial experience of his life and saw it continuing for at least three years or so, until he was more "established" as an adult. Part of his commitment, however, seemed to be based on a pseudo-alliance, in which he became compliant and passive in relation to me. Although he has a genuine wish to understand himself, his analysis has been taken up with a number of severe distortions and denials of reality.

The first two or three months were particularly difficult—given the absence of parental support—and while the transference and therapeutic alliance were only beginning to develop, he felt constantly tempted to drop out. He felt that interpretations were designed to brainwash him and rob him of his individuality, and he spent a number of sessions trying to engage me in political rather than personal discourse. I tended to respect the politics but tried to see what I could find in it that was relevant to his analysis. Nevertheless, there were many sessions in which I felt that the political propaganda was an unconscious attack on me; yet John often remained impervious to my interventions. This situation gradually changed over the first year or so. Although John was at first unable to see how his self-mutilation could be linked to his sexual and emotional life, he soon came to understand the connection. Indeed, he became somewhat too adept at interpreting his behavior and his dreams while continuing to abuse drugs and alcohol on weekends. There has been a constant and probably unconscious wish on his part to get me to collude with him and to deny (like his parents) the seriousness of his problems. It is as if he wants me to drink with him or share in the drug trip rather than face the problems they represent; yet at the same time he does not make it difficult for us to do analytic work. His constant and excited self-abuse on weekends and holidays with drugs and drinking has been a major theme and is probably related to the nature of his previous breakdowns.

He has often produced what I have called "propaganda for mindlessness," in which the drug experience becomes a means of not facing feelings of separation or dependency. There was certainly a sense, at least until after the summer break, that John had little awareness of the loss of an object, that when I was not in his presence, I was almost completely absent from his mind. In addition, he seemed at such times to be almost completely taken over by an idealized identification with a destructive and drunken father, as well as with a mother whom he felt was driving him mad. There is a considerable amount of material in the sessions; but I have often had the feeling that, although he speaks and thinks about himself, he is trying to slip out of my reach, all the while wanting me to keep pursuing him. He has thus often attempted to seduce me into colluding with him—for example, by wishing I would endorse his drug abuse or agree that homosexual feelings are no problem at all. John's turning to drugs on weekends, which has recently lessened in intensity, has also seemed to be a means of reexperiencing his breakdown in a gratifying form. That is, it could be seen as an attempt to place under ego control that which had not been under such control—for example, his fear of a break with reality or his wish to disown his male body.

Before the First Summer Holiday

Toward the end of June, John brought up some material about his fears of dependency on me and on his mother. Then one Thursday session he recounted a dream in which his mother had found a tin in which he kept condoms; there was also a tampon there. The tin was in his bedroom, although his mother usually respected his privacy and did not interfere with his things. In the dream his mother, because of the tampon, was very worried that John might be gay. In another part of the dream he was in the consulting room, but I was not there. Instead, my wife came in and then two girls were present.

John had recently told me that he had found some of his parents' contraceptives while they were absent from the house. He was shocked and surprised to learn that they still had intercourse. John associated to the first part of the dream by saying that it seemed to him to be about his fear of losing his masculinity, although he was very puzzled about his mother's concern that he might be gay. He was then led to think that what was significant about the dream was my absence and his wanting to see me, and also his feeling that no father was present. He went on to the second part of the dream and wondered about the girls. He talked a little about the tampon in the dream; without a father, he thought, he would be surrounded by his mother and all feminine things. He seemed to be anticipating the coming holiday when, without the analyst/father, he would be left alone with his feminine fantasies and his identification with a sexually provocative and intrusive internal mother. I also interpreted that the tampon in the dream perhaps represented that a part of him actually wished to be female. This was in the context of his saying that he felt much less masculine and aggressive than other boys and that he was somewhat concerned about it.

The following Friday session John began by saying that he was worried about his dependence on me and his analysis, which had come to dominate his life and his thinking. I used this opportunity to interpret that perhaps, feeling this way, he might be worried about how he was going to cope during the summer holiday when he would not be seeing me. He agreed, which led to his saying that at the same time he does not like people, tries to push them away, and has to fit in on the margins. I eventually interpreted that perhaps this was the antithesis of his extreme dependence on me—his wish to get rid of feelings of dependency outside and push them away. This made some sense to him, and we talked for quite a while about what he meant by feeling dependent. It seemed to be related to his wish to lose his individuality and to be almost submerged in the other person, which I took to have something to do with his earlier relationship with his mother. I felt at the time that this massive dependency issue was obviously an important factor that had interfered with his adolescent development.

Very soon after these sessions, one of his close friends, James, made a serious suicide attempt and was admitted to a hospital, where he became comatose. James had been a severe drug abuser and had also been in trouble with the police. For the next couple of weeks, James's suicide attempt and his condition—which in fact improved, to the doctor's great surprise—were major talking points in John's analysis, especially with the summer holiday on the horizon. On the one hand, John said, he was greatly relieved he was in analysis where, unlike James, he could deal with his worries. But on the other hand, he saw a number of his own problems reflected in his friend's behavior. He himself was becoming tempted to take LSD, and he was also thinking of "joining" his friend in a suicide pact.

He spent a couple of sessions venting his fury about the way young people were treated, saying that people like me, the analyst, were just as bad as the police and were to blame for people like James trying to kill themselves. He described how innocent and childlike and beautiful James looked when he was in the intensive care unit, and how he felt attracted to the idea of doing something similar. He also said that James's suicide attempt had reminded him of his own period of breakdown when he was in a hospital for his cuts. At that time he had felt that there was a barrier between him and other people, as if everything had broken down between him and them. He had felt overwhelmed by irrational impulses and events over which he had no control. He added that he felt slightly attracted to James in a sexual way, as James had kissed him on the mouth at a party and John had felt protected by him.

I took up John's anger with me for going off in the holiday break, pointing out that he might be feeling like taking retaliatory action. I also made conscious his identification with James's suicide attempt and suggested that he might want to be protected from his own suicidal wishes. At this point, however, such interpretations seemed to be ineffectual and were received with indifference.[1]

In the middle of July John told me the following dream: He was in Spain with a large number of people, he got them all to commit suicide, and then he followed them. The second part of the dream, also in Spain, involved his looking on after he was dead, at a festival, rather like a fiesta with Spanish dancers.

John was quick to reassure me that he was not actually feeling suicidal now and would not contemplate suicide at all, especially after having seen the effect on James and his family. However, as he emphasized, this did not stop him from having suicidal thoughts. I took up the second part of the dream, about the festivities. John talked about trying to have fun by taking drugs and drinking, although he knew this was not the best way. It certainly sounded as if he was talking about the wish to find pleasure and a sense of belonging, but it had a hollow ring as it was based on a desperate suicidal situation. I took up what I considered to be the triumph in the festivities of the dream. I eventually linked this to me and to the coming holiday, when he might be able to kill me off, as it were, forget his analysis, and feel triumphant and pleased with himself; but then this might lead to suicide. Around this time, to my relief, John managed to arrange a holiday job that would keep him occupied during the summer.

The last full week of analysis before the summer holiday began with John describing what had happened during the weekend. He had gone to a pub on Saturday and gotten drunk. Later on, he phoned the Samaritans and talked to somebody there about all the things he could not tell me. He also took some amphetamines. I interpreted his anger with me in the light of the coming holiday. First he tried to wriggle out of this, but then I took up the fact that he had gotten drunk and had telephoned the Samaritans to say that I was not available and that he could not tell me things. I pointed out that in a way he was saying, "If only I [the analyst] were like the Samaritans, always available on the telephone." John eventually agreed with my interpretation and saw that it made sense. At the same time he did not know if he could deal with the long holiday. I made it clear to him that the Centre would be available if necessary and that in fact we had arranged for a specific person to see him in a crisis.[2] But John said the Centre would not be available for him at

1. This considerably increased my anxiety. Thus it was a great relief to talk about the material and ways to deal with John within the clinical discussion group. They encouraged me to continue to take up his suicidal wishes as well as to consider seriously the possibility of a suicide attempt over the summer holidays.
2. This was actually decided in the staff discussion group.

night, so what was the point? I interpreted that it sounded as if he believed he had to discharge feelings as soon as he felt them, that he could not hold onto them and think about them. He also talked in this session about how the word *authority* had come up the previous week. I had apparently said something about John's wish to see me as his wanting authority, which had annoyed him. I linked this with his behavior—he was putting two fingers up at me as if to say that he did not want my authority nor did he want to take what I had to say seriously. At the same time, of course, he was coming to his sessions, apparently willingly. This seemed to make some sense to him.

In the next session, after a long pause, John turned once again to the coming holiday. He said he was beginning to have the feeling that he no longer needed analysis, that he had gotten to the point where there was no need to go any further. At the same time he felt that I thought he was unbalanced and, therefore, obviously did need analysis. I took up his word *unbalanced* and tried to get him to clarify what he meant; I talked (perhaps rather too abstractly) about an unbalance of forces between his destructive feelings and his positive feelings about himself. This made very limited sense to him. I also pointed out that although he might be wishing to return to drink (as in fact he had said at the beginning of the session), I was struck by the fact that he had nevertheless arranged for a job starting the next week, so that his day would have some structure. I tried to clarify what I meant by this: his analysis had been giving him structure throughout the week, on which he had been relying. His response to my interpretation was to return to his insistence that he did not really need analysis. There was also some material about his relationship with his father. John felt that he would never change his father. I tried to put this in terms of John's feelings about his father and his wish, as it seemed to me, to just come by and have a drink with me rather than analysis as such. I also said that he might feel compelled to take after his father and turn to drink in order to deal with his feelings—for example, about missing his analysis.

The following session began with his account of a dream. It was rather odd, he said, and he did not understand it. He dreamed he was having a session with me when someone knocked at the door. I then said, "Oh, that must be him; that is John wanting to leave." But in fact, the person at the door was a salesman. And there the dream ended. When John said again he could not quite understand the dream, I interpreted that it sounded as if the message was that John should never leave: whenever he left he would be coming in, so this was a kind of perpetual cycle. He agreed with this interpretation but wondered why I had said in the dream that he wanted to leave his session. I suggested that this might have been a cover-up, that it represented John's wish never to leave, especially in the summer holiday.

Although he seemed to agree with the interpretation, he then became angry about something I had said in the previous day's session. When he had talked about what he had been unable to tell me, I had apparently said that this might have something to do with his homosexual feelings. This had annoyed him very much; he accused me of being a bigot and said I just wanted to get rid of his homosexual feelings. He went on about this for a considerable time, and it was difficult to interrupt the barrage of accusations. He said that I was very subtly trying to make my point. I interpreted that this sounded as if he thought I was a subtle seducer of young men, trying to manipulate them into agreeing with my opinions; this led to my suggesting that he might have sexual thoughts about me. He was very indignant at my suggestion that he had thoughts of any kind about me, especially sexual thoughts, except of a very vague nature. He tended to see me as a disembodied voice, although I myself was usually interested in what was going on and felt quite positive toward him, in spite of his frequent acting out. It was as if he were unconsciously asking to be understood and not abandoned. In this session, he continued by saying that I might occasionally be some kind of friend, but certainly nothing more emotional than that.

We eventually turned to the destructive feelings he might experience during the holiday. I tried to link this with his wish in the dream to continue having sessions forever, and with the difficulty he might have remembering me, especially if I were just a disembodied voice. This made only very limited sense to him. But when I reaffirmed that a specific person at the Centre would be available and thinking about him over the holiday, he seemed enormously relieved. John began the following session by saying that he would not be able to come for his Monday or Tuesday session before the holiday. Later, however, I insisted that he come at least on Tuesday, and he agreed to tell his boss that he had to leave early. In fact, I had to rearrange my schedule so that I could see him in the early evening instead of at his usual morning time. Although I felt that this was a piece of acting out, I decided, after thinking about it, that it was essential to see him on the last day of the term; otherwise I felt he might act out seriously.

John was ten minutes late for the Tuesday session. He was dressed fairly smartly but all in black—shoes, trousers, shirt. He described an event of the previous night, when he had been thrown into a fish pond by someone he knew. It was apparently a lighthearted prank, for they had all drunk quite a lot. John, however, felt bad about it, and I myself was thinking that it was a description of what he might do if I did not see him again—that he might attempt a suicidal act. He said that this was the kind of thing he expected to happen to him. He then talked rather blankly and in a depressed way about his image of himself, how he felt lacking in masculinity. It was not so much a question of not being a man or a woman; rather, he felt a sense of inadequacy that would never be remedied; it made him want to kill himself. At the same time, however, he realized that he would not or could not commit suicide and had to carry on. In some ways he felt that the Catholics had it right—that suicide was against the order of God and the nature of things. In spite of this he still saw no future for himself. At least when he had analysis he had something to go to, something to keep him off the streets. I commented on all his black experiences; he seemed to be saying that he could not go on and yet he had to go on. He agreed. I think what he was really seeking from this session was an acknowledgment of his feelings and their importance.

In the next couple of sessions, the last before the holiday, John dressed rather like a thug, in shabby clothes daubed with slogans. I think he was trying unconsciously, and in bodily terms, to show me both how neglected he was feeling and how violent he felt toward me. Indeed, most of the sessions were concerned with what he thought about his violence. He said he was no longer feeling suicidal but was turning his feelings outward. For example, he felt as though he wanted to do something violent, like burn down a house or set fire to a car. I felt some fear that he was talking about my house, which he apparently admired as not being too rich, and I actually clarified that he was not. He recognized fairly easily that he was really talking about a part of himself. He also tried to reassure me—not very successfully, as it happened—that he would not try to kill himself, that he had cut down on his drinking and was trying to reform. He also talked to some extent about his new job and anticipated what it would be like.

As it turned out, John managed to survive the holiday without ringing the Centre, without making a suicide attempt, and without cutting himself. He spent most of the time successfully doing his job. He had begun to drink toward the end of the holiday, but otherwise had coped fairly well.

Discussion

I have focused in the material above on the way the analysis tried to deal with the first summer holiday and John's accompanying suicidal feelings. The issue of how he would deal with the holiday seemed first of all to center on his fear of being abandoned by the father and left with a sexually intrusive mother who would rob him of his masculinity. There were also hints of some fear of the pull toward being a girl—when he talked, for example, about being kissed by his friend, James. These fears could be understood in terms of his clinging to the pre-oedipal ties to his mother in a kind of symbiotic union in which his individuality (and hence ownership of his body) was lost. There then appeared John's worry about his loss of individuality if he recognized his feelings of dependency on me: he would be submerged in or totally dependent on another person, like a child and its mother. The suicide attempt of his friend, James, provided a focus for his own suicidal feelings. On the one hand, John tried to reassure me and himself that he would not contemplate doing anything similar; but on the other hand he felt drawn to death. It seemed crucially important for me not to be seduced into ignoring his suicidal impulses and not to agree that everything was satisfactory. That I supplied the name of a colleague at the Centre who would be able to talk to him in an emergency seemed to be a concrete sign that his disturbance was being taken seriously.

In addition, although this period was early on in the analysis, it seemed that John had basically accepted the interpretive framework and displayed some capacity to introject the analytic process; apparently this helped him cope with the break without serious acting out. But there was also a sense in which focal attention to how he was going to deal with the loss of his analysis, on which he had become very dependent, began to promote in him the idea of an absent object. Until that time he acted as if I were simply nonexistent in his mind during weekends and breaks, or else he had to blot out awareness of my presence by means of drugs and excessive amounts of alcohol. It seemed crucial, in the light of such cutting out of awareness of a relationship to me, that I be even more aware of keeping him in mind.

At this period in the analysis there were only hints of what had happened in John's previous breakdown—for example, in the material about his fears of losing his masculinity and of being left with the pre-oedipal mother. It seemed more important to attend to the immediate issue of his feelings of abandonment in the present and of his efforts to avoid awareness of feelings of dependency.

One could understand the dynamics of the analytic relationship at this time in terms of John's flight from the mother and father as a unified couple. I had the impression that as soon as I began to become a relatively nonpersecuting father in the transference, John would react by cutting off what he was saying or would act out with alcohol or drugs outside the session. I think this was related to the fact that at such moments he felt as if he were suddenly in touch with the overwhelming pre-oedipal mother. One could describe this as a "split transference," in which mother and father are not united in the patient's psyche but are constantly and strongly divided. This makes the analysis of such patients particularly difficult as they may unconsciously use the split transference to ward off interpretations.

I also think that the material points to the adolescent's attempt to deal with the reality of his mature body by trying to hold onto the image of his old, immature body. The infant's body takes a long time to develop. Lacking coordination of functions, he is dependent on others for a lengthy period. Later the child acquires an imaginary mastery of his body, linked perhaps to the ego ideal, which is an illusory image of a totally functioning body. At the autoerotic stage there is an erotic relationship to a fragmented body. Later the image of the whole body is the love object, but it is an immature image, or what one could call a nonincestuous image. This immature image is the first organized form in which the individual identifies himself.

At adolescence the wish to hold onto this immature body image conflicts with the wish to grow into a new mature body with a new mature image. Thus an attack on the new adolescent body and body image, as in self-mutilation and indeed suicide attempts, may be seen as, in part, a wish to cling to the old immature body image and the old helplessness, as well as an attack on the new sexual body. We often see the use of a particular kind of whole body image, or gestalt, underlying masturbation. This image may be either an idealized image of what the body should be or is felt to be or an *alienated* and psychotic ideal unity which cannot be reached and hence makes the subject feel incomplete. There may also be present a greater or lesser denial of the configuration of sexual desire—that is, the *entering of a female body* in the case of the male or, in the female, *being entered*.

This is, of course, far from simple and includes an ability to detach from the incestuous tie to the mother's body and enter another woman through a gap. In John's case, the prospect of entering a female body was accompanied by considerable anxiety and a sense of disembodiment. He had both a fear of losing his penis in intercourse and then losing his masculine shape and also perhaps a wish to cling onto his immature body image. John's attack on his body could be understood as a refusal to acknowledge the reality of his maturing body and seemed to be accompanied by a frequent refusal to recognize the reality of his wishes in a more general sense.

10.

Mark: Acute Paranoid Breakdown and Treatment

Mark was nineteen when he had a severe mental breakdown. His doctor referred him to the local psychiatric hospital, where he was diagnosed as paranoid schizophrenic. Although admission to the hospital was recommended, the family knew from past experience—Mark's aunt had been treated for paranoid illness with ECT and drugs—that physical treatment did not produce a lasting change. During their search for a place where he could have psychotherapy or analysis, they heard about the Centre and asked for an appointment.

When Mark came to the Centre he was barely able to cope with the demands of everyday living. He was afraid to go out of the house and could not sleep alone. He was always worried that his hands were dirty and washed them throughout the day. This anxiety was especially strong when he used the lavatory, taking extreme precautions to avoid contact with feces. He worried a great deal about whether the electrical appliances in the house were switched off, and he had to check them before he went out. Although he was enrolled at a local college, he rarely attended classes, and when he was there, he could not concentrate. Self-conscious in the company of peers, he shunned their company and limited his social life to his family. His sexual life consisted of compulsive masturbation with the help of pornographic magazines, from which he got very little pleasure. The conscious motive for his masturbation was to get rid of tension, which he believed would otherwise harm him.

On his first visit to the Centre he was too frightened to be alone with the interviewer, but on subsequent visits he overcame this anxiety. As he began to trust the interviewer, he admitted that his mind functioned in a strange way and that he was mentally ill. For the past year he had been hearing "voices" accusing him of spreading scurrilous stories about his family. He was frightened when he was not with a family member lest he give into the voices that told him to jump out of the window or otherwise kill himself. He transferred the powerful image of the family to the interviewer and asked for "counsel" on ways to fight the voices.

Before this, Mark believed he could start a nuclear war and that he was being followed by agents of the American and Russian governments. The trigger for the delusions was the discovery of an error in the accounts of a firm where he was employed. Afraid that he would be charged with embezzling funds, he stopped going to work. He was also afraid to be alone in his house and had trouble falling asleep. But those he thought were watching him came to include his family, and he became suspicious of the brother with whom he was living. One day his fear that his brother would kill him became so severe that he ran to the house of another brother, the oldest. The move helped to lessen the fears, but he still had difficulty sleeping on his own and slept in the same bed with this brother and his wife.

Although Mark had for a long time worried about dirt and had instituted elaborate rituals of hand washing, the paranoid breakdown occurred after a trip to see his parents who were living abroad. While on the holiday he visited a prostitute. The experience was so upsetting that he could remember very little of what had happened. He thought he had been cheated by the prostitute, who instead of having intercourse with him made him penetrate a "container." He was also worried about venereal diseases and went for examinations to a hospital.

Mark is the fifth of six children, with three brothers and two sisters. The difference in age between the oldest and youngest is nearly twenty years. The older siblings helped the mother care for the younger ones, and Mark was looked after by the oldest sister. He is very attached to her and even now turns to her for advice. Until the age of twelve, when a brother was born, he was the youngest member of the family. With the birth of this brother he lost his pampered position as the "baby" of the family. Throughout his childhood he slept with one of his siblings and has remained dependent on them. Such physical closeness to his siblings had serious consequences for his development, especially during puberty, when he experienced intense sexual excitement. Another factor that may have affected his development was the cramped living conditions which offered opportunities to witness the sexual activities of the parents.

Although not a great deal is known about his childhood, he has learned that he was a fretful baby who cried a great deal. He remembers being very close to his mother and would be greatly upset when she went out. During one of the initial interviews at the Centre, Mark's sister reported that at the age of six he became very anxious that, like his older brother, he had worms in his bowels, and he wanted his anus to be examined. Since that time he had worried about contact with feces, and after defecation he spent a long time wiping himself and washing his hands. His attitude toward cleanliness was, to a certain extent, influenced by the mother's preoccupation with dirt and germs. Her fear of dirt was so strong that she left the washing of dirty clothes to the children. Furthermore, she spent so much time getting rid of the dirt on vegetables that meals were always late. She had a strong suspicious streak and believed that neighbors were plotting against the family. She is highly ambitious for her children and has supervised their education very strictly.

The father, in contrast, is mild and easygoing and has protected the children from the mother's severity. He has always worried about death, however; after his own mother died, he would wake up screaming in the middle of the night, which Mark remembers terrified him.

The relationship between the parents has always been discordant, and they quarreled a great deal during Mark's childhood. Although they were never overtly violent toward each other, the mother would sometimes taunt the father to kill her, and he expressed the wish to be dead. Both parents frequently threatened to leave the home. Mark's anxiety about losing a parent was made real when the older siblings, one after the other, left home to live in Britain. The oldest brother left when Mark was nine, followed a year later by the sister to whom Mark was greatly attached.

When Mark's father was a young man, he left his native country to work in one of the colonies that was then ruled by Britain. He spent all his working life there, but on retirement decided to return to his country of birth. At that time, Mark, who was fifteen, and his younger brother, three, were living with the parents, while the older children had already settled in Britain. The parents thought that Mark would have better opportunities for studying in Britain instead of their own country, so they left him with the older children during a visit to Britain. Mark's reaction to the separation was one of extreme distress, especially because his parents took the youngest child back with them to their own country.

Soon after his arrival in Britain Mark was sent to a boarding school, where he spent two very unhappy years. His small stature and timid nature made him an object of ridicule. Although extremely unhappy, he steeled himself against painful feelings (in his words, he "outlawed thoughts" of missing his parents) but could not stop the frightening dreams. He was afraid of ghosts, especially after he learned that someone had killed himself in the school some years before. His work suffered considerably, and he then left school without completing his education.

When he rejoined his siblings his emotional state was greatly disturbed: the rituals of cleanliness had become firmly established; he was acutely self-conscious and felt persecuted. His brothers and sisters, who were busy with their own lives, paid scant attention to his distressed state. It is possible that his unhappiness reminded them of their own sadness at leaving home, but instead of comforting him, they accused him of being ungrateful for the money they had spent on his education. He started to hide his misery and pretended that he was doing well. For example, he would leave the house with the brothers and sisters, but instead of going to his new school he roamed the streets or returned home to bed, often lying there in a withdrawn comatose state until his family's arrival. The defensive maneuvers, however, were not successful in warding off the illness, and soon after his return from the holiday with his parents he showed symptoms of paranoia.

When Mark came to the Centre his mind was in a fragmented state, held together by compulsive rituals of checking and rechecking every action. The rituals, although exhausting, were not as tormenting as the anguish he experienced from the obsessional thoughts that plagued his mind. Whenever he decided to do something, the decision was challenged by a contrary thought, and he was reduced to a state of paralysis. For example, if he decided to write a letter, it was immediately challenged by its opposite—"no, you won't"—and he was helpless. Sometimes he tried to control his thoughts with the help of what he described as "security guards"; at other times he shouted at the contrary ideas to leave him alone. During these times he often heard a voice within him say, "Why don't you kill yourself?" He thought that the battles in his mind were like "industrial disputes" between management and labor. When his mind was in "dispute" he withdrew into a state of angry silence, which sometimes lasted for days. These disputes, a regular feature of his life, were often triggered when he felt humiliated.

Another activity he practiced regularly was, in his own words, "processing" or "secondment." It was a sort of mental cleansing which involved going over conversations in his mind to check that he had not said something that could be used to "blackmail" him. The "processing" had to be done scrupulously, and if he could not recall every detail, he felt extremely anxious.

The obsessional mechanisms, nevertheless, were not successful in controlling the battles in his mind, and they had to be supplemented by precautionary measures. For example, he had to sleep for eight hours, he took care not to strain his mind by overworking, and so on. None of these devices, however, was successful and most of the time his mind was flooded by ideas clamoring for attention. When the ideas were not too insistent, he could stop them by saying "yes, yes" or "later." But if they persisted, he pretended to be a traffic policeman and by raising his hand stop them.

The Analysis

Mark was pleased that he had been offered analytic help. He tried to be on time, but was often late. Worried that I might stop his analysis, he blamed the transport system or his family for his lateness. His mood was often elated, but lacked depth of feeling. For several weeks he went over his breakdown in detail; he wondered why it had happened and whether it might recur. I felt that he was saying not only that he needed help desperately but that he was still in a very disturbed state. Although his attitude toward me was deferential, his doubts about my qualifications frequently led him to ask questions about my training and experience. At times he was not sure if I really existed and checked my name in the telephone directory. He was acutely sensitive to noises outside the consulting room and worried that someone might hear what he was saying. At times he wondered if I had a tape recorder hidden in the room, and he believed that I kept a truncheon next to my chair.

Having suffered from anxiety about "contamination" for many years, he experienced analytic interventions as harmful substances that were being pushed into his mind and driving him crazy. In the early stages of the analysis his response to interpretations was either to ignore them completely or to assimilate them in his disturbed ideation and thereby make them ineffective in bringing about change. An additional difficulty arose from Mark's identification with mechanical objects such as computers and buses. Not only did he see himself as a machine, but his thinking was organized on the model of a transport system or a computer program. His thought processes were highly concretized, and he could not think in symbols.

For a long time Mark used the analysis as a place where he deposited his crazy ideas. He talked for the whole hour and filled the sessions with disconnected thoughts and stray images that I had difficulty in understanding. Most of the time he was content with getting rid of the disturbing thoughts, but occasionally he wondered what I thought of him. I was puzzled by the quality of the transference: Was it totally absent? Was it psychotic? Was it related to the analytic setting and not to the analyst? Perhaps all these were true in some way, but the most striking feature was an absence of an enduring relationship and, at times, a total absorption in his own world. Additionally, he had no idea that the cause of his disturbed state was his own thoughts and feelings, not outside agencies.

Gradually it became apparent that for his analysis to be useful I had to offer Mark a model of mental functioning that was different from the one he had constructed for himself. For example, consider this excerpt from one session: When he arrived a few minutes late, he apologized and explained that he had missed his bus. He recalled an incident during the weekend when he was refused admission to a discotheque, which puzzled him because his brother had been there the previous week. He had applied to the university for a place but had not heard if he had been accepted. The letter was to arrive at his brother's house, and he thought that his sister-in-law had destroyed it. In his next association he thought she was also responsible for his not having been admitted to the disco. In this excerpt one can see that Mark's thinking was omnipotent and paranoid, but I felt that interpreting this would not be helpful at this stage. Instead, I tried to show him that whenever he felt anxious or disappointed, he believed that it was someone else's fault and that people were against him.

I have, so far, described the disturbance in Mark's thinking; quite early in the analysis, however, it was apparent that the illness had affected most areas of mental functioning. In order to illustrate this, I will describe the intense anxiety he experienced in two areas—first, his perverse sexuality, and second, separations from the analyst.

From the very beginning of the analysis Mark talked about his compulsive masturbation, which he practiced with the help of pornographic magazines. He did not experience shame or guilt about the activity, but he worried that his hands smelled of semen and washed them repeatedly. The motives for the masturbatory activity were varied; the most significant one, however, was to get rid of the tension that, if allowed to accumulate, would lead him to rape a girl or to be raped himself. The activity of looking at dirty pictures ostensibly aroused him sexually, but the provocative poses of the models made him feel that they deserved to be raped. Additionally, by looking at the pictures of naked people, he tried to sort out his confused ideas about male and female anatomy—he believed that each sex had both male and female organs. By indulging in masturbation, he proved to himself that he was normal not only in the sexual area but in his mind as well.

The attempts at controlling the perverse impulses, however, were unsuccessful, and he was assailed by sexual thoughts about men, women, children, and animals. In a desperate attempt to prove his normality, he made friends with a young woman, hoping that sexual relations with her would free him of his perverse ideas, but he could not have intercourse because of a fear that he might penetrate her anus. The wish for a sexual relationship with a woman was also a flight from thoughts about being penetrated by the analyst, and in order to control them, he would masturbate before his session.

Mark found the separations from one session to the next or the weekend break quite disturbing, but if the contact was disrupted for a longer interval, as during the holidays, his mental state was often fragmented and confused. On many occasions he forgot the date the analysis was to start again, and he would telephone me in the middle of the holidays to find out when he was expected. I, too, worried about how he was going to manage during the holidays, and in the first year of the analysis, I always told him where I was going. He was also given the name of a colleague he could contact during the holiday if he needed to.

The anxiety during separation arose not only because of the fantasy that I did not exist any longer but also because his feelings toward me would change significantly. On the days we were meeting, his image of me was a mixed one—sometimes I was a helpful person, at other times a dangerous one. On the days when there was no contact between us, however, I would turn into a totally bad person. In his imagination he had killed me and I was going to haunt him. After a break for the Easter holidays, for example, he started a session by saying that on the way he had stopped to buy some toilet goods. While he was being served, he thought the assistant looked at him contemptuously because he had spent only a small amount on his purchases. He recalled other incidents when he had felt humiliated and had had vengeful thoughts of hitting people. I reminded him that just before the holidays he had the idea that I was not taking a holiday at all but was stopping his treatment because it was subsidized while continuing to see patients who paid. I reminded him that at that time he had felt angry toward me. He denied the feelings of anger but was reminded of a film in which a prisoner had killed a warden with the latter's truncheon. With some difficulty, he added that during the holidays he had had thoughts of killing people.

After eighteen months of treatment and as the Christmas holidays approached, his mental state began to deteriorate. The "disputes," which had been quite common at the beginning of the analysis, came back. What he was trying to control was a growing suspicion of me; he rejected all interpretations and tried to engage me in giving him advice about practical matters. One of the problems that occupied him greatly was whether he should visit his parents abroad during the holidays. Although he wanted to go, he was afraid that he might have a breakdown, as had happened after the previous trip. He wanted me to reassure him that he would not have a breakdown and dismissed interpretations of his anxiety about separation as "tricks."

He returned from the holiday pleased that he had managed the trip successfully, but the good mood did not last. His mental state was often confused, and he could not stop thinking about my penis. For example, he started a session by telling me all the things he had done during the day; after a pause, he wondered if I was thinking that he had left out something from his account. In a giggling tone, he said that he had masturbated before coming to the session. His next association was of feeling excited about a girl he had seen on his way to the session. I wondered if he had sexual thoughts about me. He was silent for a few moments and then asked me if I had watched a television program the previous evening about homosexual relationships. He became silent again; he did not want to say what he was thinking and wished that I could read his mind. He had a great deal of difficulty in speaking the next idea: he had thought of anal intercourse between two men. He became quite anxious, turned around to look at me, and was reassured that I was not masturbating. I said that he felt reassured that I was not masturbating and thinking of my penis in his anus, to which he replied that it would be terrible if it were to happen.

In the following weeks his condition worsened. He was frequently late and sometimes missed sessions altogether. He was often confused about the time of his appointment; he would arrive early and roam around the neighborhood. Once he rang my bell several hours before I was due to see him. When I met him at the door, he said that his eyes were hurting him and that he had come to wash his contact lens in the lavatory. During these days his mood oscillated between manic excitement, when thoughts rushed through his mind, and anger. Within a short time—around the second anniversary of his breakdown—he became paranoid. He thought people on the street were watching him, and he telephoned to ask me to stop them from persecuting him. One day he was too frightened to travel by public transport from my consulting room and asked me to ring for a taxi. On reaching home, he telephoned to thank me for sending him with a "friend." As his condition deteriorated, it was obvious that he would need hospitalization.

Before Mark went into the hospital, I explained to him that, since neither he nor his family could look after him, he was in need of an environment where he could be cared for. Moreover, the admission did not mean the end of his analysis, which I said would be resumed after he had left the hospital and that while he was there, I would visit him once a week. The reason I continued to see him every week was to show him that I had not gotten rid of him and that his omnipotent wishes had not destroyed me. In our discussions at the Centre, some of my colleagues agreed with my decision to see Mark in the hospital, whereas others thought it would interfere with the analysis. I felt that for the future of the analysis, contact between us had to be maintained.

The first time I went to see him I was shocked at his regressed state. He was frightened of the other patients and said that he was unable to masturbate and wanted me to examine his penis. He expressed a wish to see my penis as well, and during the interviews he mimicked my gestures and switched chairs with me.

The rage that he felt toward me for sending him to the hospital was controlled as long as I continued to visit him, but it could not be contained when I went away on a holiday for two weeks. In my absence he became violent and was sent to an isolation ward. The experience of losing control was so traumatic that even after some years he cannot recall what happened. While thinking of that time recently, he remembered that the light from the window in the room where he was kept made him think that he was in heaven.

When he returned to analysis after a stay of two months in the hospital, his mood was subdued and he was frightened that if he became overexcited he might be sent back. His thinking was confused, and he frequently lost track of his ideas. For example, while talking about the sole of a shoe, he was reminded of soul music; number two on the chart of the most popular records made him think of Jesus Christ (God was number one) and he believed he was the Savior. A striking feature of his disturbed thinking during these months was the total absence of defenses against primitive ideas. He talked openly about wanting to lick feces and pictured the naked bodies of his mother or sister.

In spite of his suspicion of me, he came to the sessions regularly. Although he could not experience his anger, thoughts like "Why am I talking to this dog?" flitted through his mind. As I put into words his feeling that I had caused his breakdown, his mental state returned to what it had been before the hospitalization. He thought I could have stopped him from having a breakdown and was disappointed in me. At times when he felt angry with me he wished he were back in the hospital. Nonetheless, there was some relatedness, albeit of a primitive kind. In one of the sessions, for example, he said that a rash on his leg was not getting better with ointment and that he might have to see a dermatologist in a hospital. When I related this to his feeling that the analysis was not helping him and that he wished he were back in the hospital, he said that he was feeling much better, although he was still afraid of being alone. He recalled a conversation in which his brother had said that doctors earned more money than people who worked in the field for which Mark was training. I said that if he were a doctor he could treat himself and would not have to depend on me. His response was that he had thought of working for a Ph.D. degree like his friend. The next association was to think of my degree, and he wondered what it would be like to be qualified like me.

In the third and fourth years of the analysis he made less use of projective mechanisms, and there was a change in his ability to experience feelings. Instead of withdrawing into a state of internal dispute, he showed irritation with me. The process of change was slow, however, and took place only after a great deal of work had been done on the manner in which he used his body to express emotions. Instead of saying that he felt angry with me, for example, he would think of ejaculating on me or of strangling me. Similarly, when angry with a woman he imagined her "cunt." Although from the context of the associations it was obvious that he was talking of an emotional experience, he had no awareness of it and showed surprise when this was pointed out. It was puzzling for me to observe that he experienced none of the emotions of guilt, anger, love, or compassion. Mark's emotional repertoire was limited to fear and shame; a primitive kind of fear was always present and he was afraid of being overwhelmed by it. When I once used the word *afraid* to describe his feelings, he became extremely upset and wanted me to take back what I had said. On another occasion, he reacted to an interpretation of his depressed mood with panic, apparently afraid that he might be pulled back into the withdrawn and comatose state he had experienced in the past.

As his ability to cope with everyday events improved, he gained confidence to speak the thoughts that went through his mind. Most of the time his mind was absorbed in ideas about automobile accidents, and he felt excited whenever he witnessed one. At other times, images of sexual organs flitted through his mind. When I tried to elicit his cooperation in understanding them, he showed surprise at my ignorance of what young men always thought of; he did not think there was anything strange about the way his mind was occupied most of the time. When I started to pay close attention to his stream of associations, I noticed that the exciting ideas occurred after an incident which one would expect to evoke a reaction of fear. For example, on arrival at a session, he said he had noticed that the bonnet, or hood, of my car was not properly shut and he thought somebody might tamper with it. The next association was a feeling of excitement he had experienced when a woman brushed against him. I said that he was thinking of exciting things because I might accuse him of damaging my car. He replied that the idea had occurred to him, but as he had not been near the car, he could not be blamed if it were damaged. In another session, he described meeting one of his female teachers of whom he was afraid because he had not done the work for her course. Jokingly, she said that he was on her blacklist for not submitting the work on time, and she invited him to join her for coffee. While they were together, she chatted in a friendly manner, but he could not concentrate because thoughts of her naked body kept going through his mind.[1]

Following the analysis of the erotization of thought processes, there was a change in Mark's mental state. An example of the change was seen in his relationship to the cat in his house. Whereas in the past he was always afraid that contact with the cat would contaminate him, he started to be friendly and was hurt when the animal spurned his overtures. Instead of feeling angry, he wondered if there was something strange about his behavior that made the cat turn away from him. Similarly, in his relationship with me, he started to complain about the limited contact, and instead of withdrawing into a confused state, he would refuse to speak. That he had become attached to me was noticed in a change in his dreams; instead of having nightmares, he could dream of coming to his session and not finding me.

Although Mark did not have conscious thoughts of suicide, he was often plagued by commands that he should jump in front of a train or crash his car against a barrier. He was so frightened by these thoughts that he had great difficulty in speaking them; when he had uttered them, he was afraid he might carry them out. He also felt angry with me for making him speak them, and he thought that I wanted him to kill himself. The externalization of the suicidal impulses apparently was to control the repressed rage against himself for the shame he brought on the family by becoming ill. He felt, however, that his mother's picture of him as a weak, dirty, and intolerable person was true and the only way he could fight this image was to think of himself as a "genius." He was unable to admit to weaknesses; he could not bear to fail and constantly tried to change things magically. Recently, for example, when he got a poor result in a degree examination, he did not speak of his disappointment but spent a long time thinking of how he could get the result altered. He could not allow himself to experience feelings of disappointment or unhappiness, as he would then wish that he was dead, and by thinking it, he might cause it to happen.

A need magically to fortify the omnipotent image of himself was noticeable in a disposition to take risks while driving a car or to indulge in petty cheating. One of his childhood heroes was Spartacus, the slave who led a

---

1. Although I was aware that these two examples at a symbolic level represented sexually exciting situations, I chose not to interpret their sexual meaning because this would have reinforced an erotization of thinking.

revolt against the Romans and was crucified. An identification with him, in addition to gratifying sadomasochistic impulses, reinforced the grandiose ideas. During the time of his overt breakdown at the age of nineteen,[2] he believed that he was Christ, an idea he had formed during his childhood. And, as a child, he indulged in orgies of killing insects with the justification that they were carriers of germs and ought to be exterminated.

Mark's infantlike dependence on his family and the analyst has been, and still is, one of the main resistances in the analysis. He sees his dependency not as a wish to be protected or taken care of but as his right. His reason for an entitlement to special consideration is the feeling that, as he was deprived of his parents' love by being separated from them when he was fifteen, all his wishes ought to be fulfilled. Underlying these attitudes is a feeling of inadequacy, which he does not recognize because it would challenge his omnipotent image of himself. Additionally, there is the intense shame that he became mentally ill—a fact he cannot accept.

The analysis of the grandiosity and the narcissistic areas of personality was not, for a long time, as successful as I had hoped. Although Mark understood the interpretations, he could not use the knowledge to change his behavior. At first I thought that his reaction was a resistance or that the interpretation was incorrect, but I then became aware that Mark's relationship to reality was an egocentric one. For example, during the time of his treatment he always made a point of going to the lavatory before or at the end of the session. Whenever I tried to interpret the meaning of his behavior, he experienced my remarks as a prohibition against his carrying out an ordinary need to empty his bowels. Recently, when we were discussing his use of analysis as a place where he looked for gratification instead of understanding, I reminded him of his regular use of the toilet. His first reaction was one of anger, followed by a feeling of helplessness—if he did not use the toilet in my office, where should he go? When I suggested alternatives, like his place of work or a public lavatory, he said those places were dirty. But after a pause he said that he had never thought of those places as an alternative because he could not delay any gratification.

Mark, now in the sixth year of analysis, has made some gains, although more work still needs to be done. He has completed his degree and is holding a responsible job. His social life has improved; he is less inhibited in initiating contacts and is not always searching for models to copy. He has started to make friends with girls, although he has not yet formed a steady relationship. Improvement in this area will depend on the working through of his

2. His breakdown at puberty will be described below.

wish to be looked after. He has been able to talk about his homosexual wishes and anal masturbation, which, for a long time, he kept out of the analysis. These wishes are not only an expression of a feminine identification but also a defense against castration anxieties, which interfere with his potency; he experiences difficulty in getting an erection and had a premature ejaculation when he tried sexual intercourse recently. Although he is working toward giving up the passive modes of functioning, he imagines a life without them as bleak. He has often accused me of expecting him to be a hundred-percent cured, whereas he himself would be satisfied with the gains he has made thus far. Although the paranoia is not as organized as in the past, Mark falls back on projective mechanisms when faced with difficulties. His affective life is no longer as restricted, although he still cannot tolerate depressive affects.

Discussion

I have described some of the features of the analysis of a very ill adolescent. In this section, I shall discuss three areas that I think are especially significant about the pathology and the treatment.

Factors That Contributed to Change

Among the factors that contribute to a process of change through analysis, interpretation of unconscious conflict is the most important. A precondition for this to happen is that the personality of the patient must be sufficiently differentiated and his capacity to form an object relationship not grossly impaired. At the start of Mark's analysis, both these factors were missing. His distorted sense of reality made it impossible for him to distinguish which thoughts and feelings were his own and which came from outside. He avoided contact with people whom he experienced as threatening. Because of these difficulties, what helped him initially was the analytic setting rather than the interpretations. The regularity of the sessions and the opportunity to share his confusion enabled him to think of himself not as a mad person but as someone who was troubled by mental states he could not comprehend.

As he became able to form an attachment to the analyst, he felt able to question the bizarre thoughts and experiences that before the analysis he had accepted as real. Furthermore, I believe there was a whole area of mental activity that he experienced concretely and could not put into words. For a long time, for example, I was puzzled by his response to interpretations. Instead of an association or a recollection, his response would be either that he had thought of something similar or that he had dreamed the same thing. At first I wondered if he was just trying to please me or, by assimilating my ideas in his disturbed ideation, was denying their validity. But I became convinced that he was borrowing my words in order to organize his inchoate ideas. Another way of describing this phenomenon would be to say that the analytic interventions helped structure the pathological ideas that, once established, could then be analyzed.

The Contribution of Adolescence to Pathology

Mark's psychosexual development was chaotic; not only was there an absence of phase dominance, but the male and female identifications were simultaneously present throughout his development. These identifications could be tolerated during childhood, but once he reached puberty a definite choice between a male and a female body image had to be made. His inability to resolve the dilemma led him to become ill.

Since childhood Mark had suffered from various symptoms: eating problems, fears of contamination, anxiety about separation, difficulties in sleeping alone. In spite of these difficulties, his development progressed; until the age of ten he was at the top of his class and was quite sociable. When he was twelve his younger brother was born and his behavior underwent a change. During the mother's pregnancy he worried about her health and prayed for her safety. His school work suffered, he started to make up stories of being tormented by other boys, and he began to cheat. The fears of contamination became stronger, and he washed his hands repeatedly. He also worried that his clothes might come into contact with those of his sisters' and he insisted that they be washed separately. (The youngest sister had at that time started to menstruate.) He became self-conscious about his appearance and worried about his small stature.

Nevertheless, he struggled to establish a male identification, noticeable in his worry during puberty about the size of his penis. Parallel to this development was an interest in female clothes and a wish to be like a girl. He remembers that he liked being dressed as a girl by his sisters and enjoyed feeling the soft texture of their garments. The analytic work has not yet resolved these conflicting identifications, but it has stood in the way of his giving into the feminine wishes.

Countertransference

During the course of the analysis I was often at a loss to understand Mark's associations, mainly because of their loose quality. Sometimes I experienced his bizarre ideas as a threat to my own relationship to reality. A relentless

exposure to affectless concrete ideas and the primitive quality of his attachment to me were sometimes overwhelming, sometimes irritating. In the early
stages I also had difficulty in interpreting the undefended impulses—partly
because I did not understand them and partly from a fear that interpretations
might bring about another breakdown. What helped me to persevere was the
patient's struggle with his illness and the support of my colleagues with
whom I discussed Mark regularly.

Ranald Urquhart

11.

George: Severe Breakdown and Lengthy Treatment

George became severely ill at the age of eighteen when he was a student. After five years of treatment he has begun to have some understanding of his adolescent breakdown. But before treatment began and for a long time during its course, he was extremely paranoid. He was, in fact, silent during nine months of his first year of analysis.

George had left high school at seventeen without passing his exams, and his parents arranged for him to attend another high school in order to retake the exams. When he began staying away from classes in his second term, his tutor discovered that he had felt depressed for several weeks, was unable to study or leave his room at home, and was contemplating taking a drug overdose. He had dropped his main subject after the first term. The tutor referred him to the psychiatric department of a nearby hospital.

He was admitted to the hospital in February and remained as an inpatient for a month; he continued to attend the hospital program all day from March to October while living at home. He told the psychiatrist of his worries: he did not like his body, he felt too small, he thought his forehead was too high, he was inferior. He secretly admired the other boys at his school and longed to be like them. But because he was shy and afraid to approach people, he had few friends. When he felt miserable he would eat a lot and then hate himself for being fat. Recently he had dieted and lost seventy-two pounds. On testing he proved to be of superior intelligence.

While George was attending the hospital program, he saw a psychotherapist weekly, who thought he was able to understand and make use of interpretations. George then became interested in the idea of further therapy.

The psychiatrist who examined him found no formal evidence of schizophrenia and thought he was not severely depressed; he was diagnosed, rather, as severely disturbed with a narcissistic personality disorder. He therefore referred George, now aged nineteen, to the Centre to be considered for analysis under its research program.

The psychoanalyst who interviewed him at the Centre was at once impressed by his curious appearance; he was corpulent with a pale face so fat as to leave his ears invisible, offering some ground for the patient's complaints about how he looked. Beyond that, however, George complained that people stared at him, laughed at him, mocked him—the entire gamut of self-conscious self-references coupled with great anger, so that he seemed clearly paranoid. In the assessment interviews he was withdrawn and tense, and when a topic painful to him was raised he might respond briefly and then lapse into silence for as long as a quarter of an hour. He hesitated to acknowledge sexual feelings and complained that his penis was too small, but would not say compared to whose. He emphasized his detachment from his own thoughts and feelings and from other people, including his family. He was later able to elaborate that his masturbation fantasies centered on men and boys; he would fantasize that he was a girl while inserting penis-shaped objects in his anus. He recalled soiling himself until he was aged ten. He would torment the family cat with an excitement he found frightening. Worried that his anger might get out of hand, he was afraid that he might attack and harm somebody.

The staff group agreed that he be offered analysis on the ground that he showed psychotic functioning in clearly paranoid thinking. George reluctantly accepted that the interviewing analyst should meet with his parents and himself as a precondition of his receiving treatment through the Centre. He was at this time still a day patient of the hospital. The meeting proved a stormy one with the mother seeking to justify herself in a highly paranoid way against expected criticism, George shouting at her in response to her belittling attitude and remarks, and the father seeming to side with George. The parents were in disagreement about the timing of events in his earlier life.

From what they said on that occasion and what they had told the hospital staff, we learned that he was the youngest by several years of four children, one of whom had died in infancy. The family had been well off and had lived abroad in earlier years, but a business failure had compelled the parents to go to work. When George was a year old they left him with impoverished relatives and came to work in England. From then until they brought him to live with them at the age of seven, they visited him perhaps three times a year.

Sometime in that period, perhaps when he was four, he had to have all his teeth removed for reasons that are unclear. At three or so, he began soiling, which went on till he was ten. His school days were unhappy: both abroad and in later schools he was isolated and performed poorly in his studies, only occasionally distinguishing himself through a piece of good work.

At the start of treatment George was a little over five feet tall and weighed two hundred pounds; he was unable to move faster than a walk. He was clean in his person and wore clean but mended and shabby clothing. His nails were deeply bitten. His eyes were always cast downward, and he avoided anyone's gaze. He was living as a recluse in his parents' lodging house, which he left only to come to his analytic sessions. He occupied himself by listening to classical and pop music on radio and records. His parents provided for him; he paid no rent and subsisted on welfare benefits, which he used to buy records and pay the fare to his sessions.

He had expressed his interest in therapy at the hospital and to the interviewing analyst at the Centre. Although he was often reticent in speech, he endeavored to ease the task of making his confused ideas and emotions understandable by bringing in complex diagrams that linked thoughts and feelings to himself with arrows. While he plainly felt uncomfortable about his anger and sense of shame, he did not have a clear idea of what treatment might do for him. He did say he felt better if he thought the interviewer was feeling concerned about him.

The Start of Analysis: Silences

In our preliminary interview to arrange session times and so on, George fell silent at the mention of his making some payment as a contribution toward his treatment, although this matter had been raised previously. The notable feature of the first week was his silence. In the first session he hesitated upon entering the room and asked, "Shall I lie on the couch?" On being told "Yes" he lay down and was still and silent. Bearing in mind that George had previous experience of psychotherapy, I said to him, "All you have to do is say whatever comes into your mind, whatever you happen to think or feel." After a pause George replied in a strangulated voice, "I don't know quite how I do feel at the moment." He then lay silent and immobile for the rest of the session, apart from some twitching of his fingers, which may have been involuntary.

I did not encourage George in the option of sitting in the chair rather than using the couch. For one thing, the interviewing analyst had already mentioned the couch, and I thought George would find it hard to sit facing me, since he had avoided my gaze. He might have felt compelled to break off treatment under the strain.

The second day he said, "I don't know what came over me yesterday. I just couldn't actually say anything." After speaking in sporadic sentences about aspects of his appearance, with occasional comments from me, he fell suddenly silent and remained so for the last twenty minutes of the session. He explained on Wednesday how embarrassed he had been that I had closed the front door just as he arrived. When I clarified that he felt shut out, that topic ended and he said no more. He was again silent throughout the Thursday session.

On Friday he explained his silence on Thursday by saying that he had felt very angry with me, that that was what had kept him silent, and that he had left the session with thoughts of suicide. He went on to say he had thought that by my silence I must be criticizing him, but at the same time I would know how readily he could feel criticized. He then started talking in a rather dogged way about areas of his life that embarrassed him—the sight of advertisements for men's underpants, looking at other men's genitals as they passed in the street and comparing them in imagination with his own, and the time when, as a child, he had been playing a sexual game with another boy and the boy noticed fecal soiling on George's underpants. He wanted to convey that two things now mainly oppressed him—his own unfavorable comparisons of his genitals with those of others and his exasperation when he found himself unable to strike a blow at a man he wanted to fight.

Meanwhile I was taking up in the transference the patient's fear of criticism, his shame and embarrassment, his fear that I would discover shameful things about him and mock him, his worry that he would be overpowered in the analysis. George amplified on this theme during the second week, describing battles of will with the hospital staff or with his father. He believed that his father had only one available emotion, anger, and said both parents expected him invariably to submit to their will. He seemed to have some limited recognition that his expectations of having to submit and of being criticized by everyone were part of his view of the analyst also. In the middle of the third week he said, "There's a thing I've noticed, that when I'm actually close to people I tend to treat them as if they're my parents; I keep thinking they're going to criticize me. It's like those two men I told you about in the hospital, I felt they could crush me like I was an ant."

His saying this seemed to indicate that he recognized some of his misperception of external reality, but since he had not mentioned the two men before, he also conveyed that he experienced the analyst as knowing what he had *not* said. When I drew his attention to his fear or terror of me which reduced him to silence, he produced a fantasy of himself pulling the emergency lever in a subway car to get help for someone who had fainted. The driver would appear and demand to know who had pulled the lever; when George admitted it was he, the driver would demand the statutory penalty of fifty pounds. He chuckled and agreed that this was an image of my making unreasonable demands on him in the analysis without regard for his feelings—even though he was only asking for help for the part of him that was hurt. After that moment he became silent in the analysis for the next two months and did not speak more than once a week for nearly nine months.

I had perhaps not given sufficient weight to the fact that on Thursday evening I had not fully unlocked the outer door, and he was unable to leave the building until I came to let him out. Because he had not seemed upset when he asked me to come to the door, I did not include this in my understanding of the subway fantasy. It could, however, have been more fully interpreted as conveying his panic at being trapped with me, a man, in a basement or underground where he had to submit to my wishes and, moreover, was expected to pay for my services—both lending further color to his passive homosexual fears. Nevertheless, although the further interpretation might have been more correct, its absence hardly explains the length and obduracy of the ensuing silence.

The silent sessions at this stage of the analysis were tense but fraught with the expectation that he might speak. He would respond to my "Good evening" with "Hello," and to my "Good night" with "Goodbye." His gaze did not meet mine. On the couch he lay utterly still; infrequently he raised a hand to scrutinize his deeply bitten nails. The patient after him, with long experience of working in a mental hospital, complained of the menace in George's gaze.

While his silence and regular attendance seemed to convey only his wish and need to come and be with the analyst, and his seeming efforts to speak suggested a wish to make use of the time, the quiet tone he used in greeting seemed to support my feeling that he needed the experience of such containment as the session afforded. Throughout these silent sessions I persisted in making speculative comments, four or five times in a session, about his mental state. The comments were as varied as possible in form and content and were based on a variety of assumptions about why it was difficult for him to speak: he was embarrassed at his thoughts; he was angry with me, angry with himself; he preferred to hear me speak; he wanted me to speak first, or not at all; he felt I might intrude into his thoughts. None of these comments, however, elicited the faintest stir. I also bore in mind what he had said about feeling that his parents constantly intruded into his life.

It was not, therefore, a matter of my simply waiting hopefully or patiently for something to turn up. It was necessary to give close attention to him at all times, using the very limited nonverbal clues he gave that might convey shifts in his mood. He would clench his fist, for example, and cover it or not with the other hand. It was also necessary to convey that I was not deflected from the task of maintaining my analytic stance, even when it was tempting to be impatient or reassuring, critical or casual. Such patients are acutely sensitive to the analyst's mood or intention, and any such deviation can end the treatment.

The invitation to conjecture in interpretation that his silence gave also had to be resisted as potentially far too intrusive; indeed, while his sense of reality was evidently shaky, it would have risked confusing him utterly or invited a spurious dialogue. The efforts I did make to return to the subway fantasy for some further clue to its meaning brought no response. Although I cannot be sure what the effect would have been, for example, of focusing on the fact of his presenting only his body and leaving the words to me, I think he might have heard this as criticism and at best taken it as an area for argument or, more likely, been compelled to leave. From what transpired later, when it became clear that he had no useful sense of ownership of his body, I think that the attempt to link his posture or gestures to my perception of his feelings would not have been understandable to him at this stage and would clearly have been too conjectural.

Breaks in the setting, on the other hand, did seem to allow him to speak. Once his mother telephoned me, and when I told him this, he spoke at length in a quiet, reasonable voice about how his silence was an attempt to control me as he felt controlled by his parents. If he made no payment as a contribution to the cost of his treatment, he said, I would not be paid—again a way of controlling my life. He felt driven to speak when the setting was threatened from outside, for he was perturbed that he might be denied his sickness benefit and compelled by authority to take a job. This moved him to interrupt seven months of virtually uniform silence and say that if he had a job he would be unable to see me for help with his fears of people.

In November I once arrived twenty minutes late, which apparently allowed him to speak again. He explained that his silence was the result of his being angry. These were his words, not the repetition of a phrase I might have used. He added further that what had frightened him so much in the February session about the subway fantasy was that he had heard my voice as actually his father's. Separately or together, these ideas could offer only a beginning of an account of how he had been feeling, but they also conveyed how fragmented his thinking must be. He then said that during the months of silence, he felt better when I said something; thus my approach of speaking to make my presence and analytic persistence known to him was acknowledged as to some extent useful to him. It is, of course, less clear that anything I said mattered of itself. It is an open question whether he had needed the silence as a period of regression and would have profited if, for instance, instead of living at home, he had been an inpatient at a hospital and received skilled psychiatric nursing while coming for analysis. It should be noted, however, that while he was an outpatient his disturbance did not appear as floridly psychotic as it appeared later. Now, in this session, George made clear that he felt toward me the same murderous rage he felt toward his father, which had led George to throw him down the stairs in a fight three months before analysis began. This was far from the last of his silences, but from then on he spoke in most of his sessions, voicing his omnipotence, anger, paranoia, and homosexual fears.

I will now summarize the thinking about this patient's first year and the approach taken to his silence. My intention was to provide containment for him and to avoid intrusion in or assumptions about what he said that might go beyond the evidence available within the analysis. George's continuing attendance and the subsequent clearer focusing of his omnipotent rage on me seem to have resulted from this. The view I had of him was that his omnipotence and paranoia constituted the central issue and that although he may have had a wish for help, primarily he had a primitive need to experience a reliable object. His particular complaints about his body and his homosexual concern were side issues; they were split off or disconnected, so that he spoke of them with rapid intellectual ease and without any available feeling. It should be clear from what has been said about maintaining an analytic stance that I was not simply involved in being as passive as the patient, nor was I enacting some passive role for an omnipotent fantasy of the patient; rather, the patient's wishes to control were being gradually and consistently interpreted.

I also recognized that the appearance that George's body only and not his mind came to the session was a defensive one. I therefore had to refuse to allow my own mental activity, or the evidence of it in speech, to be brought to a standstill that would match that of the patient, for however many months this might go on. Later in the analysis George employed other strategies to interfere with communication—equivocation, confusion, incoherence, denials, distortions—which had similar defensive intent.

It seemed to me and still does that at least in the first year of his treatment George lacked a clear sense of differentiation of himself from me and needed to spend this time coming to a recognition of me as in a measure separate from him. The experience of breakdowns in the setting—my arriving late and the other threats to the continuity of the treatment—illustrated his need for the experience of safety; what he did say made it clear that the important area of difficulty lay not in neurotic conflict but in his omnipotence and paranoia, and therefore that interpretation directed to later levels of development would have been unlikely to be understood or used. What this approach afforded by way of safety was an opportunity, either shielded or provided by interpretation, to move at his own necessarily slow pace toward the identification and naming of his affective experience in relation to an object only gradually perceived.

Only the beginnings of this process of achieving a separate identity were alluded to in the material of this first year—for instance, when George said he felt better so long as I spoke. It was not until the third year of his analysis that he began to try to induce me to tell him how to think or that he could begin to debate his relationship to his own anger, as intimations of a sense of separateness and discrimination of himself apart from me. He once said that in the past he could not answer questionnaires because of the feeling that he had no "I" to have an opinion. He was making it clear that what might have passed for secondary process thought had for him borne only an uncertain relationship to a continuing sense of self. Similarly he is still working to assimilate the experience of aspects of his body, as the following section describes.

Breakdown and the Beginnings of Recovery

George's history, as we have seen, included major difficulties in his early life. Around three years of age his weight loss was so severe that his mother briefly took him back from abroad to fatten him up. Removal of all his milk teeth at about four left him deeply ashamed until his permanent teeth came in. Because of his soiling himself, he was given enemas from the age of seven until ten, when the soiling stopped. When he failed to learn to read in school, his mother coached him for months with evident success.

At the onset of puberty around twelve he now remembers withdrawing and wanting to be a baby, but also reading endlessly. At thirteen he took to urinating on the carpet, which his parents understandably resented. By sixteen he was withdrawn and considerably obese, although he went through a period of dieting, keeping fit, and resolving to go out. Because of his poor performance at school, he left without qualifications. By the time he was referred from his second high school to the psychiatric department of the local hospital, he had abandoned his aim of following a career. He was burdened now by his fears of people, preoccupied by adverse thoughts about his body, and, as the first year of his analysis made clear, filled with murderous rage. Thus the leading features of his adolescent breakdown were his withdrawal, his paranoid fears, his humiliating thoughts about his body, his concomitant abuse of his body by gaining so much weight and receiving satisfaction only from anal masturbation, and his overt abandonment of his mental capacity as shown in his academic failure.

The process of recovery has been a slow one but has lately accelerated to the point where he can begin to reconstruct and understand his breakdown in adolescence. Change in his external life, from the potential recluse or long-term psychiatric casualty he was, has been gradual but considerable. The omnipotence, rigidity, and secretiveness that were characteristic of him had long prevented access to large areas of his mental life, so that, for example, only glimpses have been given so far of his masturbation fantasies.

During the first year of the analysis, he did not speak of food or dieting or mention his weight loss. For want of verbal reference, one must assume that the weight loss, or lessened need to eat, indicated a decreased need for food as a comforter since he had come to rely on the analyst and the sessions for comfort. It is possible that other motives played a part and may yet emerge in treatment. He may have been engaged in a secret effort at self-cure, for he attributed for a long time any forward steps he saw himself making to a scheme of intellectual development he practiced from a series of self-help books.

The sessions at this stage were furious battles in which he strove with me (ostensibly the father or mother) over who should assume the right to speak first in the session. If I spoke first, I had in his terms usurped the position of parental power and yielded to his silence. If he spoke first, he had submitted to my demand that he speak but had also assumed power. At the same time he came to acknowledge breaks as painful. He would wish for tenderness or cuddling from me and would be tearful about his feelings of abandonment at weekend or holiday breaks. In the third year he described how he could use some of his daydream thoughts, though these were not revealed, to comfort himself as a substitute for food. Only in the fourth year of analysis did he begin to mention his eating on the way to the session when upset, or binging afterward if he found the session disappointing, equating the session and my words with food.

His explicit anger with me began in November of the first year. During the Christmas holiday, when his father suggested that the analysis was doing no good and he ought to stop, George had a stand-up fight with him and again threw him down the stairs. The next day he left home to stay with a relative. In the more usual analysis material might have been available to give some understanding at the time of what this incident had meant, but beyond the bald statement of fact, there was nothing more. He continued in the sessions in a state of furious anger. He would rebuke me if I had not spoken, as if he were the analyst rebuking the patient, and took every word I spoke or did not speak, every sneeze or cough, as the ultimate expression of my contempt for him. Every session he threatened to leave the couch, smash up the room, and beat me to a pulp. In his infrequent calmer moments, which tended to come in sessions in the middle of the week on Wednesdays or Thursdays, he could hear me more clearly. It emerged then that he felt that, like his father, I always saw him as small, dirty, and useless. In a session the next September, when he seemed on the point of beating me up, I told him that if he did so I would not be able to continue his treatment. He was dismayed, saying, "I always thought that no matter what I did, my mother would always have me back." I in turn was taken aback by his reply. Although relieved at having prevented his attack, I had no answer in the heat of the moment, for the reference to his mother had come out of the blue, and I could find nothing to connect it with. He accepted this limitation of his behavior in the treatment, but he resented it and complained about it for another couple of months.

It may be relevant to observe at this point that working with so unpredictable and disturbed a patient imposes on the analyst tasks different from the ordinary. The analyst has to be prepared to maintain his view of the patient and his own composure for years, if need be, against the patient's open attack and the more insidious unconscious subversion. At the same time, painful countertransference feelings can be aroused, which make for difficulty in recording accurately and in reporting such a patient. A group of analysts at the Centre with whom this patient was regularly discussed shared my difficulty in enduring the uncertainties and pressures to which I was exposed. Although the views such a group contributes may conflict with the line taken by the analyst and to that extent add to his burden, those working with patients of comparable difficulty can more readily recognize the patient's need; even if they themselves might choose to work differently, they can allow for the analyst's preferred technique of fostering the analytic process.

Alongside his paranoid rage and fears of attack and intrusion, George was beginning by degrees to show some trust in me and in himself. His voice changed from a rasping attack to a gentler tone he used for reflective thoughts, which would last for minutes at a time or even a session or two. Eventually there were hints that he could accept and allow change in himself and in his life; he nerved himself, for example, to patronize a different fast-food shop near home.

The following notes made after a Monday session at the beginning of the third year of his treatment illustrate many of the themes of the second two years. Being unedited they include my errors and uncertainties. George was on time, as he had been most days since the New Year. His manner was brisk, and he shut the door firmly. I said "Good evening," and he lay silent. After a bit I said I wondered whether he might be waiting to hear me speak after the weekend. After a brief interval he replied, "Look who's flattering himself," adding, "I never said anything of the kind." I left that for a bit and then said, "You were saying that you resented my not seeing you Saturday and Sunday." "Ah," he said, "but that's not the same thing."

Then with difficulty he set out to describe to me his state of mind during the previous week, saying that he was in a position where he felt "Why should I speak anyway?" I was bound to interrupt him, to pick on some minor aspect of what he was saying. "Now, don't interrupt," he said, and then paused and asked, "What was I saying?" I told him. He went on explaining that he could begin on a train of thought but then lose it. I pointed out that he kept expecting to be interrupted, to be criticized, and to have me misunderstand him.

He continued worrying at the problem, saying that once he got in that mood there didn't seem any way out of it; it seemed perfectly valid. I agreed that, for him, once he felt that way, of course, his thoughts traveled in the same direction, but then equally, it seemed, that when he thought he was going to be interrupted, that prevented him from thinking, as had happened just now. He then gradually came round to saying that it was, of course, as it was with "him" (his father) and not "now and then," as I had phrased it. But most of the time he would feel his father was bound to cut in and be continually angry with him, and so the only time he could feel all right was when there were no thoughts of equality or inequality in his mind. Maybe that was it last week, or at the beginning of last week if it was, he said. I pointed out to him that it wasn't just that he was feeling like hitting me, but that he was feeling that I was just about to hit him or interrupt him, which might come down to much the same feeling. He now tried to catch me out in my words, to quote something at me that proved his point, but he couldn't remember what it was that he was trying to tell me I had said, and said so. He said that I had said something on Friday that did make sense, that, of course, it did not matter what he said. The point was not actually to say something; if it was said in an angry mood, then that was it, that it was possible to say it. He hadn't really understood that until Friday, or rather he had known it but hadn't felt it to be so. He now declared that that made sense to him.

I should interpolate that in ordinary terms these remarks fall short of making sense but illustrate his difficulty in thinking, in self-observation, in being aware of or naming his feelings as distinct from expressing them. He then reminded me of how it felt to him when he had been going to hit me on the head, and I pointed out that it wasn't quite that so much as that he was feeling that that was exactly what I was going to do to him, that I was going to say, "I've had enough of this." I was going to punch him or something of the sort. He added, "Or you will say that it is time," meaning that I would choose to end the session.

I pointed out that behind all this the issue for him was that he felt his father's sexual equipment was bigger and better than his. George replied, "Well, his equipment *is* bigger." I observed that it hadn't felt that way the time he thumped his father, that it wouldn't have appeared that way to any- body looking on. George laughed and reminded me that as he had done so his towel had fallen off and anybody could see that George's equipment was no- where near as big as his father's. I said, however, that to George at that mo- ment it had not mattered what size his equipment was; power, not size, was the issue. George then wondered if that was what was happening when he— the other Friday, was it?—had spoken out on his ideas about politics. Maybe it was since then that, having put himself on a pedestal, he hadn't felt so sure. I wondered in return whether he was feeling that, having spoken as he did on Friday, he might have exposed himself to vengeance, but George didn't find that plausible or valid. Nevertheless I maintained that something of the sort might have been happening. At the end of the session I found myself pointing out to him that the difficulty he had been looking at that day, among others, was that, while he could talk this way at the time, a few hours or twenty-four hours later, it would seem or feel different. Here the notes end for that session.

As I understood the session at that time, George was wrestling with understanding himself, but was handicapped by his need not to admit that he could not fully do so unaided. Beyond that he had difficulty both in accurate recall and in formulating ideas. He began the session scoffing both at the thought he might want to see me after the weekend and at my processes of thought. He then set up a situation where, having forbidden me to do so, he could make me at least seem to interrupt him. Having established his superi- ority over me by getting me to reply and tell him what he had been saying, rather than interpret, he could feel able to expound further, to the point where he talked of equality and inequality.

I would sometimes be unaware of being caught in George's traps, but I would also allow myself to answer or comply, as in this instance, when his underlying intent was not wholly clear. The limited range of his affective expression and his need to control resulted in a great restriction of topics and vocabulary. The purpose of what might seem to have been a knowing collusion with the patient's unconscious designs was to allow clearer expression of what he had in mind and the opportunity for me to experience and examine in the countertransference what he was intending, with a view to more accurate interpretation later. The particular instance in this session was an operation whereby one person knows what is going on or thinks he does, and the other is the sucker or makes out that he is. It took a long time for George to recognize or accept that this went on and then to identify the origin of the maneuver in his childish way of dealing with people. I say "people" rather than the father of whom he mostly spoke in this connection. It was a defensive pattern with many variants, with the analyst initially representing not simply father or mother but an undifferentiated figure. Only gradually did it become clear that there were different refinements applying to the father and the mother and other childhood figures.

When I returned to reminding him of his underlying anger at me and its projection, the interpretation unsettled his idea that his thoughts were better than mine and evoked the defense of trying to shift out of the session to the previous week as an escape from the nature and intensity of his current angry feelings. He turned then to more open attack, again from an omnipotent standpoint. He tried to use my words against him but was unable to recall them and went on to ferret about in the muddle of his recollections. Not having said anything new or conclusive, he made out that he had done just that, and that something made sense to him. This was not, however, insight, only part of the struggle with his omnipotence. He was enormously grandiose and full of rage and destructiveness, which he constantly projected. But if the image of himself available to me was grandiose, it was torn with anxiety and fear of the return of the projections. It did seem that his perception of reality was interfered with to the extent that he kept to a very narrow routine in his day, as if to protect himself from danger. He spoke outside the analysis to only four people during the week, if that. A glance from a passerby, the giggle of a child overheard, could make him detour a whole block in fear or become filled with violent rage. His fantasy life at this stage was not otherwise available; he has mentioned only one or two dreams in all the years of his treatment.

From the session I have just recounted it will also be clear that following or recalling verbatim what he said was not possible through the thickets of his confusion. One result of that may be that what the analyst recalls himself as having said, deprived of the full context, can sound as arbitrary or as ill conceived as the patient's thinking.

It was in that same week that George first reported his self-observation that he would adopt different postures on the couch for speech and silence, making clear in his description, however, that he discerned this with his eyes; so, therefore, should the analyst. He had no seeming internal perception of any feeling state other than his anger. He wondered if other people's gestures similarly matched their intentions and might serve as signals for anger.

At this stage of the analysis it appeared that George was trying to take my more ordered thinking as a model for his own and also was making use of my tolerance to vent and experience the intensity of his feelings. It was important to him that I not fail by allowing my countertransference to take over in irritation or other forms of failure. More than a few times I was late, even by as much as ten minutes, and once I was for a moment irritated by George's twisting of an interpretation. His response to these events was a mixture of panic and fear that he had destroyed me, with a compensatory crowing triumph. But my usual consistency allowed the construction in George's mind of a reliable object and thereby a more reliable sense of himself and of his own feelings.

As the year went on, with the analytic work focused on his projective mechanisms, George became less withdrawn, able to help out with jobs in the house and outside the house with relatives, able to go to the employment exchange, even if unsuccessfully. Along with these changes in his external life he was beginning to recognize that other people might have feelings, that I might, and that he and others might have the same *kind* of feelings; he could begin to explore the meanings of fantasies and their function for him.

In the autumn an important fantasy surfaced: of a gray river steamer that was entirely nice; all the people in it had neat haircuts; there was no litter; even the farts smelled nice; on the upper deck were wild animals that were all benign. Examination of this fantasy clarified the compensatory aspects—that it dealt by reversal with his sense of shame that he had soiled and smelled, that his aggression, represented by the animals, was contained, and that on board he was not being looked at. The destination of the steamer was a fair he had been taken to twice by a woman outside the family, a reminiscence in an idealized form of the years of his separation from his parents.

Another important recognition now was the function of his pursuit of intellectual development by a scheme akin to Pelmanism, involving diagrams and acronyms. This went along with thoughts of himself as a genius, a master politician, a virtuoso, a tycoon, always at first wronged and misunderstood, but finally, by his own efforts, triumphing, vindicated, and universally applauded. The transference operated in subtle ways, however. It was never so simple as that if the patient was a genius, then the analyst was an idiot, and vice versa, which might seem clear enough and was to an extent the case. The patient would be pretending to be an idiot while secretly a genius, and he would, of course, believe that the analyst was playing the same involved deception. It has continued to be an important theme in the analysis.

As these fantasies emerged and were worked on, and George became able to communicate his secrets more directly to me, he started taking another, direct-travel route to his sessions, enrolled full time in a course that could lead to well-paid work, and completed the course the following spring. The summer was spent in unsuccessful attempts to get a job with prospects in a prestigious company. He settled for a job as a clerk the following autumn. Having worked at that for a year and gaining promotion, he enrolled at another school for a course potentially leading to higher education and did extremely well. He got himself a flat and lives independently. He has a modest social life with a group of friends from secondary school days, going to parties and entertaining in his flat.

Now after six years of analytic treatment five times a week, he feels dependent on me and apprehensive about how he might manage without analysis. He has become able to make constructive use of his intellect and has a place at a university. He can see that his obesity was part of his flight from sexuality in adolescence. His figure has been trim for a long time and he can engage in competitive sport. He remains somewhat shy and has not yet approached a girl, but he can go to parties and is on easy terms with his parents.

He has been able to do quite an amount of work on understanding his breakdown in adolescence. This has included his recalling the impact of the beginnings of puberty, which entailed at the age of twelve a period of general withdrawal and a wish to be a baby again. Then at thirteen a brief spell of independence and self-assertion was brought to an end by his parents refusing to recognize his growing up and belittling him repeatedly. These memories and others have come to him linked to still other memories from early childhood. Although he can make better sense of himself, the picture remains shadowy: even if he can use treatment more effectively, he has not fully dealt with his infantile rage, nor are his sexual fantasies sufficiently available. But he has now at least the possibility of pursuing an independent well-paid career, whereas without treatment he would likely have been an unemployable, severely disturbed recluse.

I think it would have been a mistake to see his problems in sexual terms from the start. He needed help first with his omnipotence and paranoia, and for this a lengthy period of analysis was required. I had to work within George's limitations of thinking, feeling, and vocabulary, until he could acquire a useful sense of his own identity. The severity of his adolescent breakdown could then begin to be understood in relation to the painful vicissitudes of his upbringing.

III.

Clinical and Theoretical Implications

M. Eglé Laufer

12.

The Dynamics of the Transference

As the clinical material has demonstrated, the transference relationship in the treatment of the severely disturbed adolescent appears to be experienced with a particular intensity by both patient and analyst. The quality of these experiences has become clear in the accounts of the analyses, which contain the only "reliable" information on which to base an understanding of the meaning of the adolescent's psychopathology.

The nature of the transference in the treatment of adolescents has been the subject of much controversy. One issue centers around whether the analyst represents the oedipal objects from whom the adolescent needs to feel he can become libidinally independent, or whether he represents a new object who, in allowing the adolescent to become dependent on him, helps him feel less dependent on the original objects. In our view, the detachment of the libidinal tie to the original objects, although crucial, has to take place simultaneously with the development of a change in the relationship to the physically mature sexual body. Breakdown in this aspect of development does not imply a static state; rather it fluctuates dynamically. The adolescent relates to and experiences his sexual body in many differing ways—by the use of negation, projection, displacement, or physical attacks on the body—as he struggles with the constant demands coming from within his body and from changes in the outside world's view of him as a sexually mature person. We have observed that defenses used by these adolescents result in areas of psychotic functioning in which the adolescent may be forced to change his relationship to reality by giving up the relationship to real external objects or to his own body. This dynamic process becomes central within the analytic process and can be observed by examining the meaning of the transference. Regardless of whether the analyst is unconsciously perceived as the oedipal parent or as a new sexual object, what becomes of central importance for the adolescent is how he responds to what he believes to be the demands of the relationship and how these demands influence his response to his own body, to the analyst, and to his external reality.

The analyst becomes part of the inner struggle in which the adolescent feels himself involved. The wishes and demands he experiences within the transference create anxiety and a need to force the analyst to relate to him in a way that he feels will relieve the anxiety. For instance, the adolescent may demand that the analyst deny the abnormal nature of his sexual wishes or collude with them (expressed in perverse fantasies of gratification based on early pre-oedipal fantasies); he may want the analyst to participate in the adolescent's own need to destroy or attack his sexual body; or the demand may be that he be allowed to remain in a passive or submissive role toward the analyst. The analyst, by remaining neutral in the face of these demands and by maintaining the structure and continuity of the analytic setting, allows the adolescent to experience the warded-off anxiety while offering him the opportunity to gain an understanding of its source and of his own active role within it.

As long as these conflicts continue to be part of an active analytic experience and can be kept in the forefront of the analytic work, the therapeutic process can be thought of as ongoing, however difficult it may be. The defensive measures that led to the original developmental breakdown at puberty now stand in the way of development toward normal adulthood. By helping the adolescent feel less reliant on these defenses, the developmental process can be kept open and foreclosure in development may be prevented from taking place.[1] When there appears to be a recurrent threat to the continuation of the analysis, we have understood this as representing the possibility of pressure within the adolescent to give in to the wish to establish a pathological solution to his conflicts—that is, foreclosure. Other adolescents feel so overwhelmed by their anxiety that it makes them feel quite helpless; such adolescents may need to be temporarily admitted to a hospital so that analysis can be either continued while they remain in the hospital or resumed after the acute crisis is over.

These situations, together with the analyst's awareness of the possible

---

1. By "developmental foreclosure" we mean the establishment of a premature but fixed pathological solution to relieve the pressure of anxiety. See Laufer and Laufer, 1984, p. 181.

dangers of the adolescent's self-destructive actions, create very special countertransference problems. The analyst can be placed in the position of unconsciously colluding with the adolescent's need to avoid experiencing anxiety because of his own anxiety at being confronted by the adolescent's destructiveness. But in doing so, the analyst is giving in to the adolescent's unconscious wish to destroy the analysis and the possibility it offers of psychic change.

In the nine cases described, there was often a real danger that this would occur at times of an approaching holiday, when the adolescent's anger and sense of rejection and worthlessness were at their height. These were times when it was especially important to work through the adolescent's anxiety rather than avoid it by assuming that he had found his own answer. The weekly discussion meetings of analysts treating the adolescents provided opportunities for the analysts themselves, alerted by the group, to become more aware of the possible dangers contained in the adolescents' "answers" at such times. Such discussions could ensure that the hidden and "secret" ways of acting out in the transference and in the countertransference could be confronted rather than avoided. They provided a safeguard without which it might not have been possible to have kept these adolescents in analysis.

Our experience has confirmed that every analysis of the severely disturbed adolescent contains an element of risk: risk of failure; of serious acting out of destructive or self-destructive impulses; of a temporary psychotic breakdown. But, as these cases demonstrate, it is only by the analyst's being prepared to involve himself in areas where the conflict is at its most intense and evokes the greatest anxiety, and the risk is at its height, that the adolescent can begin to hope that the conflicts and the mental pain do not have to remain negated, split off into action, or repressed. In order to counter the adolescent's fear of being out of control the analyst has to be able to feel that he is in control of the treatment and to feel free to question the adolescent's actions so that the underlying fantasies and affects can be brought into the analysis.

If the adolescent feels out of control of his feelings or thoughts, he can experience himself as mad. He may feel that the only way to achieve relief from his anxiety is through taking control once more by carrying out an action that involves his body, an action in which physical excitement or pain can be used to negate thoughts or feelings. The specific choice of behavior or action always has a special symbolic significance to the adolescent related to the content of the thoughts or feelings that are being avoided, but the action itself is a means of enabling the adolescent to avoid the experience of giving in passively to his feelings and to becoming "mad." Inasmuch as the analyst's task is to give meaning and content to the action on which the adolescent depends at such moments, the analyst is also experienced as depriving him of his sole means of defending himself against dependency on the analyst. The action may be a suicide attempt, self-cutting, drug taking, or bulimic stuffing, as was the case for some of our nine adolescents. For these adolescents analysis was always unconsciously experienced as the demand by the analyst that they give up what they felt enabled them to feel in control and to avoid having to feel dependent on others. In the initial stages of the analysis the adolescent's implicit question to the analyst, "Why should I depend on you to help me?" always contained a belief in his own omnipotence.

The analytic treatment, although helping the adolescent to allow himself to be confronted by external reality, challenges his unconscious belief in the omnipotence of his sexual body. At the same time he comes to understand the anxiety he now has to face of feeling totally helpless without the use of his pathological solutions. We described in the first chapter how the central masturbation fantasy represents the adolescent's unconscious belief that it is only through living out this particular fantasy within an object relationship that he will be able to experience gratification of both his libidinal and his narcissistic needs. This fantasy must represent a specific way of relating to his sexual body so that it continues to maintain the image of the body he feels he must possess in order to realize the fantasy. For the severely disturbed adolescent this fantasy may be very far from reality—for example, a male adolescent may have an unconscious fantasy of having a female body so that he will be able to be penetrated passively. (This particular unconscious wish was present in a number of the male adolescents in our study.) Such a *distorted* body image can eventually, if it becomes integrated as part of the final sexual organization, represent a giving up of the relationship to a part of external reality—as in giving up the potential for having a heterosexual relationship—as well as to a part of the reality of the person's own body. This may then form the core for an established perversion or a psychotic area of functioning in adult life.

For the severely disturbed adolescent the compelling need to live out the central masturbation fantasy not only is motivated by the wish for gratification of libidinal or narcissistic wishes, as in normal development, but is used *primarily* as a means of relieving the anxiety of reexperiencing the pubertal breakdown. For the normal adolescent the central masturbation fantasy also contains the means of maintaining the idealized prepubertal body image as well as the means of gratifying the new sexual potential. But for the severely disturbed adolescent, the anxiety of the earlier experience at puberty that led to the original breakdown remains the compelling force behind the continuous need to bring the prepubertal aspects of the central masturbation fantasy into the transference relationship and the unconscious attempts to force the analyst to participate in its realization within the transference.

The adolescent's struggle to feel in control of the analyst and his need to try to force the analyst to participate with his unconscious wishes is most readily displaced onto a struggle within the analytic setting. Not lying down on the couch, not coming five times a week, not coming at the requested times, or not ending the session at the precise time can all be used in the struggle to feel in control of the analyst—as if, through remaining in control, the patient can still force the analyst to fulfill his wishes. Holiday breaks assume the added significance of emphasizing to the adolescent his actual helplessness. The need to restore the fantasy of being in control can then become the basis for a fantasied attack on the analyst or the analysis or a real attack on himself. It can, as mentioned earlier, lead to a renewed dependence on the use of psychotic mechanisms and to a breakdown in relation to reality, which may then require the adolescent's hospitalization. At such times, the analyst must constantly keep in mind the adolescent's hatred of him for being in omnipotent control of him, as he experiences it. By making the adolescent aware of this, the link can be made to his hatred of his own body, thereby helping him feel less dependent on destructive actions against his body as a means of attacking the analyst in his fantasy.

The Analytic Case Material

In preceding pages we have described the critical role played by destructive impulses in ongoing conflict, and how this becomes an essential part of the transference relationship. In this section we will use the descriptions in part II to discuss the different ways in which these destructive impulses were actually expressed or lived out in the transference situations.

In general the adolescents fall under three headings (although some have to be considered under more than one heading):

The First Group: The adolescent's relationship to the analyst is characterized by the analyst's growing awareness of his own fear that actual violence may be directed at him or at others. George and Sam both belong to this group. Mary should also be included during the initial phase of her analysis preceding her suicide attempt.

The Second Group: These adolescents made the analyst feel as if he had to be constantly on the alert to the possibility of self-destructive attacks. They included Cara, Kevin, John, Charles, and Bill.

The Third Group: The destructiveness of these adolescents appeared to be reflected in the analyst's constant vulnerability to feeling helpless or confused rather than feeling threatened by actual violence. The analysis itself was threatened with destruction either by the adolescent's wanting to leave the analysis or by his destroying the analyst's capacity to use his understanding or by his becoming unable to function in his day-to-day life and needing to be hospitalized, thus making the analyst appear unable to help him. This group included Cara and Bill from the second group, Mary from the first, and Mark.

The First Group

George was silent for most of the first nine months of his treatment. During this period the analyst was constantly made aware of the threat of violence contained in George's relation to him. George started analysis complaining that he was too fat and too small—people looked at him and laughed at him. In order to try to control these thoughts it was evident that he had sought to detach himself from the people in his environment and to isolate himself in his own inner world, where he could feel able to avenge himself in fantasy for the humiliations he felt he had had to suffer. He talked in the initial sessions of his embarrassment that his actions and thoughts were being observed by the analyst. This led to violent anger with the analyst alternating with thoughts of attacking himself through suicide. He linked how he was feeling now with the humiliations he had experienced when he had soiled himself as a child and talked of feeling murderously violent toward men, his father in particular. He described his father as someone who wanted George to submit to him. His only defense against this conflict, reexperienced within the transference, seemed to be by remaining silent.

The analyst was left feeling helpless without a sense of reality regarding his own function or that of the analysis, while having to respond to George's demand that he be treated as "sick" "because [he] could not work because of [his] fear of people." George's silence enabled him to feel that he was not submitting to the analyst but also that he was unable to work in the analysis and should not be expected to do so (in the same way that he had stopped work in his day-to-day life). When the analyst was eventually forced to confront George with the warning that he would not be able to continue analysis if George became violent toward him, George's surprise made it clear that his inactivity and silence had enabled him to deny totally the reality of his potential violence against the analyst, as if he could be conscious only of his own fear of the analyst. During the long period of silence the analyst was left to struggle with his own anger and anxiety at feeling helpless. Here the group discussions were important in supporting him in his capacity to go on giving meaning to his observations of George and to use them to continue to communicate with him despite George's withdrawal.

It seemed to the analyst that George's ability to remain silent in the sessions reflected his need to feel that he would not lose control over his wish to attack the analyst. George's anxiety about losing control of his violence arose from seeing the analyst as a man to whom he presented his body daily to be looked at; this to him meant allowing the analyst to humiliate him. Any comments by the analyst could be taken by George as proof of the analyst's wish to humiliate him. The compelling quality of George's silence seems to have indicated that inflicting violence on a man had become an essential part of his central masturbation fantasy. George had already lost control of his violence once when he attacked his father. He seemed to feel that he needed to show his power to destroy the father in order to allow himself to feel that he had a sexual body that could serve purposes other than to humiliate him further.

As he began to lose weight it appeared that he was developing some hope about what he could do for himself without the analyst's help, which enabled him to feel less persecuted by the fantasy of the analyst's contempt for him. In the fantasy he reported in the first week of treatment before he became silent—of traveling in a subway train and pulling the alarm signal— he appeared to be telling the analyst how compelled he felt to do something extreme, both when he broke down at school and now, because the situation of the analysis was one in which the analyst was in control, like the driver of the train. His only means of regaining control had been by bringing his life to a dead stop, as he was doing to the analysis via his silence.

The anal masturbation, about which he was later able to tell the analyst, represented his belief that he could not use or own his penis with a woman since this could only further humiliate him because of its inferior size. But in his anal masturbation he could live out the fantasy of being in co:trol of a penis while his body was identified as female. In the same way he could let the analyst help him as long as he felt completely in control of the analyst, similar to his control of the object he used for anal masturbation. Fantasies of relationships with women apparently had been totally repressed; George used homosexual fantasies of submitting to a man's attack in order to avoid experiencing the anxiety about the violent fantasies associated with fulfillment of his wish for a relationship to a woman as well as to avoid his violent fantasies toward men. By identifying his body with that of a woman, he could experience his masturbatory activity as a revenge on his mother, showing her that he did not need women. The anxiety against which he needed to defend himself was the reexperience of being left by a woman and feeling worthless and shamed, as his mother had made him feel when she left him as a child.

The analyst's interpretation could be experienced by George in his fantasy as if the analyst was attempting to enter his mind as well as his body—a fantasy that became clearer when George became preoccupied with finding means to develop his brain on his own in order to deny his wish for penetration. The anxiety provoked by such a fantasy could be interpreted as George's fear of allowing the analyst to have the power and the control to use his own penis (the analyst was male), instead of George's being able to maintain the unconscious belief that, as in his anal masturbation, it was he, not the analyst, who was in control of his mind.

Although George gave up using silence as a weapon after the first year, he continued to use confusional thinking and avoidance of thinking, making it extremely difficult at times for the analyst to make meaningful interpretations. George could then triumphantly taunt him for not getting things right. The fantasy of the analysis as an underground train of which the analyst was in control and in which George felt in danger gradually changed to his fantasy of a gray river steamer on which he was being taken for a treat—an idealized fantasy of feeling safe with the analyst, like a child with its mother. Any event that acted as a reminder of his feeling abnormal or inferior, however, continued to evoke an attack on the analyst's capacity to help him.

Sam also came to the Centre when he had broken down in his ability to function in the outside world. He had become totally dependent on his parents, needing to feel that they could both tolerate and survive his destructive attacks on them and their home. The fear that brought him to the Centre and into analysis was that of going mad, not the fear of his violence. As in the case of George, it was the analyst who was made anxious and frightened by Sam's potential for destructiveness and violence. Like George too, Sam needed to feel in control of the analyst—but he did so by constantly and relentlessly provoking the analyst to think of him as disgusting, hateful, and unbearable. In this way he tried to maintain his view of the analyst as the powerful and dangerous object who had to be kept under control or destroyed, while at the same time being able to deny experiencing guilt or shame about his actions.

During the first months the analyst was made to feel bored and deadened by Sam, and as if only the parents were interested in Sam's coming to his treatment. Following the first holiday break, however, Sam brought all the sexual excitement that he had felt unable to control at home, and that made him feel mad, into the transference relationship. It was as if the fantasies he had been driven to enact as a young adolescent came into the transference as an excitement that needed to be shown to the analyst. By forcing the analyst to share in the excitement related to his sexual fantasies, Sam could avoid feeling left alone with them. In this way he showed how terrified he was of feeling alone with his disgust of himself. When he felt he had failed to force the analyst to respond during the session, he experienced the ending of the session as the analyst's reacting to his fantasies and to him as he felt he would be compelled to do to himself when left alone. That is, he would reject and rid himself of his body as a dirty object—identified by him as a piece of feces.

Sam, like George, also had used anal masturbation to live out his wish for passive submission through anal penetration and in this way to enact the fantasy of being the victim—passive and female—rather than the active male perpetrator. Sam talked of feeling excited by sexual fantasies about dead women, as if he felt that he would need a dead woman in order to be male and potent. Only then could he feel it safe to risk using his penis, without the woman's having the power to shame him by seeing his dependence on her. In the transference this meant that he saw the analyst as the one who was allowed to possess a penis—but only as long as Sam felt he could be in control of it by making him respond in ways that he dictated, as he tried to do to his parents at home. To experience the analyst as separate and not under his control made him feel that he would have to kill the analyst because he now knew of Sam's secret masturbatory activities and fantasies and therefore had power to shame him. He had delusions about whether he actually possessed a penis. When he was a young adolescent he had run naked through back gardens, compelled to exhibit himself, as if he were trying to stop the mad thought that he did not have a penis, which arose from his anxiety of perceiving himself as a sexual male.

The breakdown that brought him into treatment had followed his first attempt at sexual intercourse, when he found that he was impotent. Following this experience he had become more violent and out of control at home. The provocations reported by the analyst represented Sam's attempt to provoke him into revealing excited interest in Sam's "dirty anal thoughts." But in contrast with George, Sam demanded the analyst's direct involvement with his body. Sam, unlike George, had conscious heterosexual fantasies and was aware of his hatred for women, who he felt had the power to make him impotent and helpless as his mother had done by making him frightened about her death. His anxiety, as well as the analyst's, was that when the analyst was not with him and in control of his violence, Sam might feel compelled to find a woman with whom to have sexual intercourse but whom he would have to kill in order to deprive her of the power to frighten him.

George, unlike Sam, had found a way to avoid anxiety about his potential violence through his breakdown at school. This had led to his withdrawing from the external world and isolating himself within the inner experience of his body, through his masturbation and his compulsive eating. The violence could remain split off from his experience and was perceived as coming from the external world. Sam, on the other hand, had maintained his relation to the external world through his renewed dependence on his parents and in this way had also kept a tenuous relationship to his sexual body, including his penis. But this left Sam more vulnerable to feeling alone with his mad violence, hating himself and his body for shaming him through his dependence on his external objects. Analysis for George was initially a terrifying experience since it demanded that he give up his defensive withdrawal. For Sam it meant giving up his dependence on his parents and feeling totally dependent on the analyst to control his violence.

Mary belonged to the first group in the initial phase of the analysis, before her suicide attempt. Although the analyst was not directly concerned with her violence, it was clear that Mary herself at times failed to control it. She had hit her mother and had reported other incidents that occurred mostly on weekends at home. In the beginning of the analysis, the analyst experienced her violence in the transference only by the way she felt bombarded by Mary's communications and her insistent attempts to compel the analyst to participate in her belief in her mother's madness and destructiveness while denying her own problems or destructiveness.

What Mary could make clear was her fear of being left and becoming overwhelmed by her anxiety each weekend. She became aware each Friday that she could not control the analyst—in contrast to her belief during the sessions that she could control the analyst's thoughts. On weekends she felt left alone with the fear of her own madness and violence. When the analyst responded to her anxiety by offering her extra sessions, Mary could not make use of the offer and instead tried to use her friends' homes as a support. Her anxiety at being left by the analyst was related to her fear that she could not contain her violence when alone with her mother. She enacted this by making a suicide attempt at the time scheduled for her Monday morning session. Choosing this time meant blaming the analyst for making her feel out of control, while directing the violence at her own body instead of at the analyst. The analyst then had to find a way of enabling the analysis to continue by arranging for Mary to be hospitalized.

The Second Group

Cara, Kevin, John, Charles, and Bill had all, at one time before they began analysis, made a suicide attempt. Some were also attacking their bodies by cutting themselves or through self-inflicted vomiting. John, Charles, and Bill also depended on drugs to enable them to deal with their anxiety. These adolescents made their analysts aware of their dependence on self-destructive actions or drugs to deal with their anxiety and of the continued availability of these means whenever they felt the analyst was failing to protect them from the anxiety. Carrying out an action involving their body enabled them to feel once more in control of their body and hence of the source of their anxiety; at the same time, the action could be used to express hatred of the analyst, by whom they felt abandoned.

In the initial phase of the analysis, all these adolescents were unable to show any awareness of the analyst's existence outside the session—as if they could not feel that the analyst existed during a holiday break or weekend. Their inner experience at these times was one of being totally alone with their anxiety. These were also the times when there was a marked danger of self-destructive attacks on their bodies or, as in the case of John, Charles, and Bill, of needing drugs to deaden any potential wish for the object.

Cara had talked of wanting to die and had made a suicide attempt some time before beginning analysis. She told her analyst that she thought of suicide at the times when she compulsively stuffed herself with food. Once she had made herself vomit the food, she could feel "alone and calm." It was as if she lived out her sexual excitement in the relationship to food: first in the stuffing, but then followed by the self-enforced sight of the vomit which confronted her with what she could do to the object of her excitement. She felt that suicide was the solution to her hatred of her sexually destructive body. In the transference her anxiety at feeling that she might have to kill herself compelled her to provoke the analyst into attacking and hating her, as if this would keep her from having to be aware of her wish to attack herself. Stuffing could then remain a source of excitement that enabled her to feel independent rather than in need of the analyst.

Despite the analyst's continued efforts to maintain the treatment in the face of Cara's provocation, Cara eventually became unable to attend her sessions. Instead she used the analyst to allow her to remain alive and to live out in her stuffing the fantasy of having a means of gratification available that allowed her to feel independent of the analyst and her mother. She could live out the sense of triumph over the analyst which she had been afraid of living out in relation to her mother. Cara felt responsible for keeping her mother alive and well; to her, this meant allowing her mother to be the giver who was responsible for satisfying all her needs. She said her mother spoke of her as a child "who had taken everything," as if this would be the mother's reproach should Cara show that she no longer wanted to be totally dependent on her as she had been as a child.

At puberty, the reality of having a female sexual body meant to Cara that she now had something belonging to her that could make her mother, and later the analyst, feel not needed or wanted by her. She now had her own sexual powers to enable her to find someone other than her mother to satisfy her. It also made her feel that she could exclude the mother from her relationship with the father. The anxiety aroused by this sense of power made Cara feel that she had to try to destroy her body for containing the potential for destroying her mother. The analyst was made overtly aware throughout the period Cara remained in analysis that Cara could not tolerate feeling that the analyst was able, or wanted, to help her, as if she needed desperately to show the power she had to destroy any such possibility. This she was able to do by forcing the analyst to focus attention on her binging and vomiting and by unconsciously wanting the analyst to hate Cara for what she was doing. By focusing the analyst's attention on what Cara could do, Cara felt she could also deprive the analyst of the satisfaction of showing Cara what she, the analyst, could do to help her. Showing the analyst that the analysis was useless was like triumphantly showing her vomit to her parents. But the hatred of herself and her body for feeling able to enact the fantasy of destroying her mother made her feel that she should die.

The analyst was made helpless through the immediacy of the experience that Cara put in place of the analysis, at the same time having to be aware of the self-destructive dangers contained in this activity. Eventually Cara's need to hold onto this precarious defensive balance of using her body to live out her destructive fantasies made her unable to continue coming to her sessions. The analyst, instead of being experienced as someone she needed to help her, had to become useless and helpless in order for Cara to be able to leave her. By leaving she could also maintain the fantasy of the analyst as someone who was trying to take her away from her mother and thus someone who could unconsciously be blamed for the destructive attack on her mother which Cara felt so afraid of wanting to make herself. The analyst, by having to focus her attention on what Cara was doing to her own body in this process, was forced into showing the anxiety that Cara herself wanted to deny—that is, of the compelling need to attack and destroy her own female sexual body. As Cara became more aware that she could not give up her behavior, she became terrified and felt she would fall apart. This seemed to represent her awareness that despite her crazy behavior the analyst remained unharmed and "didn't cry" as her mother had, thus putting Cara more in touch with the reality of what she was doing to herself.

Three of the four male adolescents in this group—Kevin, John, and Charles—similarly appeared to live with the unconscious fantasy that their male sexual bodies, when used actively by them, had the potential to destroy their mothers. This was expressed in the content of the central masturbation fantasy which contained giving up the active role as a means of gratification. The passive nature of their sexual fantasies then became the source of the anxiety they experienced because of the attack it represented on their male sexual body. In the transference they could hold their analysts responsible for their own passive wishes by seeing them as someone who was forcing them to submit to their demands. By attacking the analyst in the transference they could then live out the fantasy of ridding themselves of the hatred of their own passive wishes instead of needing to experience the hatred of their own body for the failure in being an active male.

Kevin, in the first few months of the analysis, appeared to see the analyst as like his mother—someone who needed him to talk to, rather than someone he needed. He was terrified of being abandoned by the analyst, but it was as if he himself did not relate to the analyst with any needs or feelings of his own. Instead, he could unconsciously use the fantasy of her need of him to feel that he had to stay alive for her, as for his mother. The analyst was made aware of the intensity of Kevin's anxiety through his talking in a way that made her feel flooded by him and left her not knowing what to respond to—but at the same time feeling that she had to be careful about how she responded in order not to seem seductive to Kevin in the transference.

Kevin's fear of going mad when he was cutting himself related to a fantasy of being overwhelmed by his destructive feelings and taken over by them. He appeared, however, to welcome the dizzy spells he experienced, when he felt out of control of his body. They allowed him to feel that he did not have to be in charge of his body but, rather, could give in to something more powerful than himself. In the transference he tried to appear in charge while enacting his wish to be passively overwhelmed by the analyst. On weekends, when he could no longer maintain the fantasy that he was just passively submitting to the analyst's wish to be talked to, the anxiety relating to his active wishes made him seek out ways of being a passive victim, beaten up or raped by a man who could then be made responsible for Kevin's violent wishes while he could remain passive. His fantasy was of wanting to be a girl or a child so that he would not have to attack his own body or allow himself to be beaten up. He had lived out this sexual fantasy in a homosexual encounter in mid-adolescence, and it continued to be present in his conscious fears and wishful fantasies in relation to his brother, who he feared would come home to beat him up or rape him.

In the transference it was expressed initially in a compelling need on weekend breaks to get involved in fights and be beaten up by a man, while consciously feeling preoccupied with thoughts of how he could find a girl with whom to have a relationship. While involved in a fight with a man he was able to deny the anxiety of having a male sexual body capable of inflicting damage on a woman. Instead, he could feel abandoned by the analyst and able to think of finding a woman to replace her. He told the analyst how he used to burn himself before holidays and of wanting to come to the session in bandages. He was angry with her because she did not react. Before a holiday he told her of his fantasy of starting a fire somewhere "in order to hurt others" but also to hurt himself. Kevin needed to frighten the analyst with the fantasy of his male sexual excitement, as he remembered his mother having been frightened by his father while wanting her to reassure him that she did not take his violence seriously and was not frightened by it.

Kevin's wish to die, which was related to his fear of losing control of his destructive body and of becoming mad, could also be related to a fear of giving in to the wish to remain with his mother, united in death, rather than becoming separate and alone. His mother had told him that she had wanted to kill herself while pregnant with him after his father left. The fantasy of death could thus express the wish to submit to his mother's wish to keep him inside her womb as a baby forever, while also representing the punishment for his oedipal sexual wishes to possess her as a man. At the time of puberty Kevin had had an epileptic episode, similar to one his older sister had when she reached puberty. It appeared as if Kevin was able to use this symptom as confirmation that he could become instead a girl like his sister.

For Kevin, to be a man was to become like his father, someone able to inflict violence on women. In the transference, he could begin to feel that his wish to be separate from his analyst did not mean that he had to give up his male sexual body and become a girl in order to avoid the punishment of death or madness for the damage he was doing to the analyst. Kevin's anxiety of losing control over his male body and his fear of risking death were reflected in the analyst's initial feeling of extreme caution about what could be talked of safely in the analysis. By cutting himself or banging his head, he was able to deny his fears of damage while at the same time showing his analyst the power of the violence he felt was contained in his body.

John had made a suicide attempt following puberty and two more in the year before he started analysis. The last time he had cut his wrist following a rejection by a girl. John talked of a fantasy that cutting himself and then smearing himself with the blood allowed him to identify his body with that of a menstruating woman. Once he could experience himself in this state he would be able to keep his hatred repressed for what he felt as his inadequate male sexual body. Instead of having to die as he had intended, he could then allow himself to remain alive, as he showed when he asked his mother for help and phoned for an ambulance. Having a male sexual body, which he could only perceive as weak and inadequate, made him aware of his hatred of it and afraid of becoming compelled to destroy it. He had to find ways of isolating himself from the experience of his male sexual body in order to control his destructive impulses against it. He used the feeling that he could shock people by being different to deny his belief that his penis was too insignificant for anyone to notice him as a man.

Cutting himself was a way of shocking both himself and others. The analyst describes him as being a "good patient" during the week, but feeling on weekends as if the analyst had lost touch with him and his needs. He would then turn to drugs or alcohol, with the fantasy that they enabled him to create a "barrier" between his feelings and his body. He could thus avoid the anxiety of feeling his need for the analyst to remain in touch with him in order to feel the reality of his body. Just before a holiday break in the analysis, he told the analyst about a friend of his who had made a suicide attempt, and he talked of his envy of his friend for doing something he too would like to do. His fantasy was that by attempting suicide he could look "innocent and young," as his friend had when he visited him in hospital. He saw the analyst's presence as necessary in order to prevent him from needing to return to a prepubertal state in which he had felt safe and loved. In his fantasy the analyst would then have to love him instead of leaving him, and he would not be left alone with his hatred of his inadequate body. He seemed afraid that feeling rejected by the analyst would cause him to reexperience the rage and the violence toward his body he had felt in the past after being left by his girlfriend. John talked of feeling on weekends as if a glass barrier existed between him and his ability to feel that he had a normal sexual body. But he had to maintain this barrier against awareness of the reality of his sexual body by inducing an illusional state with drugs. Cutting himself both expressed his anxiety of feeling unreal and allowed him to experience his body as real through maintaining the fantasy of being a menstruating woman. The use of drugs also expressed the unconscious hatred he felt for his male sexual body and the wish to destroy it. In the transference the wish to be male and the wish to be female were seen as in constant conflict. On the one hand he showed a wish to compete with the power of his male analyst in a destructive way—he would then be able to feel adequate—but on the other hand, he made the analyst aware of his longing to submit passively to him. This was lived out in the transference when he could feel attacked by the analyst's interpretations. On weekends, when he could not live out the fantasy of being attacked by the analyst and was afraid of his hatred of his body he used drugs to re-create the barrier.

Charles, together with his mother and sister, had been left by his father when he was a child. His mother had been in the hospital, diagnosed as schizophrenic, and Charles was sent away to school. Reaching puberty meant to him that he now had a penis which could enable him to stop his mother from sending him away because he could now use his powerful penis to take active possession of her body; he would now also be able to leave her as his father had done. But being able to replace the absent oedipal father made him feel that he had to become responsible for his father's absence and therefore that he could now be blamed by his mother for her illness. It also carried the risk of his incurring his father's anger.

Soon after reaching puberty Charles enacted the fantasy of the risk he felt having an adult penis entailed. He enacted his fear of being found out by stealing the key to a forbidden locked cupboard at school and climbing inside it. When he was caught and confronted by a teacher, he made the first of his ten suicide attempts. Following this attempt, his mother once more was admitted to a hospital. For Charles this could have been a confirmation of his fantasy that he had made his mother ill by being a man who could leave her as his father had done.

In the transference the analyst was constantly alert to the way Charles attempted to maintain the fantasy of the stolen penis (key) which was not really his, and for which he could be caught and punished, through the use he made of his relationship to his motor bike. As described by the analyst, the motor bike represented his penis given by or stolen from his mother, which, like the key, were he to feel the excitement of owning it himself, had to contain the potential for destroying his or someone else's body. He seemed constantly to need to keep the analyst in a state of anxiety about his harming himself or others with his motor bike, while at the same time wanting the analyst to be strong enough to catch him. The analyst was also alert to the danger of Charles's using the bike to live out the fantasy of submitting to a stronger man in order to be damaged or killed as punishment for the excitement he was able to experience on the bike.

In the transference he constantly attacked the analyst in order to provoke him into showing him his powerful interpretations—which in his fantasy he could then make his own by submitting to him. This fantasy expressed his central masturbation fantasy that he could avoid the punishment of castration by his father, or his mother's wish to keep him for herself, only if he used a "stolen penis" and kept his own penis hidden. The dangers of the incestuous potential of possessing and owning his penis made him feel that it really should go on belonging to his mother and now to the analyst. Although he was able to have sexual relationships with women, he used these mostly to protect himself from the anxiety of feeling abandoned by the analyst at weekends through the fantasy of sharing in the analyst's activity by becoming identified with him. He showed his hatred of the analyst for leaving him by becoming helplessly dependent on a woman when the analyst was not there and then rejecting the woman when he had the analyst available once more. The fantasy he had of the woman who would be able to excite him, and whom he would not reject, was of a woman with big breasts; he could use the sight of the big breast unconsciously to represent the woman's penis in the way he used his motor bike. The wish for a woman who possessed a penis of her own represented a longing to feel safe from the fear that otherwise she would want to steal his. He believed that if a woman had a penis as well as a breast, she would then possess something that would make him want to stay with her instead of leaving and rejecting her. He perceived his own penis as something dead and unexciting, and all his fantasies of what he would do if he experienced his penis as alive were displaced onto the fantasies surrounding the motor bike.

As with the other adolescents, the danger of self-destructive actions involving his motor bike or of a suicide attempt was greatest during weekends or holiday breaks. For Charles, weekends represented the loss of the excitement he could unconsciously live out in the fantasy of sharing in the analyst's power in the session by submitting to his penis/breast in the transference. The fear of feeling his own penis as dead when he was alone led to Charles's compelling need to seek excitement either with a girl or through his motor bike. Alternatively he also relied on drugs, as John did.

Charles also used money to defend against his violent and incestuous fantasies. For a period in his analysis he withheld payment of his contributions for his treatment, on the excuse that he needed it to repay his mother for his motor bike. In this way he could make what the analyst was offering him seem valueless compared to what he was allowed to share with his mother. At the same time he was able to deny the secret excitement related to the fantasy that the analyst wanted to castrate him by depriving him of his stolen "penis," the motor bike, in retaliation for Charles's withholding the contribution and devaluing the analyst's breast/penis. In the transference the analyst was aware of the potential danger of allowing Charles to feel able to excite him into showing that he wanted to possess the money Charles had from his mother, since this would confirm his fantasy of why he could not risk possessing his own penis.

Bill had made a suicide attempt at fourteen. Following this event he became involved with another boy whom he described as a sadistic bully, with whom he had a submissive relationship and with whom he could sexually identify himself. When he failed to progress academically he left home and became involved with his physical development via dieting and body building. He was referred to the Centre following a very serious suicide attempt at the age of eighteen, which included cutting his wrist. He was still in a very disturbed state when seen at the Centre and was advised to enter a hospital; he was told that analytic treatment would be available to him after his discharge. He expressed great doubts, however, that analysis could help him. In the transference he lived out these doubts by continuing to use the hospital and drugs as alternatives to the analyst's help. His fear of the analyst, as someone who would control him, was expressed by his attempts to control the analyst by demanding changes in the frequency of sessions, according to what he felt he needed, or changes of session times.

Following a holiday break in the analysis, Bill broke down again and had to return to the hospital. He repeated the experiences with the sadistic bully that had followed his first suicide attempt by getting himself attacked by a man on the way from the hospital to his session—as if he could return to the sessions only when feeling that his violence was under a man's control. In the sessions he became too anxious to lie on the couch and had to sit up. It was as if the actual experience of being left by the analyst, a woman, revived all the violence he felt capable of and from which he had been trying to detach himself through the use of drugs. Coming to the session, he needed to submit his body once more to a "sadistic bully" in order to feel that his violence against the analyst for leaving him was under a man's control, as if he felt that the analyst would not be able to prevent him from attacking her. Bill wanted analysis to make him feel less mad. But in order to succeed he had to perceive the analyst as sufficiently powerful in his fantasy to enable him to gratify his wish to submit to attack by this more powerful and sadistic object with whom he could then also feel identified. Being "less mad" meant to Bill giving up the experience of "a private, powerful inner feeling which made [him] feel mad with racing thoughts." He felt that being mad enabled him to live out in his own thoughts the powerful excitement he feared experiencing in his body, which he could experience only by identifying with a powerful object to whom he submitted. By feeling that he had his "own powerful thoughts" as a source of excitement, Bill was also able to feel that he had no need for his body or the analyst, but also that the analyst's wish to make him less mad would deprive him of his own source of excitement.

He could use drugs to feel in control of his thoughts while the hospital could be used to look after his body, which he experienced as worthless and as something he wanted to rid himself of. Unconsciously he felt his body contained all the physical violence he could direct against his mother and the analyst; he could protect the analyst only by killing himself or by finding a man powerful enough to submit his body to. Following the analyst's canceling of a session, his denial of his need for the analyst broke down once more. This event repeated for Bill, in the transference, the actual experience that had preceded his last suicide attempt, when his mother had had to cancel a meeting with him in order to attend an important funeral. He responded to the cancelation of his session by being confused and feeling out of touch with reality. He said he felt he could not distinguish the analyst from his mother any more, that the analyst had become like his mother, an unbearable frustrating reality. His only defense against his violence was by feeling out of touch with her. He had responded to the cancelation by showing how dependent he felt on having available his own powerful, mad thoughts and feelings. It left him confused and bewildered as he may have felt as a small child when he had experienced being left by his mother.

His fear of the violence contained in his body, which he felt afraid of wanting to use to prevent the analyst from leaving him, was also expressed in the fantasy of losing touch with it, for then he would not have to feel responsible for what he did. This was, perhaps, similar to his "wandering off" from his parents as a child: he could not feel them as wanting to look after his body, so he had to go and look for someone else to take care of him for fear of having to be responsible for himself. He used his need for hospital care when he was angry with the analyst for leaving him and when afraid of losing touch with reality. Thus he could destroy his perception of the analyst's capacity to help him and deny his wish to be cared for by her while showing her she could not stop him from giving in to his own powerful thoughts, which made him feel he was going mad and would have to leave the analyst.

In the transference the analyst felt that Bill needed her to be under his complete control; any proof that she was able to act or think independently could lead to his breaking off the treatment because of his anxiety. The destructiveness contained in the wish to use the analyst as if she were part of him and not separate made him and the analyst feel that the treatment was constantly endangered by his destructiveness. It seemed as if he believed he would inevitably be destroyed by the analyst if he gave in to his wish to sub-

mit to her so that he could then become part of her. In order to protect both
the analyst and himself he had to find ways of avoiding involvement in the
analytic relationship—to the point where eventually he broke off analysis. It
was as though he had to reexperience the analyst's failure to make him feel
safe so as to confirm his belief that only those who could be part of his private fantasy life, and therefore under his control, like drugs, were safe and
dependable. This repeated the way he had used his teddy bear as a child to
feel part of him when he felt alone. The conflict he experienced in the analysis contained his wish to enact the fantasy of having the analyst as part of
himself and his fear of destroying her or himself if he succeeded in doing so.

The Third Group

Cara and Bill are included here because they broke off analysis prematurely.
Mark and Mary also repeated their adolescent developmental breakdown
within the transference relationship, leading to a transference breakdown in
the analysis. Both needed to be hospitalized as a result, but, unlike Cara and
Bill, they were able to continue with their treatment. Mary had never been
hospitalized before, but this became necessary when she made a suicide attempt soon after beginning analysis. Mark, who had been diagnosed at a hospital as suffering from a paranoid schizophrenic disturbance, was advised to
enter the hospital for treatment. He came to the Centre instead and began
analysis, using his family as additional outside support.

Mary had, in the weeks preceding her suicide attempt, made it clear
how out of control she was feeling and how she saw her parents and others as
people she could not trust and from whom she had to get away. When she felt
that her mother was involving herself too closely with her, Mary said she was
unable to control her mad thoughts and had hit her. The violence she was
unable to control made her feel hopeless and rejected, and eventually compelled her to attack her own body. After her suicide attempt she agreed to the
analyst's condition that she should stay in the hospital so that her analysis
could be continued.

Mark had never made a suicide attempt or shown any violent behavior
toward himself or others. His anxiety when he came for help was related
more to his dependence on omnipotent fantasies of being able to deceive
others so that they would see him as potent, strong, and normal. His terror
was of being blamed, found out and abandoned, and left to die as a helpless
child. He broke down at eighteen following an attempt at intercourse where
he failed and had felt deceived and infantilized by the woman. Later he de-

veloped paranoid ideas when a possible fraud was being investigated at the office where he worked, and he could not rid himself of his belief that he would be caught and blamed. His breakdown in the course of the analysis followed a holiday and repeated the original adolescent breakdown at puberty. He became terrified, begged the analyst to help him and stop people from persecuting him, and was in a state of complete dependency on the analyst (as he had felt when his parents sent him away earlier).

At the same time he was suspicious of the analyst and had the fantasy that the analyst could have changed his (Mark's) body into that of a girl. He wanted to look at the analyst's penis, as if wanting to reverse his fear of the analyst's seeing Mark's weak penis. He enacted the omnipotent fantasy that he could change his body and take over the analyst's penis as his own by sitting in the analyst's chair in the session. Having to go into a hospital and being confronted with the reality of his illness made him less suspicious of what the analyst was doing to him. He could once more acknowledge his dependence on the analyst and his need for treatment and was able finally to return to analysis. At times, however, he would revert to his suspicions of the analyst and blame him for his breakdown.

When Mark began analysis, he complained of hearing voices that told him to kill himself. He expected the analyst to rid him of the voices but made no link between them and his feelings about his body and his sexual activities. He dissociated himself totally from his own violence and heard it as coming from outside himself. In the transference he demanded that the analyst protect him and tell him what to do; yet, at the same time, he continued to feel suspicious of what the analyst might be doing to him. He spoke of needing to rid himself of his feces and semen in order to keep his body from being harmed by these substances. He needed to feel he could keep his body safe from contamination by substances with destructive powers; by ridding himself of them he could feel free of all violence. He masturbated compulsively and was preoccupied with his anal activities—defecating or scratching his anus—as a way of living out his magical belief in his ability to keep himself uncontaminated while continuing to treat the analyst's interpretations with suspicion.

When he was afraid of his omnipotent belief that he could rid himself of the analyst, whom he experienced as threatening to contaminate him, he turned the conflicting words of the analyst and himself into "disputes" that took place in his mind and from which he wanted to be freed by the analyst. He did not confront the analyst with threats of violence or with self-destructive actions. Instead Mark had succeeded in destroying any emotions associated with the thoughts and fantasies he communicated to the analyst.

The anxiety the analyst experienced was of responding to Mark's communications in a similarly mechanical way and, in doing so, losing touch with reality. As long as Mark continued to feel that he had no feelings, he could experience the analyst's attempts to introduce feelings into his thoughts as attempts to contaminate him.

The analyst described his task as one of helping Mark gradually to feel that it was safe to take over responsibility for the way he chose to communicate with the analyst, as well as for his actions, without the terror of feeling blamed for the dirty, contaminating activities he might be engaged in. Like George and Sam, Mark depended on anal activities as his source of excitement, but he used the excitement in his fantasy to allow himself to feel that he had magically been given a girl's body and did not possess a penis. It was this fantasy that he repeated in his transference breakdown when he alternated between believing that he was being made into a girl and that he could acquire the analyst's magical powers and make himself into a girl.

Mary had shown her conflict about accepting the need for treatment from the outset. Although she said she could no longer continue with her life as she had been doing until then, any attempt to help her change was felt as a threat. The analyst had been concerned from the start with the possibility of a suicide attempt since Mary made it clear how desperate she felt at the end of each week. But she also enacted, in relation to the analyst as well as outside the analysis, her compulsion to reject any help offered to her. This repeated the conflict she was experiencing between her wish to return home to her mother and her hatred of her for being unable to care for Mary. When she was at home with her mother she became aware that it was not only the mother who was out of control and "mad," as she thought, but she herself. This failure of the attempt to deny her own mad feelings then led to her suicide attempt and rejection of the analyst.

Once Mary was in the hospital she could displace some of the hatred she felt for the analyst onto the hospital staff, and this allowed her to begin to experience the analyst as someone she could relate to safely and without losing control. The analyst traveled some distance to see Mary three times a week at the hospital. Yet, at first, Mary made herself unavailable for sessions by being asleep when the analyst came, using this as a defense against her fear of losing control once more.

Gradually she began to feel safer in the transference relationship and to make more use of the sessions. When plans were being made for Mary to leave the hospital and move to a hostel, she began once more to attack verbally the people responsible for providing her with a suitable home—they were useless and failing her. When she left the hospital, she was no longer able to deny her dependence on the analyst. During holiday breaks from treatment she had tried to deny her dependence by involving herself in a sexual relationship with a male patient. This expressed her wish to prove to herself and to the analyst that she was not sexually abnormal and therefore did not need the analyst. Each time she felt she had failed in her attempts to prove herself capable of a normal sexual relationship, she reacted with anger and despair. The analyst describes how Mary would then have to find someone other than the analyst who could be blamed for not having made her into what she had hoped.

One example involved a hairdresser who had cut Mary's hair in a way she disliked. She reacted with complete despair because the unbecoming haircut made her feel that she could not change her body into what she wanted and that she would therefore have to attack her body. Her birthday, the birthday of her younger sister, and the date of Mary's suicide attempt all remained linked in her mind with the sense of her failure to change herself into what she wanted instead of having to depend on the analyst to help her change. The analyst describes the gradual lessening of the sense of threat that Mary brought into the transference at these anniversary times. In the fantasy accompanying masturbation, Mary could maintain the omnipotent belief that she could change her body into one that was neither male nor female but could be both.

In the transference she continued to attack the analytic setting—being late, changing sessions, lapsing into long silences—as a way of feeling able to control what the analyst was doing to her. Unconsciously she needed to feel that she could prevent the analyst from giving her what she did not want—a female body instead of the one she felt she could give herself. The analyst describes her as "nullifying her interpretations and analytic nurturing"—in this way rejecting her need of the analyst and attacking the food offered by the analyst. It was as if she still blamed her mother for having given her the wrong food and thus making her change into something she did not want to be—the older child when the younger sister was born. By her silences and by withholding of herself from sessions she could continue to live out the fantasy of punishing the analyst by not giving her what she believed the analyst wanted.

Gradually she began to give up rejecting her female body and knew she could enjoy being a woman. The central masturbation fantasy which allowed her to believe that she could give herself the body she wanted, both male and female, was expressed in her delusional experience after taking the overdose. At that time she said she felt herself to be liquified, and that this could mean "that her and her parents' liquid would become mingled." This thought had filled her with "rage and revulsion." It was as if she felt that the rage and the revulsion against her body that led to her suicide attempt had been caused by her inability to keep the parental intercourse separate in her mind from her own existence; this had made it impossible for her to see her female body as a source of pleasure in a sexual relationship.

Discussion

Apparently the analysts of the first group of adolescents were being put into the position of participating in the adolescents' use of destructive fantasies to live out their sexual excitement, as in a perverse sexual relationship. With the adolescents of the second group, where their violence was directed at their own bodies, their destructive sexual fantasies were lived out in relation to their own body rather than within the transference relationship. The third group of adolescents, where the analyst had to be more directly involved in preserving the treatment situation, can be thought of as including those who felt compelled to live out the adolescent developmental breakdown within the transference, wherein the threat then appeared to be of its repetition in a transference breakdown.

The first group of adolescents, compared to the second, had moved much closer in their pathological development toward effecting a split in the internal reality of the representation of their sexual body by the use of projective mechanisms. They experienced the analysis as a threat to their ability to maintain this split. As long as the split could be maintained, they experienced the external world and objects, rather than their own body, as the source of their persecution and anxiety.

The second group felt the persecution as coming from within their own bodies and were more consciously involved in the conflict resulting from having to find a way of psychically integrating their newly matured genitals. When they felt compelled to do something destructive, they directed the action against their own bodies. They could then continue to deny the attack on the analysis and the analyst implied in such an action. With these adolescents the analyst had to force his way into the arena where the central masturbation fantasy was being lived out rather than being forced to participate in it directly, as with the first group. There also appears to have been a greater capacity in the adolescents of the second group to keep repressed any feelings aroused within the relationship to the analyst in the initial stages. This may again have been the result of the adolescent's consciously thinking of his own body as the source of his fantasies and feelings and thus the object of his hatred. These adolescents were not so dependent on feeling in control of the external world as were those in the first group, but they were more compelled to control their own body even if it meant attacking or destroying it. The analysts' task with the first group was to stand in the way of a pathological process which, by attempting to integrate a perverse organization, would also integrate a distorted sexual body image. The task of the analysts of the second group was to prevent the integration of a relationship to the sexual body which contained the hatred of that body.

The third group of adolescents included two of the second group, Cara and Bill, both adolescents who broke off analysis prematurely. Bill used his dependence on psychiatric drugs to replace the analyst, and Cara used her addiction to binging and vomiting as a substitute for attending her sessions. The developmental breakdown was repeated in the breaking off of the analysis. The other two adolescents, Mark and Mary, needed to go to the hospital and were dependent on the analyst to ensure that this did not mean the breaking off of the analysis. Mark and Mary can be said to have been able to use the actual breakdown of the analysis and the reliving of the developmental breakdown that took place at puberty to recognize the existence of their illness and their need for help.

Both Cara's and Bill's analysts were forced to give in to the adolescents' need to maintain their own ways of functioning. The problem for each analyst came from his awareness that this need contained the adolescent's attack on himself as well as the wish that the analyst should experience the failure of the analysis as his failure.

It also seemed that these adolescents felt that as long as they could make the analyst feel abandoned or alone through missing sessions, they could feel safe from having to acknowledge what they were doing to themselves. The analyst's task was to try to show the adolescent how he was destroying his own hope of change as well as the analysis by staying away. But for both Cara and Bill, this only led to more desperate attempts to find ways of feeling they had a substitute for the experience of the sessions—Cara's stuffing and vomiting and Bill's drugs. Unconsciously, they were living out the fantasy of having found an alternative to being totally dependent on the mother. Leaving analysis meant becoming independent of the analyst and could thus represent an alternative to feeling compelled to kill themselves as a way of becoming independent of the mother. Mark and Mary, in contrast, needed to become quite helpless and totally dependent on the analyst in order to reestablish the relationship to an internal caring mother which had been lost as the result of the developmental breakdown. Before a transference relationship could be established with these adolescents, the analysts had to take on a more directly caring and protective role.

Moses Laufer and M. Eglé Laufer

13.

Commentary and Implications

We began this study with two assumptions: (1) that among a certain group of adolescents a breakdown in development takes place at the time of puberty—that is, at the time of physical sexual maturity; and (2) that this developmental breakdown manifests itself in the adolescent's relationship to his body. We had previously observed that adolescents who were showing signs of severe disturbance, however this was made manifest, always showed signs of disturbance in their relationship to their body as well—whether by direct attacks upon it or by the use they made of it. We thought, therefore, that understanding the different meanings of the use made by the adolescent of his body—and the feelings and attitudes about the body that this represented—would eventually enable us to differentiate better among the various pathologies, as well as to be more precise about the significance of these pathologies as forerunners of some of the mental disorders of adulthood.

Of the nine adolescents described in this book, five had attempted suicide before seeking help through the Centre (Cara, Charles, Bill, Kevin, John),[1] three were included in the study because of behavior that we believed indicated psychotic functioning or possible psychosis (Mary, Mark, George), and one was included because of behavior that might be a sign either of perverse development or of psychotic functioning (Sam).

---

1. Of these five, four (Cara, Bill, Kevin, John) would have been included in the study even if they had not attempted suicide before coming to the Centre; Cara and Bill showed signs of psychotic functioning, and Kevin and John showed signs of perverse development.

The data obtained from the treatment of these adolescents confirmed our hypothesis that a developmental breakdown at puberty had preceded the breakdown in functioning for which the adolescent sought help at the Centre. We found that, by the time the adolescent came for help, we were seeing the result of a serious disruption in his efforts to integrate the sexual body as part of the new image of his body. An important aspect of the assessment of the breakdown for which the adolescent sought help was the interference or damage present in his relationship to the external world. We could begin to see this as an indication of the interference or damage in the adolescent's relationship to his own body, and to use this to predict the seriousness of the risk to his life and his future mental state.

Although our clinical evidence is by no means conclusive, it seems that the direction and the severity of the developmental breakdown—that is, the rejection of the sexually mature body and the disruption of the relation to external reality—depend on whether the acute breakdown takes place at the time of puberty or whether the response at puberty is the result of, or a reaction to, a pathological oedipal resolution that has led to the establishment of a distorted body image. In order to assess the degree to which a distorted body image has already been integrated—and, therefore, the difficulty we might face in any therapeutic efforts to help the adolescent to change—we took into account any special external pressures that may have been present at puberty and have contributed to the difficulty in effecting a change in the body image. Factors such as loss of a parent, separation of the parents, the birth or illness or death of a sibling were all viewed as especially relevant in hindering the adolescent in his efforts to change the body image from puberty onward through the use of the oedipal identifications.

With our adolescents it was possible, although still speculative, to identify those for whom the prepubertal distortion of the body image meant that puberty and the period of adolescence must act as a confirmation that the sexual body is foreign, dangerous to one's narcissistic equilibrium, and a threat to one's established relationship to the oedipal objects and to the prepubertal means of gratification that had been used to live out certain fantasies. For these adolescents, the availability of physically mature, functioning genitals acted as an organizer toward a perverse or psychoticlike solution—a solution used defensively to contain the overwhelming anxiety aroused by pubertal development. For them, confrontation with the real presence of their mature male or female genitals was experienced as an attack and a potential destruction of the idealized but distorted body image—a body image before puberty that in fantasy contained the perfect but pathological solution.

The clinical data can help us understand why, for some of the adoles-

198 • *Clinical and Theoretical Implications*

cents in our study, certain changes were possible which, in prescribed ways, transformed their lives. Although there is evidence that these adolescents have not been able to give up all dependence on the distorted body image, thus still leaving open the possibility of the need to establish perverse sexual relationships, the belief that they can make an object relationship—a belief that was lost to them before treatment (Sam, Mary, Mark, George)—has been reestablished. Their lives were transformed by restoring their ability to work or study, to establish and maintain relationships with people, to function intellectually and in ways that conveyed some direction and organization in their thinking. It is likely that the danger of severe psychopathology is less than before treatment because their previous feeling of being compelled to behave in certain ways is now under conscious control (thereby lessening the feeling of helplessness). It is important to note that none of the four listed above had attempted suicide before they came to the Centre, although Mary did so soon after she began treatment.

Of the five adolescents who had attempted suicide before seeking help at the Centre, three (Cara, Bill, Kevin) made only marginal use of their treatment, which they decided to end early. They remain vulnerable to future trouble, but there is some clinical evidence to show that even the limited treatment period enabled each of them to have a less helpless relationship to his psychopathology and to feel more in charge of his present and future life. Although they could not risk giving up their dependence on their solutions, treatment made conscious the conflict about the need to hold onto these solutions and allowed them to experience the self-destructive meaning of this.

It was different for Charles and John. Charles, who had attempted suicide ten times and who before treatment felt hopeless and was convinced that his life would end by suicide, was able to reorganize his educational and work life and, with some difficulty, to establish and maintain a heterosexual relationship. This was also true for John, who, before seeking help, had attempted suicide and had begun also to cut himself on various parts of his body.

An associated observation is that none of the adolescents in the study killed him- or herself. This fact has a range of theoretical and clinical explanations; one is that treatment for these adolescents meant that we were able to convey our hope that something could be done to help, and that they experienced the Centre's commitment to them as our belief that they were not worthless and that we were not frightened of their hatred of themselves or of the hatred they felt for their fantasied enemies. Their responses to the offer of treatment by the Centre and to the seriousness of our undertaking to help them indicated they understood we wanted them to go on living. This implies that their attempts to kill themselves before they came to the Centre meant that conflict about the choice of a pathological solution was still active in them and that they did not want to die. Instead, it was more likely that the timing of the suicide attempt represented their feeling that they deserved to die because of their abnormal fantasies or as a punishment for their fantasied crimes.

If some of these clinical findings are correct, they have diagnostic and prognostic implications. It may be that the adolescents who attempted suicide were, in fact, less ill than were those who did not attempt suicide but who removed themselves from their physically mature sexual body through perverse or psychotic solutions. It may be that the adolescents who attempted suicide were still battling with the abnormal solution represented by their distorted body image, but it was a solution that had not yet resulted in their removal from a relationship to their sexual body or in their giving up the hope or wish to establish a relationship to a longed-for object. This may be less true of the adolescents who did not attempt suicide. For them, it may be that the conflict was less active; the behavior or fantasies they were compelled to live out gratified a perverse wish while perpetuating a relationship to a distorted but idealized body image—that is, one that did not include genital sexuality. Their sexuality was more autoerotic, and they felt less dependent on objects.

One of the factors common to all of the adolescents was the part played by violence in their relationships to themselves, to objects, and within the transference. By violence we do not mean destructive attacks on people or property, but rather attacks on their own body or mind (as in attempted suicide, self-cutting, bulimia, psychotic functioning, or the use of their own body for the expression of perverse wishes). Such destructive potential had to become a central feature in the transference because it contained the expression of the adolescent's relationship to his sexual body and to the internalized oedipal objects, while at the same time he lived out fantasies that were integral to the breakdown. An important aspect of this violent potential is that its expression was also available to the adolescent as a vehicle for maintaining the pathology and the status quo. In other words, the adolescent, wishing for change, came for help. But at the same time a force existed that stood in the way of change and tried to protect the pathological answers that had been found and that were present in the breakdown at puberty and in the pathological adaptations found during adolescence.

We knew from the start of the study that treating adolescents who had experienced a breakdown in development would be difficult at best, possibly involving risk and danger. We were aware that the development of the transference *must* mean dealing with the adolescent's distortions and his violent intentions directed at himself and at the analyst as a transference object. We also knew that such an undertaking would most likely include crises that could endanger the adolescent's life or at the least jeopardize the treatment. But we knew that to avoid recognizing these issues, and thus be taken by surprise, would mean not tackling the pathology and the consequences of the developmental breakdown. It was only during the development of the treatments that we began to understand the overwhelming strength of their compulsion to behave in certain prescribed ways to deal with their paniclike anxiety and their helplessness to change it. We realized that this had to become an integral part of the transference if the pathology was to be understood and changed.

If it is correct that the final sexual organization is established by the end of adolescence, this treatment would be their last chance to do something about their present and future lives. We were aware that we could not guard against the failure of treatment if the adolescent felt compelled to destroy his chance of giving up his distorted body image and the pathology that supported and maintained it. But we knew also that understanding certain transference and technical issues was critical to the treatment, and we were able to plan for some of these. As our experience with these adolescents accumulated, and as we became more aware of the quality of the anxiety with which they lived, we also became better able to deal with these issues and crises in therapeutically important ways.

The analytic data enable us to see that there are certain common features in some of the clinical issues. The destructive and violent qualities these adolescents brought into the relationship to the analyst were discussed in the previous chapter. In order for them to feel more in touch with the reality of their sexual body, it was necessary to try to make conscious the fantasy that forced them to attack or disown their sexual body, a process that enabled them also to feel in some control, not driven by anxiety. Clinically, this meant that the adolescent had to be confronted with that which made him feel that the destructiveness was not under his control, as if he had no choice in its expression. This internal battle could be displaced onto a range of external problems—the adolescent's conflicting commitments, times of the sessions, parental demands to discontinue the treatment. Ultimately the adolescent could then become aware that he was making the choice, even if he did not yet know the meaning of making such a choice. This was true of self-destructive or self-damaging behavior (self-cutting, attempted suicide, drug taking, starving, overeating), and even of regression into confusional or depersonalized states. It was only by keeping to such an emphasis that the analyst could remain separated from the adolescent's feeling of helplessness in the face of the internal pressure he was experiencing. Giving meaning to the adolescent's actions enabled him to feel that he had not made the analyst helpless; it also conveyed to him that the analyst did not share his belief in his madness. This remained central throughout the treatment.

The analyst's own responses during treatment can be an important obstacle to this therapeutic task. We refer to the analyst's wish or need to deny the destructive threat posed to himself, to his capacity to continue to function as analyst, or to the continuation of the treatment by the adolescent's behavior (Rosenfeld, 1987). In this regard, working with colleagues and discussing one's own and others' clinical problems become essential. Colleagues can make it possible to identify issues that are being avoided or sidestepped by the analyst and/or the adolescent, something the analyst may not be able to do in the session, when involved in the relationship to the adolescent patient. Regular meetings with colleagues can offer the support the analyst needs to confront the destructive and violent enactments of the adolescent, while at the same time feeling in charge of the treatment without risking being blamed for the consequences.

The analyst's own anxiety during the treatment of such adolescents should not be considered a reflection of his "blind spots," but be understood instead as a predictable response to a patient whose pathology unconsciously relies on destructiveness or violence. It is critical to help the analyst guard against losing his belief in his capacity to help the adolescent change while the adolescent may have to go on trying to destroy the treatment or himself. During such times of discouragement the analyst may mistakenly turn to various other means of helping rather than continue to rely primarily on his interpretive work, which would lead to understanding and change. To do so risks destroying the treatment because of the adolescent's belief that the analyst's compromise is equivalent to his destruction of the analyst—a transference situation that arouses unbearable anxiety in the patient. It is therefore essential to plan to help the analyst in such an undertaking through the way in which the clinical work is organized.

Another part of the organization of the clinical work is the framework for treatment. This has been discussed earlier, but from our experience with these adolescents we now know other factors that can help the continuity of the treatment in times of crisis. It is predictable that some patients who have experienced a developmental breakdown during adolescence will have to be admitted temporarily to a hospital or will find it necessary to move from home to some other accommodation. It is advisable for arrangements to be made, as part of the setting up of treatment during the interviewing period, with hospitals or hostels where the adolescent can be admitted or can live without jeopardizing the treatment. This also conveys to the adolescent and his family that the disturbance is being taken very seriously. It may be advisable for the treatment to continue while the adolescent is in a hospital, and such an arrangement should be made, if at all possible. Similarly, it would be advisable to arrange with a hostel for the adolescent to live there, with the hostel's knowledge and agreement that the treatment can be continued without interruption.

One additional and important issue is that of contact with parents. They may have ample reason to be very anxious about their adolescent child; their concern should not be viewed as interference. It may be necessary for the analyst to see the parents at times, but it should be made clear to them and to the adolescent that his treatment remains confidential. In his contact with parents the analyst should not embark on trying to alter the family structure or address the problems of one or both parents. In our view, such help should be undertaken separately by the parents, preferably arranged by themselves and at a different service. Our primary commitment is to the adolescent, and his treatment must be protected. To undertake to help the parents as part of the treatment of the adolescent encourages the view that the parents are responsible for their child's present disorder, with the added danger that his need to blame his parents is made more real.

The adolescents we have described are not unusual or special but represent many adolescents who are in serious trouble now and who will carry their pathology into their adult lives. Our clinical experience shows repeatedly that pathology never appears out of the blue, that there are always earlier signs of the presence of severe or potentially severe disorder. It is disastrous for the life of the adolescent to isolate the manifest signs of disorder— anorexia, the wish to die, perverse activities that seem to be transitory, sudden uncharacteristic behavior, physical attacks on oneself or on a parent— without seeing them as part of a comprehensive picture of the adolescent's internal life. We are often mistakenly relieved when such serious signs seem to disappear, only to reappear later in adolescence with much more severe consequences.

It is also clear to us that we need to address further the relationship between breakdowns in adolescence and the psychotic organization that often becomes manifest during adolescence or in early adulthood. We know that the period of adolescence is used to select and to organize, but we still need to learn about the factors that become critical during this period in the selection of pathological ingredients and in the organization of a psychotic adaptation to oneself and to the external world.

Bibliography

Abraham, K. (1949). A short study of the development of the libido, viewed in the light of mental disorders. In *Selected papers of Karl Abraham*. London: Hogarth Press, pp. 418–501. (Original work published 1924)

Adatto, C. P. (1966). On the metamorphosis from adolescence into adulthood. *J. Amer. Psychoanal. Assn., 14*, 485–509.

Aichhorn, A. (1951). *Wayward youth*. London: Imago. (Original work published 1925)

Arlow, J. A. (1953). Masturbation and symptom formation. *J. Amer. Psychoanal. Assn., 1*, 45–58.

Bak, R. C. (1939). Regression of ego-orientation and libido in schizophrenia. *Int. J. Psychoanal., 20*, 64–71.

Baker, R. (1984). Some considerations arising from the treatment of a patient with necrophilic fantasies in adolescence and young adulthood. *Int. J. Psychoanal., 65*, 283–294.

Banks, I. (1985). *The wasp factory*. London and Sydney: Futura Publications.

Bender, L. (1959). The concept of pseudopsychopathic schizophrenia in adolescents. *Am. J. Orthopsychiat., 29*, 491–509.

Beres, D. (1956). Ego deviation and the concept of schizophrenia. *Psychoanal. Study Child, 11*, 164–235.

Bernfeld, S. (1938). Types of adolescence. *Psychoanal. Q., 7*, 243–253.

Bibring, G. L. (1959). Some considerations of the psychological processes in pregnancy. *Psychoanal. Study Child, 14*, 113–121.

Blatt, S. J., & Wild, C. M. (1976). *Schizophrenia*. New York and London: Academic Press.

Blinder, B. J., & Cadenhead, K. (1986). Bulimia: A historical overview. *Adolescent Psychiatry, 13*, 231–240.

Blos, P. (1962). *On adolescence*. New York: Free Press.

————. (1966). The concept of acting out in relation to the adolescent process. In E. Rexford (Ed.), *A developmental approach to problems of acting out.* New York: International Universities Press, pp. 153–182.

————. (1967). The second individuation process of adolescence. *Psychoanal. Study Child, 22,* 162–186.

————. (1972). The epigenesis of the adult neurosis. *Psychoanal. Study Child, 27,* 106–135.

————. (1977). When and how does adolescence end: Structural criteria for adolescent closure. *Adolescent Psychiatry, 5,* 5–17.

Bruch, H. (1977). Anorexia nervosa. *Adolescent Psychiatry, 5,* 293–303.

Brunswick, R. M. (1940). The pre-oedipal phase of the libido development. *Psychoanal Q., 9,* 293–319.

Burch, C. A. (1986). Identity foreclosure in early adolescence: A problem of narcissistic equilibrium. *Adolescent Psychiatry, 12,* 145–161.

Burgner, M. (1985). The oedipal experience: Effects on development of an absent father. *Int. J. Psychoanal., 66,* 311–320.

Buxbaum, E. (1958). Panel report: The psychology of adolescence. *J. Amer. Psychoanal. Assn., 6,* 111–120.

Calogeras, R. C. (1967). Silence as a technical parameter in psychoanalysis. *Int. J. Psychoanal., 48,* 536–558.

Chasseguet-Smirgel, J. (1981). Loss of reality in perversions—with special reference to fetishism. *J. Amer. Psychoanal. Assn., 29,* 511–534.

Clower, V. L. (1975). Significance of masturbation in female sexual development and function. In I. M. Marcus & J. J. Francis (Eds.), *Masturbation.* New York: International Universities Press, pp. 107–144.

Deutsch, H. (1932). On female homosexuality. *Psychoanal. Q., 1,* 484–510.

————. (1942). Some forms of emotional disturbance and their relationship to schizophrenia. *Psychoanal. Q., 11,* 301–321.

————. (1944). *The psychology of women.* Vol. 1. New York: Grune & Stratton.

————. (1945). *The psychology of women.* Vol. 2. New York: Grune & Stratton.

————. (1968). *Selected problems of adolescence.* New York: International Universities Press.

Dewald, P. A. (1978). The psychoanalytic process in adult patients. *Psychoanal. Study Child, 33,* 323–332.

Dibble, E. D., & Cohen, D. J. (1981). Personality development in identical twins: The first decade of life. *Psychoanal. Study Child, 36,* 45–70.

Eissler, K. R. (1958). Notes on problems of technique in the psychoanalytic treatment of adolescents: With special remarks on perversions. *Psychoanal. Study Child, 13,* 223–254.

Ekstein, R. (1978). The process of termination and its relation to outcome in the treatment of psychotic disorders in adolescence. *Adolescent Psychiatry, 6,* 448–460.

Emde, N. (1982). Anaclitic depression: A follow-up from infancy to puberty. *Psychoanal. Study Child, 37,* 67–94.

Erikson, E. H. (1956). The problem of ego identity. *J. Amer. Psychoanal. Assn.*, *4*, 56–121.

———. (1959). *Identity and the life cycle: Psychological issues.* Mono. 1. New York: International Universities Press.

Erlich, H. S. (1978). Adolescent suicide: Maternal longing and cognitive development. *Psychoanal. Study Child, 33,* 261–277.

Esman, A. H. (1973). The primal scene: A review and a reconsideration. *Adolescent Psychiatry, 28,* 49–81.

———. (1985). A developmental approach to the psychotherapy of adolescents. *Psychoanal. Study Child, 12,* 119–133.

Federn, P. (1952). *Ego psychology and the psychoses.* New York: Basic.

Feigelson, C. I. (1976). Reconstruction of adolescence (and early latency) in the analysis of an adult woman. *Psychoanal. Study Child, 31,* 225–236.

Ferenczi, S. (1950). On the part played by homosexuality in the pathogenesis of paranoia. In *Sex in psychoanalysis.* New York: Basic, pp. 154–186. (Original work published 1911)

———. (1952). Stages in the development of the sense of reality. In *First Contributions to Psycho-Analysis.* London: Hogarth Press, pp. 213–239. (Original work published 1913)

Fraiberg, S. (1982). The adolescent mother and her infant. *Adolescent Psychiatry, 10,* 7–23.

Francis, J. J. (1968). Panel report: Masturbation. *J. Amer. Psychoanal. Assn., 16,* 95–112.

Francis, J. J., & Marcus, I. M. (1975). Masturbation: A developmental view. In I. M. Marcus & J. J. Francis (Eds.), *Masturbation.* New York: International Universities Press, pp. 9–52.

Freud, A. (1937). *The ego and the mechanisms of defence.* London: Hogarth Press.

———. (1949). Aggression in relation to emotional development: Normal and pathological. *Psychoanal. Study Child, 3* (4), 37–48.

———. (1949). Some clinical remarks concerning the treatment of male homosexuality. (Abstract) *Int. J. Psychoanal., 30.*

———. (1958). Adolescence. *Psychoanal. Study Child, 13,* 255–278.

———. (1965). *Normality and pathology in childhood.* New York: International University Press.

———. (1968). Acting out. *Int. J. Psychoanal., 49,* 165–170.

Freud, S. (1905). Fragment of an analysis of a case of hysteria. *S.E.,* 7:3–122.

———. (1905). Three essays on the theory of sexuality. *S.E.,* 7:125–243.

———. (1906). My views on the part played by sexuality in the aetiology of the neuroses. *S.E.,* 7:271–279.

———. (1910). Contributions to a discussion on suicide. *S.E.,* 11:231–232.

———. (1911). Psycho-analytic notes on an autobiographical account of a case of paranoia (dementia paranoides). *S.E.,* 12:3–82.

———. (1912). The dynamics of the transference. *S.E.,* 12:99–108.

————. (1913). On the beginning of treatment (Further recommendations on the technique of psychoanalysis, I). *S.E.*, 12:123–144.

————. (1914a). On narcissism: An introduction. *S.E.*, 14:69–102.

————. (1914b). Remembering, repeating and working-through. *S.E.*, 12: 145–156.

————. (1917). Mourning and melancholia. *S.E.*, 14:239–258.

————. (1919). A child is being beaten. *S.E.*, 17:177–204.

————. (1920). Beyond the pleasure principle. *S.E.*, 18:3–64.

————. (1923). The ego and the id. *S.E.*, 19:3–66.

————. (1924a). Neurosis and psychosis. *S.E.*, 19:149–153.

————. (1924b). The dissolution of the Oedipus complex. *S.E.*, 19:173–179.

————. (1924c). The loss of reality in neurosis and psychosis. *S.E.*, 19: 183–187.

————. (1927). Fetishism. *S.E.*, 21:147–157.

————. (1931). Female sexuality. *S.E.*, 21:223–243.

————. (1937). Constructions in analysis. *S.E.*, 23:255–269.

Friedman, M., Glasser, M., Laufer, E., Laufer M., & Wohl, M. (1972). Attempted suicide and self-mutilation in adolescence: Some observations from a psychoanalytic research project. *Int. J. Psychoanal.*, *53*, 179–83.

Galatzer-Levy, R. M. (1985). The analysis of an adolescent boy. *Adolescent Psychiatry, 12*, 336–360.

Galenson, E., & Roiphe, H. (1980). The preoedipal development of the boy. *J. Amer. Psychoanal. Assn.*, *28*, 805–827.

Geleerd, E. R. (1957). Some aspects of psychoanalytic technique in adolescence. *Psychoanal. Study Child, 12*, 263–283.

————. (1961). Some aspects of ego vicissitudes in adolescence. *J. Amer. Psychoanal. Assn.*, *9*, 394–405.

Gillespie, W. H. (1940). Fetishism. *Int. J. Psychoanal.*, *21*, 401–415.

————. (1964). Symposium on homosexuality. *Int. J. Psychoanal.*, *45*, 203–209.

Glasser, M. (1979). Some aspects of the role of aggression in the perversions. In I. Rosen (Ed.), *Sexual deviation* (2nd ed.). Oxford: Oxford University Press, pp. 278–305.

————. (1985). The weak spot—some observations on male sexuality. *Int. J. Psychoanal.*, *66*, 405–414.

Glover, E. (1933). The relation of perversion formation to the development of reality sense. *Int. J. Psychoanal.*, *14*, 486–97.

Greenacre, P. (1953). Certain relationships between fetishism and the faulty development of the body image. *Psychoanal. Study Child, 8*, 79–98.

————. (1958). Early physical determinants in the development of the sense of identity. *J. Amer. Psychoanal. Assn.*, *6*, 612–627.

————. (1960). Further notes on fetishism. *Psychoanal. Study Child, 15*, 191–207.

————. (1969). The fetish and the transitional object. *Psychoanal. Study Child,* *24,* 144–164.

————. (1975). On reconstruction. *J. Amer. Psychoanal. Assn., 23,* 693–712.

Greenson, R. R. (1968). Dis-identifying from mother. *Int. J. Psychoanal., 49,* 370–374.

Gurwit, A. R. (1976). Aspects of prospective fatherhood: A case report. *Psychoanal. Study Child, 31,* 237–271.

Haim, A. (1969). *Adolescent suicide.* (English trans., 1974). London: Tavistock Publications.

Hall, G. S. (1916). *Adolescence.* 2 vols. New York: Appleton.

Harley, M. (1961). Some observations on the relationship between genitality and structural development at adolescence. *J. Amer. Psychoanal. Assn., 9,* 434–460.

————. (1970). On some problems of technique in the analysis of early adolescents. *Psychoanal. Study Child, 25,* 99–121.

Hartmann, H. (1953). Contribution to the metapsychology of schizophrenia. *Psychoanal. Study Child, 8,* 177–198.

Hoffer, W. (1950). Development of the body ego. *Psychoanal. Study Child, 5,* 18–24.

Hollender, M. H. (1975). Women's use of fantasy during sexual intercourse. In I. M. Marcus & J. J. Francis (Eds.), *Masturbation.* New York: International Universities Press, pp. 315–328.

Horney, K. (1933). The denial of the vagina: A contribution to the problem of the genital anxieties specific to women. *Int. J. Psychoanal, 14,* 57–70.

Hurry, A. (1977). My ambition is to be dead. Part 1. *J. Child Psychotherapists, 3* (4).

————. (1978). My ambition is to be dead. Parts 2 and 3. *J. Child Psychotherapists, 4* (4).

Jacobson, E. (1954). Contribution to the metapsychology of psychotic identifications. *J. Amer. Psychoanal. Assn., 2,* 239–262.

————. (1961). Adolescent moods and the remodelling of psychic structures in adolesence. *Psychoanal. Study Child, 16,* 164–183.

————. (1964). *The self and the object world.* New York: International Universities Press.

————. (1971). *Depression.* New York: International Universities Press.

Jones, E. (1948a). Some problems of adolescence. In *Papers on psychoanalysis.* London: Ballière, Tindall & Cox, pp. 389–406. (Original work published 1922)

————. (1948b). The early development of female sexuality. In *Papers on psycho-analysis.* London: Ballière, Tindall & Cox, pp. 438–451. (Original work published 1927)

————. (1948c). The phallic phase. In *Papers on psycho-analysis.* London: Ballière, Tindall & Cox, pp. 452–484. (Original work published 1932)

Katan, M. (1950). Structural aspects of a case of schizophrenia. *Psychoanal. Study Child, 5,* 175–211.

———. (1954). The importance of the non-psychotic part of the personality in schizophrenia. *Int. J. Psychoanal., 35,* 119–128.

———. (1969). A psychoanalytic approach to the diagnosis of paranoia. *Psychoanal. Study Child, 24,* 328–57.

———. (1975). Childhood memories as contents of schizophrenic hallucinations and delusions. *Psychoanal. Study Child, 30,* 357–374.

Kernberg, O. F. (1980). Developmental theory, structural organization and psychoanalytic technique. In R. Lax, S. Bach, & J. A. Burland (Eds.), *Rapprochement.* New York: Aronson, pp. 23–38.

———. (1984). *Severe personality disorders.* New Haven and London: Yale University Press.

Kestemberg, E. (1986). Adolescent pathology: Commencement, passage, or catastrophe. *Adolescent Psychiatry, 13,* 455–466.

Klein, M. (1948a). Early stages of the Oedipus complex. In *Contributions to psycho-analysis 1921–1945.* London: Hogarth Press, pp. 202–214. (Original work published 1928)

———. (1948b). The Oedipus complex in the light of early anxieties. In *Contributions to psycho-analysis 1921–1945.* London: Hogarth Press, pp. 339–390. (Original work published 1945)

———. (1958). On the development of mental functioning. *Int. J. Psychoanal., 39,* 84–90.

Klumpner, G. H. (1978). A review of Freud's writings on adolescence. *Adolescent Psychiatry, 6,* 59–74.

Kramer, P. (1954). Early capacity for orgastic discharge and character formation. *Psychoanal. Study Child, 9,* 128–141.

Kris, E. (1951). Some comments and observations on early autoerotic activities. *Psychoanal. Study Child, 6,* 95–116.

———. (1956). The personal myth. *J. Amer. Psychoanal. Assn., 4,* 653–681.

Ladame, F. (1987). Depressive adolescents, pathological narcissism, and therapeutic failures. *Adolescent Psychiatry, 14,* 301–315.

Lampl-de Groot, J. (1950). On masturbation and its influence on general development. *Psychoanal. Study Child, 5,* 153–174.

———. (1960). On adolescence. *Psychoanal. Study Child, 15,* 95–103.

———. (1962). Ego ideal and superego. *Psychoanal. Study Child, 17,* 94–106.

Laufer, M. (1964). Ego ideal and pseudo ego ideal in adolescence. *Psychoanal. Study Child, 19,* 196–221.

———. (1968). The body image, the function of masturbation, and adolescence: Problems of the ownership of the body. *Psychoanal. Study Child, 23,* 114–137.

———. (1976). The central masturbation fantasy, the final sexual organization, and adolescence. *Psychoanal. Study Child, 31,* 297–316.

————. (1978). The nature of the adolescent pathology and the psychoanalytic process. *Psychoanal. Study Child, 33,* 307–322.

————. (1981). Adolescent breakdown and the transference neurosis. *Int. J. Psychoanal., 62,* 51–59.

————. (1982). The formation and shaping of the Oedipus complex: Clinical observations and assumptions. *Int. J. Psychoanal., 63,* 217–227.

————. (1986). Adolescent psychopathology and aims of treatment. *Adolescent Psychiatry, 13,* 480–492.

————. (1986). Adolescence and psychosis. *Int. J. Psychoanal., 67,* 367–372.

Laufer, M., & Laufer, M. E. (1984). *Adolescence and developmental breakdown.* New Haven and London: Yale University Press.

Laufer, M. E. (1981). The adolescent's use of the body in object relationships and in the transference: A comparison of borderline and narcissistic modes of functioning. *Psychoanal. Study Child, 36,* 163–180.

————. (1982). Female masturbation in adolescence and the development of the relationship to the body. *Int. J. Psychoanal., 63,* 295–302.

————. (1986). The female Oedipus complex and the relationship to the body. *Psychoanal. Study Child, 41,* 259–276.

Lewin, B. D. (1933). The body as phallus. *Psychoanal. Q., 2,* 24–47.

————. (1950). *The psychoanalysis of elation.* New York: Norton.

Lichtenstein, H. (1961). Identity and sexuality. *J. Amer. Psychoanal. Assn., 9,* 179–260.

Limentani, A. (1966). A re-evaluation of acting out in relation to working through. *Int. J. Psychoanal., 47,* 274–282.

————. (1977). The differential diagnosis of homosexuality. *Brit. J. Med. Psychol., 50,* 209–216.

Little, M. (1958). On delusional transference (transference psychosis). *Int. J. Psychoanal., 39,* 134–138.

Loewald, H. W. (1971). The transference neurosis: Comments on the concept and the phenomenon. *J. Amer. Psychoanal. Assn., 19,* 54–66.

————. (1979). The waning of the Oedipus complex. *J. Amer. Ps,choanal. Assn., 27,* 751–775.

Loewenstein, R. M. (1935). Phallic passivity in men. *Int. J. Psychoanal., 16,* 334–340.

McDougall, J. (1979). The homosexual dilemma: A clinical and theoretical study of female homosexuality. In I. Rosen (Ed.), *Sexual deviation* (2nd ed.). Oxford: Oxford University Press, pp. 206–242.

Mahler, M. S. (1963). Thoughts about development and individuation. *Psychoanal. Study Child, 18,* 307–324.

————. (1974). Symbiosis and individuation: The psychological birth of the human infant. *Psychoanal. Study Child, 29,* 89–106.

Mahler, M. S., Pine, F., & Bergman, A. (1975). *The psychological birth of the human infant.* London: Hutchinson.

Marcus, I. M. (1980). Countertransference and the psychoanalytic process in children and adolescents. *Psychoanal. Study Child, 35,* 285–298.

Masterson, J. F. (1978). The borderline adolescent: An object relations view. *Adolescent Psychiatry, 6,* 344–359.

Milrod, D. (1982). The wished-for self image. *Psychoanal. Study Child, 37,* 95–120.

Modell, A. H. (1968). *Object love and reality.* New York: International Universities Press.

Mogul, S. L. (1980). Asceticism in adolescence and anorexia nervosa. *Psychoanal. Study Child, 35,* 155–175.

Moore, W. T. (1975). Some economic functions of genital masturbation during adolescent development. In I. M. Marcus & J. J. Francis (Eds.), *Masturbation.* New York: International Universities Press, pp. 231–276.

Peto, A. (1959). Body image and archaic thinking. *Int. J. Psychoanal., 40,* 223–231.

Reich, A. (1951). The discussion of 1912 on masturbation and our present-day views. *Psychoanal. Study Child, 6,* 80–94.

———. (1960). Pathologic forms of self-esteem regulation. *Psychoanal. Study Child, 15,* 215–232.

Reiser, L. W. (1986). Denial of physical illness in adolescence: Collaboration of patient, family and physicians. *Psychoanal. Study Child, 42,* 385–402.

Reiser, M. F. (1984). *Mind, brain, body.* New York: Basic.

Rinsley, D. B. (1981). Borderline psychopathology: The concepts of Masterson and Rinsley and beyond. *Adolescent Psychiatry, 9,* 259–274.

Risen, S. E. (1982). The psychoanalytic treatment of an adolescent with anorexia nervosa. *Psychoanal. Study Child, 37,* 433–460.

Ritvo, S. (1971). Late adolescence: Developmental and clinical considerations. *Psychoanal. Study Child, 26,* 241–263.

———. (1976). Adolescent to woman. *J. Amer. Psychoanal. Assn.* (supp. 24), *5,* 127–138.

———. (1978). The psychoanalytic process in childhood. *Psychoanal. Study Child, 33,* 295–305.

———. (1981). Anxiety, symptom formation and ego autonomy. *Psychoanal. Study Child, 36,* 339–364.

———. (1984). The image and uses of the body in psychic conflict. *Psychoanal. Study Child, 39,* 449–469.

Ritvo, S., & Solnit, A. J. (1958). Influences of early mother-child interaction on identification processes. *Psychoanal. Study Child, 13,* 64–85.

Roiphe, H. (1973). Some thoughts on childhood psychoses, self and object. *Psychoanal. Study Child, 28,* 131–145.

Roiphe, H., & Galenson, E. (1981). *Infantile origins of sexual identity.* New York: International Universities Press.

Rosenfeld, H. (1964). An investigation into the need of neurotic and psychotic patients to act out during analysis. In *Psychotic states*. New York: International Universities Press, pp. 200–216.

———. (1987). *Impasse and interpretation*. London: Tavistock Publications.

Sandler, J. (1960). On the concept of superego. *Psychoanal. Study Child, 15,* 128–162.

Sands, D. E. (1975). The psychoses of adolescence. In. A. H. Esman (Ed.), *The psychology of adolescence*. New York: International Universities Press, pp. 402–413. (Original work published 1956)

Sarnoff, C. A. (1975). Narcissism, adolescent masturbation fantasies, and the search for reality. In I. M. Marcus & J. J. Francis (Eds.), *Masturbation*. New York: International Universities Press, pp. 227–304.

Schafer, R. (1960). The loving and beloved superego in Freud's structural theory. *Psychoanal. Study Child, 15,* 163–188.

Schilder, P. (1950). *The image and appearance of the human body*. New York: International Universities Press. (Original work published 1935)

Schur, M. (1955). Comments on the metapsychology of somatization. *Psychoanal. Study Child, 10,* 119–164.

Segal, H. (1964). *Introduction to the work of Melanie Klein*. London: W. Heinemann.

———. (1977). Psychoanalytic dialogue: Kleinian theory today. *J. Amer. Psychoanal. Assn., 25,* 363–370.

Sherfey, M. J. (1966). The evolution and nature of female sexuality in relation to psychoanalytic theory. *J. Amer. Psychoanal. Assn., 14,* 28–128.

Sklansky, M. (1972). Panel report: Indications and contraindications for the psychoanalysis of the adolescent. *J. Amer. Psychoanal. Assn., 20,* 134–144.

Solnit, A. J. (1959). Panel report: The vicissitudes of ego development in adolescence. *J. Amer. Psychoanal. Assn., 7,* 523–536.

———. (1983). Obstacles and pathways in the journey from adolescence to parenthood. *Adolescent Psychiatry, 11,* 14–26.

Stern, D. N. (1985). *The interpersonal world of the infant*. New York: Basic.

Stewart, W. A. (1963). An inquiry into the concept of working through. *J. Amer. Psychoanal. Assn., 11,* 474–499.

Stoller, R. J. (1965). The sense of maleness. *Psychoanal. Q., 34,* 207–218.

———. (1969). *Sex and gender*. London: Hogarth Press.

———. (1975). The transsexual experiment. In *Sex and gender*. Vol. 2. London: Hogarth Press.

———. (1986). *Sexual excitement*. London: Maresfield Library.

Strachey, J. (1934). The nature of the therapeutic action of psychoanalysis. *Int. J. Psychoanal., 15,* 127–159.

Sugar, M. (1979). Therapeutic approaches to the borderline adolescent. *Adolescent Psychiatry, 7,* 343–361.

———. (1983). Sexual abuse of children and adolescents. *Adolescent Psychiatry, 11,* 199–211.

Tanner, J. M. (1962). *Growth at adolescence.* Oxford: Oxford University Press.

Tausk, V. (1951). On masturbation. *Psychoanal. Study Child, 6,* 61–79. (Original work published 1912)

———. (1948). On the origin of the "influencing machine" in schizophrenia. In R. Fliess (Ed.), *The psychoanalytic reader.* New York: International Universities Press, pp. 31–64. (Original work published 1919)

Tylim, I. (1978). Narcissistic transference and countertransference in adolescent treatment. *Psychoanal. Study Child, 33,* 279–292.

Wallerstein, R. S. (1986). *Forty-two lives in treatment.* New York and London: Guilford Press.

Wexler, M. (1965). Working through in the therapy of schizophrenia. *Int. J. Psychoanal., 46,* 279–286.

Wilson, C. P. (1986). The psychoanalytic psychotherapy of bulimic anorexia nervosa. *Adolescent Psychiatry, 13,* 274–314.

Winnicott, D. W. (1953). Transitional objects and transitional phenomena: A study of the first not-me possession. *Int. J. Psychoanal., 34,* 89–97.

———. (1958). The capacity to be alone. *Int. J. Psychoanal., 39,* 416–420.

———. (1960). Counter-transference. *Brit. J. Med. Psychol., 33,* 17.

Index

Abandonment, fear of: in bulimic patient, 46; father and, 117; in fetishism case, 64, 65, 71; holiday breaks and, 119, 187; transference and, 61. *See also* Separation, fear of
Achievement, external, 72–73
Adolescence: developmental function of, 10–14; end of, 11, 13–14, 15, 200; pathology and, 11, 13–14, 15, 151
Aichorn, A., 3*n*
Alcohol, use of, 126, 127, 129, 132, 133
American Psychiatric Association, 14n
Anal activities, 33–34, 35, 191, 192
Anal masturbation, 36, 150, 154, 161, 177–78, 179
Analyst: breakdown patient's reliance on for comfort, 161; in case with necrophilic fantasies, 32–41; danger of adolescent's self-destructive attacks and, 180–90; danger to, of patient's violence, 175–80; denigration of, 37, 38, 39–41, 47–48, 49, 50, 115; helplessness as response of, 176–77, 178, 182, 190–94; independence of, 40, 78, 181, 189; obsessive thoughts about, 145, 146; as part of adolescent's struggle, 172; task of, 162, 195, 201; weekly staff meetings and, 5, 15, 39, 132*n*, 201. *See also* Countertransference; Holiday and weekend breaks; Interpretation; Responses of analyst; Transference
Analytic treatment: aims of, 20–23; in case of acute paranoid breakdown, 142–50; in case of severe breakdown, 155–68; destruction

of, 48–53, 201; framework for, 23–24, 201; gratification and, 149; patient's feelings of helplessness and, 198; period of assessment and, 18–19; premature termination of, 48–53, 71–73, 78, 89; recognition of feelings and, 107, 135; resistances to, 22–23, 88–89, 128; selection for, 25; suitability of, for adolescents, 24–25
Anger, 158–59, 161–62, 165, 166
Anorexia, 108, 109, 116, 118, 121. *See also* Bulimic symptoms
Anxieties of analyst, 4–5, 15, 172–73, 184; in case of severe breakdown, 81, 84; patient's violence and, 33, 34, 175–80; as predictable response, 201; staff discussion group and, 5, 15, 39, 132*n*
Anxiety: aroused by sexual power, 181–82; castration, 61–62, 65, 68, 69, 71, 150; about dirt, 138, 139, 140, 141; disintegrative, 82; external reality as source of, 194, 195; about losing control, 176–78, 184; pre-oedipal, 61, 71
Assessment period, 18–19
Attempted suicide: adolescent's experience of, 112–13; clinical material on, 74–90, 108–24, 125–37; clinical material preceding, 111–12; crisis pattern in, 117–24; external reality and, 9–10; severity of illness and, 199; splitting and, 112, 113, 120; as treatment category, 15. *See also* Death, desire for; Suicidal fantasy; Suicide